The
GAY
100

ALSO BY PAUL RUSSELL

Sea of Tranquillity
Boys of Life
The Salt Point

The
GAY
100

A Ranking of
the Most Influential
Gay Men and Lesbians,
Past and Present

Paul Russell

A Citadel Press Book
Published by Carol Publishing Group

A Citadel Press Book
Published by Carol Publishing Group
Citadel Press is a registered trademark of Carol Communications, Inc.

Editorial Offices: 600 Madison Avenue, New York, NY 10022
Sales and Distribution Offices: 120 Enterprise Avenue, Secaucus, NJ
    07094
In Canada: Canadian Manda Group, P.O. Box 920, Station U, Toronto,
    Ontario M8Z 5P9

Queries regarding rights and permissions should be addressed to:
Carol Publishing Group, 600 Madison Avenue, New York, NY 10022

Carol Publishing Group books are available at special discounts
for bulk purchases, sales promotions, fund-raising, or
educational purposes. Special editions can be created to specifications.
For details, contact: Special Sales Department, Carol Publishing Group,
120 Enterprise Avenue, Secaucus, NJ 07094.

"Love Song of Alice B." is reprinted from *Bee Vine Time and Other Pieces* (New
Haven: Yale University Press, 1952) courtesy of the estate of Gertrude Stein.

Translations of Hafiz are from *Hafiz of Shiraz: Thirty Poems,* by Peter Avery
and John Heath-Stubbs. London: John Murray, 1952.

Passages from Tacitus and Petronius are from *The Satyricon,* translated by
William Arrowsmith. Ann Arbor: University of Michigan Press, 1959.

Passages from Marcel Proust are from *Remembrance of Things Past,* translated
by Terence Kilmartin. New York: Random House, 1981.

Manufactured in the United States of America
10 9 8 7 6 5 4 3 2 1

Library of Congress Cataloging-in-Publication Data

Russell, Paul Elliott.
    The gay 100 : a ranking of the most influential gay men and
lesbians, past and present / by Paul Russell.
        p.   cm.
    "A Citadel Press book."
    ISBN 0-8065-1591-0
    1. Gays—Biography.   2. Gays—History.   I. Title.
II. Title: Gay one hundred.
HQ75.2.R87   1994
305.9'0664'0922—dc20

94–12607
CIP

To Karen
Reluctant Queenmaker

CONTENTS

ACKNOWLEDGMENTS

I wish to thank my editor, Bruce Shostak, who first proposed this project; my agent, Harvey Klinger, who thought it a fine idea; the National Endowment for the Arts, for a grant that allowed me time to research the material; the Sojourner Truth Library of the State University of New York at New Paltz, whose shelves held virtually everything I needed; Jim Brain for many roast chickens and fish stews; Tom Heacox and David Bass for all that brainstorming on the front porch one cloudy day in August; Ann Imbrie, Scott Mendelssohn, and Sherry Williams for some invaluable suggestions along the way; and Michael Somoya, who kept me on track.

There is no doubt that if it became widely known *who are* the Uranians, the world would be astonished to find so many of its great or leading men among them.

—EDWARD CARPENTER, 1908

INTRODUCTION

The Premise

In 1593 the playwright Christopher Marlowe was accused of having, among other things, concocted a list of famous sodomites. He was neither the first to do so nor the last. I believe that gay people have always made such lists—secret histories of the world passed down through time, sometimes made public, more often kept private and close to the heart.

One of the ways by which gay men and lesbians have survived through the centuries is by recognizing one another in the various disguises we have worn. We have survived on the consolation of knowing there were others like ourselves. We have been given courage by the rare example of someone like ourselves who has burned brightly in the imagination. We have been fed by the creative dreams and visions of our comrades, widely scattered and persecuted and all but silenced though they may be.

The men and women whose names were secretly whispered, repeated, cherished as homosexual helped create and sustain that amorphous phenomenon we know today as gay culture. These people have signaled who we were, who we might one day be. Their example has answered the world's calumny, has put the lies and stereotypes to rout, has enhanced our sense of possibility.

In this book I have ranked the one hundred gay men and lesbians, past and present, who have been the most influential in their contributions to modern gay/lesbian identity.

What Do I Mean by "Influential"?

A friend of mine once told me a story. He was visiting Paris and met a young man in a cafe. When the young man discovered my friend had done graduate work in philosophy, he insisted on taking him to the cemetery where the existentialist philosopher Jean-Paul Sartre lies buried beside the feminist intellectual Simone de Beauvoir. Two simple graves. Sartre's was bare, unadorned, neglected—but de Beauvoir's bloomed with flowers, trinkets, candles, notes from admirers who had come halfway around the world to see her final resting place.

Whether tangible or intangible, evidence that a person's legacy continues in the world, luminous and alive, is what I have sought in attempting to gauge the extent of his or her influence. By influence, then, I mean the ability to effect change, to reconfigure the parameters, to leave in one's wake a set of challenged assumptions and transformed lives. For the purposes of this particular ranking of influence, I have asked myself a twofold question: How has the individual in question, specifically as a gay man or lesbian, contributed both to history in general and to gay/lesbian identity in particular?

The well-known case of Alexander the Great can serve as an example of what I mean. For better or worse, Alexander left his world a profoundly changed place. He altered the cultural landscape of both the Greek and Persian worlds. He was perhaps the greatest military genius this planet has seen (or endured). That is all without question, regardless of his sexuality. My judgment regarding Alexander's influence takes into account all that and then also considers the role his homosexuality has played in the world's imagination in the 2,300 years since his death.

History is full of influential military men who loved men: one thinks of Julius Caesar, Richard the Lion-Hearted, Frederick the Great of Prussia, T. E. Lawrence, the World War II hero Bernard Montgomery. Nevertheless, it has been the name of Alexander that has been invoked, for hundreds of years, whenever anyone wanted to challenge the assumption that gay men are necessarily effeminate or weak-willed or passive. It is not because Alexander the Great was a military genius who happened also to be gay that he earns his ranking on this list; rather, it is because, historically, there has been such a well-known and much-circulated tradition about his homosexuality. His love of men has been an indelible part of his allure. It is thus as a military commander *but also as a man who loved men*, the two legacies inextricably intertwined in the single individual, that Alexander is influential for the purposes of this ranking.

I do not, of course, presume to judge whether it has necessarily been a good thing for the world to have Alexanders, whether gay or straight, traipsing around continents at the head of their marauding armies. I simply acknowledge that such activities have greatly influenced the world we live in today.

In many of my entries I have indicated other contenders for the particular ranking in question and have suggested why I believe the particular gay man or lesbian I have chosen for that ranking is appropriate. Clearly, with such a wide range of individuals represented, I have had to weigh the relative significance of different kinds of influence, though basically two kinds of influence surface in this ranking. One manifests itself in those figures whose influence stems from the fact that they are well-known as lesbians or gay men and as such contribute an invaluable visibility to our accomplishments. These include many writers, artists, musicians—for the simple reason that it is in these fields, to a large extent, that gay/lesbian culture has been created and transmitted from one generation to the next. The imaginative worlds these men and women have offered us propose new and transforming ways of thinking about our identities, our desires, our hopes. The other type of influence—represented by less familiar names such as Magnus Hirschfeld, Karl Heinrich Ulrichs, and Edward Carpenter—is seen in people who were active in the gay rights movement, and whose specific and invaluable contributions to gay/lesbian existence have outlived their name recognition. Some of these more forgotten figures have, ironically, been the most influential of all, and I have ranked them accordingly.

Figures in the sciences, especially the so-called hard sciences, are less well represented, in large part because contributions to mathematics or nuclear physics have little immediate bearing on gay/lesbian identity (though a friend of mine insists the person who gave all those queer names to subatomic particles must have been gay). The great mathematician Alan Turing's presence on this list is due not so much to the brilliance of his work as to the anguished predicament of his double life as a gay man and a scientist doing top-secret research for a homophobic government.

I have—of necessity—limited my notion of influence to late-twentieth-century American/European gay and lesbian identity. Many important gay people are left out—for instance, the great Sufi poet Jalal ud-Din Rumi or the Han dynasty emperor Aidi, whose sacrifice of the sleeve of his robe in order to allow his lover Dong Xian to sleep undisturbed inspired the term *duanxiu*, "the cut sleeve," to signify male homosexual love in the Chinese language—because, for better or worse, they have had little or no practical influence on contemporary American/European gay and lesbian identity.

What Do I Mean by "Gay/Lesbian Identity"?

To talk about an influential person presupposes someone else who is influenced. For the purposes of this book, I have assumed a certain community of gay and lesbian individuals living in the late twentieth century in (for the most part) North America and Western Europe. Within that community there are, however, such vast differences of race, class, ethnicity, religion, taste, desire, etc., as to render the very notion of community virtually meaningless. From the wealthy white male weekenders of Fire Island to the economically underprivileged lesbian Chicanas of California to the black drag queens of the house balls to the women's softball teams of Omaha, Nebraska, there are countless gay and lesbian communities, overlapping cultures whose boundaries are in constant flux, whose codes and fashions and meanings are inherently unstable, always evolving.

About the only people who believe in a single, monolithic, coherent gay/lesbian culture (or "lifestyle," another favorite term) are the enemies of that culture, homophobes like the religious right who, in their paranoid worldview, imagine the existence of that vast, well-organized, threatening phantom known as the "gay agenda." As anyone who has ever attended any kind of lesbian/gay political meeting can wearily attest, gays and lesbians have a hard enough time figuring out a mutually agreeable time for the next meeting, let alone anything like a "gay agenda." It is not without good reason that the emblem of the rainbow has been adopted by gay activists as an expression of the range and richness of our affiliated communities.

Despite all this great and daunting diversity of ours, I have had to do some thinking, for the purposes of constructing this list, about what—if any—common denominators might unite gay men and lesbians across the rainbow in anything remotely resembling a shared culture. What I have come up with is this: that we have all, whatever our varying circumstances and stories, been collectively and variously characterized by mainstream culture as deviant, sick, sinful; that we have been constructed as a beleaguered minority, as perpetual outsiders, rebels, exiles; that we have often used that outsider status to question, subvert, and sometimes transform the mainstream culture; that against all odds, laws, taboos, and prejudices we have persisted in loving those whom society has said we should not love; and that we have been hated because we loved. These things, I believe, compose the common language of our experience.

The people on this list represent some of the many ways in which we have reacted to the rampant hostilities arrayed against us, the many ways in which we have rethought our identities and retold our histories, the many ways in which we have explored the vast potentialities of our forbidden desire, given voice to "the love that dare not speak its name." These one hundred gay men and lesbians have enabled, either by example or tangible activity, the rest of us to take our place in the world.

What Do I Mean by "Gay Men and Lesbians," Especially in the Context of 2500 Years of History?

History is not a costume drama. The ancients were not people just like ourselves who wore togas instead of business suits. Instead, as has often been said, the past is another country. That is to say, its customs are different, as are its habits and perspectives and prejudices. Nothing escapes the shaping forces of culture, including sexuality. As cultural parameters change, so do sexual attitudes, practices, and even identities. At the same time, there are certain broad currents of experience, the raw stuff of desire and need and taste that is shaped by different times and cultures in different ways. One of these currents, present everywhere, though in differing disguises, is same-sex love. Same-sex love has existed in all times and all cultures, as far as we know—just like its equivalent, opposite-sex love. Still, both same-sex and opposite-sex love have taken different forms over the years.

For most of human history, our modern distinction between "heterosexual" and "homosexual" would not have made much sense. The term *homosexuality* wasn't coined until 1869, and the term *heterosexuality* some time after that. If things are not named, do they exist? The French philosopher Michel Foucault has argued that we name things when the need to identify them arises. Thus, the invention of our modern distinction between homosexuality and heterosexuality points to some new configuration of human sexuality that arose sometime in the last two hundred years or so. Before that time, sexuality was configured differently, and other ways of thinking and talking about it sufficed.

All of this is simply to say that I am aware, in constructing a list that begins in the sixth century B.C. and traverses 2,500 years to the present, that I am attempting to yoke together a vast variety of sexualities that have perhaps only this in common: that they are same-sex loves. To take one example of what I am talking about: In ancient Athenian society, male sexuality was organized in ways that would seem utterly bizarre and alien to most of us today. As far as free adult male citizens were concerned, the following individuals were considered "women," i.e., they were appropriate *passive* sexual partners for an *active* male: women, boys, slaves, and foreigners. Within that range of possible objects of desire, some men chose mostly women, some mostly boys, while others ranged freely among their culturally prescribed options.

What was unthinkable to the ancient Athenians was the idea that sex should be reciprocal, or that active partners should ever become passive (or *vice versa*). Sex was something perpetrated by an active member on a passive one as a private expression of the public hierarchies of society. In the act of having sex, the two partners no more entered into a mutual relationship than a burglar and his victim might be said to form a mutual relationship. Furthermore, the notion that one would be attracted for the duration of one's lifetime exclusively to one sex—either the opposite or one's own—made very little sense to the ancient Athenians. In the context of such a culture, to speak of homosexuality and heterosexuality in any modern sense is to miss the mark. Nevertheless, there were in Athenian society men like Socrates whose primary erotic attraction seems to have been to boys. The terms *gay* or *homosexual* would have meant nothing to them (though the term *paiderasteia* may have); nevertheless, I think we are entirely justified in placing them within a "gay" continuum.

In light of our own fairly rigid sexual categories, many of the people on this list would be considered bisexual rather than strictly homosexual. Many on this list married and had children and had affairs with members of both sexes. It is essential to keep in mind the vastly different cultural presumptions, expectations, and opportunities many of the men and women on this list had available to them.

That said, I wish to stress how important it is for us to record for ourselves—again and again—the persistence of same-sex love throughout history. Since the writing of history is for the most part controlled by heterosexuals, the tendency is to assume that all the important people of the past were securely heterosexual. The fact that throughout history people have loved people of their own sex in rich and complex ways tends again and again to get erased. One of the things I hope to accomplish with this list is to remind lesbians and gay men of their heritage. At the same time, I wish to correct the distortions introduced into the historical record by heterosexist assumptions. Or in the words of a poster showing some famous gay faces: "Sometimes scholarship has gotten its facts a little *too* straight."

While doing my research, I became acutely aware of the pressing need for a book like this one: time and again I saw how the subject of homosexuality is still silenced in the biographies of famous men and women. If you were to look up the lesbians and gay men on this list in standard encyclopedias, you would for the most part never guess that any of them were lesbian or gay. On the subject of their sexuality discreet silence or, worse, coy euphemism is still all too often the rule. Marlowe becomes "unconventional," Jane Addams "never married," Rimbaud and Verlaine were "very close friends." It is vitally important that people—especially young people who are still struggling with feelings of isolation and solitude—be made aware of the presence of gays and lesbians throughout the historical record.

Though the presence of certain people on this list may surprise you, I have not "outed" anyone: the historical facts are all there in the record, though you sometimes have to prowl around a bit before you find them. I think it's a good sign, though, that I didn't have to get myself to a specialized library to write this book: I was able to do virtually all my research at the fairly modest Sojourner Truth Library of the State University of New York at New Paltz. The information I present here may not be common knowledge, but it is certainly no longer secret. Recent biographies, many of which I list in the select bibliography at the end of this book, have been invaluable in beginning to break the veil of silence that prevailed for too long. I have tried, wherever possible, to name names, to provide specific glimpses into my subjects' loves as well as their accomplishments. The accomplishments you can read about in any standard reference work; what I wish to do here is make the sexuality of my gay and lesbian subjects as profound and integral a part of their lives as the sexuality of straight people is whenever *their* biographies are written.

Why Aren't There More Lesbians?

Although this ranking may seem weighted toward gay men—there are sixty entries for men, thirty-eight for women, and two entries shared by men and women—I believe I have done a reasonable job of constructing a list that is representative but that also takes into account the inequities of the historical record. The simple, deplorable fact is that the record for most centuries before the nineteenth does not contain lesbians who correspond in influence to Alexander the Great, Michelangelo, or Shakespeare. Nevertheless, I have attempted to recover the lesbian past wherever possible. At first this seemed a daunting task.

When I began researching this project, I was troubled that I could find so few lesbians before the twentieth century. Between Sappho in the sixth century B.C. and Gertrude Stein in the twentieth century A.D., there seemed a great silence with regard to the existence of lesbians—at least lesbians as we know them today. But as I researched more, I came to understand that I was applying a false standard in looking for lesbians *as we know them today*. If I went looking for women who met the twentieth century's definition of a lesbian, I simply wasn't going to find them—because they weren't, in fact, there. The twentieth-century lesbian is a product of the twentieth century. Nineteenth- or eighteenth-century lesbians are going to look different because the culture was different. By the same token, if I had gone through history trying to find women whose lives and identities resembled those of a late-twentieth-century middle-class heterosexual suburban American housewife, I would have had an equally hard time coming up with them. Of course, nobody sifts the historical data looking for such women, and there's no political reason to get upset by their absence. The twentieth-century heterosexual suburban housewife isn't somehow compromised just because we can find no fourteenth-century equivalent. All we do is look for her predecessors: women whose marriages were arranged as economic alliances between families, for example, rather than freely chosen on the basis of that relatively recent Western concept, "romantic" love between men and women.

This discovery was liberating for me. I began to realize more and more the revolutionary importance of Adrienne Rich's concept of the lesbian continuum. According to Rich, the lesbian continuum is "a range, through each woman's life and through history—of woman-identified experience; not simply the fact that a woman has had or consciously desired genital sexual experience with another woman. If we expand it to embrace many more forms of primary intensity between and among women, including the sharing of a rich inner life, the bonding against male tyranny, the giving and receiving of practical and political support; if we can also hear in it such associations as *marriage resistance*...we begin to grasp breadths of female history and psychology that have lain out of reach as a consequence of limited, most clinical, definitions of "lesbianism."

I began to see that, given the constrictions of eighteenth- and nineteenth-century society, especially with regards to women, same-sex affections necessarily took different forms than they do today. The option of genital sexual contact between women was very probably just not there much of the time, culturally or psychologically or practically, before the sexologists of the late nineteenth and early twentieth century invented modern sex—both the heterosexual and homosexual varieties. We have been taught to want the fulfillment of genital contact in our romantic loves, whether homosexual or heterosexual. But this has not always been the case. Those passionate romantic friendships between nineteenth-century women—which many scholars have been quick to assure us, with great relief, were not "sexual" in a twentieth-century sense—were nonetheless often the only available channels for erotic same-sex affection that in the twentieth century would be able to express itself in sexual contact. Far from arguing that those romantic friendships were a kind of affection between heterosexuals that—for some mysterious reason, perhaps the fear of that new invention "lesbianism"

—has disappeared in our day, I would argue that such friendships were precisely the form that lesbian sexuality took in the days before it had found its modern means of expression. Denying the lesbian implications of those passionate friendships is a convenient way of silencing lesbian history.

I am of course hardly the first to reclaim these women for lesbian history. My initial reluctance to do so, based on the fear that I didn't have enough "evidence" that they were lesbians, illustrates how pervasively our ways of thinking about the lesbian past have been conditioned by homophobic anxieties. We are trained to suppress the possibility of even considering a rich range of lesbian existence in any era but our own. When I began this project, I worried that my evidence for some of the lesbians on this list was too flimsy because it didn't conform to our narrow modern definition of what it means to be lesbian in the 1990s. Now I have come to believe that the evidence we possess for women like Mary Wollstonecraft, Emily Dickinson, Jane Addams, or Florence Nightingale is already entirely sufficient for us to recognize them, not as twentieth-century lesbians, which they are not, but as embodiments of some of the various options that were open in the nineteenth century to women-identified women. Furthermore, each of these women played an influential and undeniable role—whether social, artistic, or political—in creating the conditions that, in the twentieth century, would allow the existence of those women we do recognize as lesbian.

A Challenge

Such a ranking as this will always be vexed, but that's part of the intellectual challenge of the undertaking. I invite you to be challenged. I invite you to quarrel, to construct your own ranking, to think about the nature of gay and lesbian identity and the forces that have shaped it, the influences that have determined its tone and texture, the way we perceive ourselves, the way we live today.

Everyone's list will, of course, be different. The important thing is not my list but yours. Mine is simply offered here as a stimulus to your own thinking about these issues.

The
GAY
100

1

Socrates

469-399 B.C.

When we returned from the play I went to bed and began to read my Cary's Plato. It so happened that I stumbled on the *Phaedrus*. I read on and on, till I reached the end. Then I began the *Symposium;* and the sun was shining on the shrubs outside the ground-floor room in which I slept, before I shut the book up....

Here in the *Phaedrus* and the *Symposium*—in the myth of the soul and the speeches of Pausanias, Agathon and Diotima—I discovered the true *liber amoris* at last, the revelation I had been waiting for, the consecration of a long-cherished idealism. It was just as though the voice of my own soul spoke to me through Plato, as though in some antenatal experience I had lived the life of a philosophical Greek lover.

...I had touched solid ground. I had obtained the sanction of the love which had been ruling me from childhood. Here was the poetry, the philosophy of my own enthusiasm for male beauty, expressed with all the magic of unrivalled style. And, what was more, I now became aware that the Greek race—the actual historical Greeks of antiquity—treated this love seriously, invested it with moral charm, endowed it with sublimity.

So wrote the pioneering nineteenth-century homosexual rights advocate JOHN ADDINGTON SYMONDS [10] in his *Memoirs*. This record of his discovery at age seventeen of Socrates's teachings gives eloquent testimony to the influence the ancient Athenian philosopher has exercised on the gay imagination for the last 2,400 years. More compellingly and enduringly than anyone else, Socrates gave moral authority to homosexual love. In so doing, he has enabled gay men and lesbians to discover themselves in profound and life-changing ways.

Socrates was born in 469 B.C. in the Greek city-state of Athens. His father was Sophroniscus, a sculptor, and his mother, Phaenarete, was a midwife. We know little about his early years, though it is recorded that at seventeen he was a favorite and disciple of the philosopher Archelaus, who had been a pupil of Anaxagoras, Athens' first philosopher. During the Peloponnesian War (431–404 B.C.), Socrates served as a hoplite (a foot soldier) in the Athenian army and at the battle of Potidaea saved the life of his famous pupil Alcibiades. In order to maintain his spiritual independence, Socrates lived a life of such self-imposed austerity that the commentator Antiphon observed, "A slave who was made to live so would run away." Completely neglecting his personal affairs, Socrates spent his days sitting in the shade of an olive tree and discussing philosophical questions of justice, virtue, piety, and the soul with well-born youths. As a teacher and lover of young men, he was the embodiment of the Athenian institution of *paiderasteia*, or boy love.

Socrates left no writings, and our knowledge of his teachings and personality come from the dialogues of his most famous pupil, Plato, and from the memoirs of another student, Xenophon, both of whom knew Socrates during the last ten years of his life.

Even in his own day, Socrates was regarded as the wisest among men. In fact, the great Oracle at Delphi had even declared this to be so. The object of all his dialogues, Socrates claimed with characteristic slyness, was to test the oracle. To "convict the god of falsehood," he set about to discover someone wiser than himself. The conclusion he came to, however, was that he was indeed wiser than others—because he was aware of his own ignorance. This formed the basis of Socrates' famous irony: his constant refusal to claim to know anything for himself. He had no firm philosophical doctrines of his own: his role was to serve as "midwife" to others' ideas. Hence the celebrated Socratic method: by asking his students a series of questions and then examining the implications of their answers, he brought forth the wisdom that was latent in his students' souls. His goal was self-knowledge, a goal enshrined in such famous injunctions as "Know thyself" and "The unexamined life is not worth living." Since no one knowingly does wrong, Socrates argued, knowledge of one's true self necessarily leads one to the virtuous life.

Socrates is credited with refocusing philosophy away from science and toward ethics, and with introducing a concern for method in philosophy. His enormous influence on Western thought is measured by our use today of the term *pre-Socratic* to describe his predecessors.

Socrates' criticism of Athenian political and religious institutions made him many enemies. In 399 B.C. he was tried on charges of corrupting the morals of Athenian youth and for religious heresies. It is now believed that his arrest stemmed at least in part from his influence on Alcibiades and Critias, two who had betrayed Athens during the oligarchy of the Thirty Tyrants (404–403). At his trial, Socrates steadfastly refused to admit to any wrongdoing, and in fact argued the opposite: that he should be honored as a public benefactor for his role as a teacher. This claim incensed the court, and he was condemned to death. The sentence, however, couldn't immediately be carried out because the sacred ship sent once a year to the island of Delos had not yet returned. During his time in prison, Socrates continued to receive friends and discourse with them about philosophy. His student Crito engineered an escape plan, but Socrates declined, apparently wishing to confront the Athenians, in one last moral lesson, with the injustice of their accusation. When given the cup of poison hemlock, he drank willingly. Socrates' trial and death are eloquently described by Plato in the *Apology, Crito,* and *Phaedo.*

It is through Plato's *Symposium* and *Phaedrus* that Socrates has exercised his most potent influence on the gay imagination. In these two dialogues, Socrates examines how love begins in the erotic passion of an older man for a beautiful boy. The passion of a man for a boy is a kind of divine madness—in its grip, we neglect our material needs, we act generously, without regard for mercenary calculations. But this passion should not remain physical. Rather, by loving the beautiful boy the older man pays tribute not to the boy but to the philosophical beauty the boy embodies. The madness of passion is closely connected with the madness of poetry and philosophy. It moves us from our preoccupation with the particular to a more disinterested—and hence philosophic—consideration of the universal. It is beauty, as embodied in a boy, that leads us from one divine madness to the other.

This is the essence of what has become known as platonic love. Through it, the older man becomes the teacher as well as lover of the beautiful boy. As Socrates says in Plato's *Phaedrus:* "Every lover wants his beloved to resemble his own god, and when he has won him, he leads him on to walk in the ways of this god, and after his likeness, patterning himself on that god and giving counsel and discipline to the boy. There is no jealousy or petty spitefulness in his dealings, but his every act is aimed at bringing the beloved to be like himself and the god of their worship. So therefore glorious and blissful is the endeavor of true lovers in that mystery rite."

Although philosophers have—even to this day—studiously attempted to ignore the forthright homosexual love that is the basis of the *Phaedrus* and the *Symposium,* gay readers have always found their way to these texts. What they have discovered there has often struck them with the force of revelation. I rank Socrates as the most influential gay person in history because of the essential philosophic underpinnings he provided—and has continued to provide—for gay men and women's search for identity and self-knowledge. Who we are, in a sense, began with him.

2

Sappho

Flourished early sixth century B.C.

Sappho was born on the Aegean island of Lesbos off the coast of Asia Minor, probably in the early sixth century B.C. We know virtually nothing about this woman whose very name, along with the name of her island home, has come to denote women who love women. She is said to have been married to a wealthy merchant named Cercolas, to have had a daughter named Cleis, and to have plotted against the tyrant Pittacus and been banished to Sicily for a time. That she spent most of her life on Lesbos is probable.

It is thought that on Lesbos in the sixth century women of the aristocracy gathered in informal societies to compose and recite poetry. Sappho was the head of one of these societies—an ancient salon of sorts—and attracted admirers, some of whom journeyed from abroad to hear her. She wrote in the Aeolian dialect, in many different meters, one of which, the sapphic, is named for her. Primarily concerned with her relations with other women, enmities as well as attractions, Sappho's lyrics are passionate and simple, vernacular rather than literary. Atthis, Anactoria, Gongyla, Mnasadica: the names of some of the women she loved survive.

Although no complete poem of hers exists today, we do have lovely fragments, the longest a mere twenty-eight lines. She was generally regarded by the ancients, however, as the greatest of the early Greek lyric poets. Plato named her the tenth muse, and her work greatly influenced the Latin poets Catullus and Ovid, among others.

Though the evidence in her work that survives today is tantalizing at best, ancient writers who had access to a substantial body of her work described her in terms we would construe as lesbian. Maximus of Tyre, for example, deemed her relationship with girls analogous to Socrates' pederastic relationship with beautiful boys.

How Sappho's work was published or circulated during her lifetime is unknown. What we do know is that by the third or second century B.C.—three to four hundred years after her death—what remained of her work was collected into ten books: nine of lyrical verse and one of elegiac verse. Copies of this edition survived until the Middle Ages, but then were lost or destroyed. By the ninth century A.D., the only traces of Sappho's work were to be found in quotations by other writers.

Sappho's name—and what she stood for—did not so easily disappear, however. To homophobes, she was anathema. Only a generation after her death, the Greek poet Anacreon was already imputing an origin on the island of Lesbos to women whose sexual inclinations he wished to disparage. In the eighteenth century, we find Marie Antoinette accused of being "at the Head of a Set of Monsters call'd by each other *Sapphists*, who boast her example." On the other hand, the ideal of a band of women-loving women, poetic and passionate, managed to survive as well. One of the most famous literary hoaxes of the nineteenth century was *Les Chansons de Bilitis*, a collection of erotic lesbian love poems by Pierre Louÿs which purported to be translations from the ancient Greek of one of Sappho's disciples. "This little book of ancient love," Louÿs wrote, "is respectfully dedicated to the young women of the future society." The work—even after it was discovered to be a hoax—was taken to heart by a generation of women who were just beginning to think of themselves as lesbians. Writing in 1902, NATALIE BARNEY [43] sang the praises of Sappho in her *Cinqs Petits Dialogues grecs,* and she and her lover Renée Vivien made a pilgrimage to Lesbos in the hopes of founding a school of poetry based on sapphic models. In the 1950s American lesbians, casting about for a name for their nascent organization, decided to call themselves the Daughters of Bilitis in homage to Sappho's fictitious disciple. In 1972, a pioneering and immensely popular book of lesbian liberation by Sydney Abbott and Bernice Love was titled *Sappho Was a Right-On Woman.* JUDY GRAHN [91] traces a lyric-erotic tradition directly from Sappho through such lesbian poets as Amy Lowell, H.D. [70], ADRIENNE RICH [47], and Olga Broumas.

Sappho thus stands at the very dawn of an immensely long lineage—a mysterious, haunting, still resonant presence among us 2,500 years later, all but silenced and yet eloquent still. With her the history of lesbian existence may be said to begin.

3

Oscar Wilde

1854–1900

The world's first modern homosexual, Oscar Wilde was born Oscar Fingal O'Flahertie Wills Wilde on October 16, 1854, in Dublin, Ireland. His father was a famous eye and ear surgeon who, in his spare time, wrote books on archaeology. His mother was a folklorist and poet.

From 1864 to 1871, Wilde attended Portora Royal School in Enniskillen, and after that received scholarships first to Trinity College, Dublin, and then to Magdalen College, Oxford, from which he graduated in 1878 with honors. At Oxford, Wilde established a reputation not only as an aesthete and dandy whose gorgeously decorated rooms and discomfiting wit were the talk of the college, but also as a serious classics scholar and a talented poet (his final year at university, he won the prestigious Newdigate Prize).

Moving to London, Wilde continued his flamboyant ways, soon earning himself caricatures in the satirical magazine *Punch* and a character (Bunthorne) based on himself in Gilbert and Sullivan's comic opera *Patience*. All this attention was just fine with Wilde, who had published a first book of poetry and was eager for publicity. To further this aim, he undertook a lecture tour of the United States and Canada in 1882 to widespread critical hooting in the American press, and skeptical but large audiences across the country. Dressed in a dark purple velvet jacket with a frill of lace at the wrists, knee breeches, black silk stockings, and shoes with bright buckles, he preached his doctrine of aestheticism, the worship of art and beauty. In Camden, New Jersey, he met with WALT WHITMAN [6], saying, "I come as a poet to call upon a poet." The meeting was cordial, and Whitman later remembered Wilde as "a fine handsome youngster." Wilde took in other American sights along the way, tossing off those bons mots for which he was justifiably famous. Characterizing Niagara Falls as "endless water falling the wrong way," he averred, "Niagara will survive any criticism of mine. I must say, however, that it is the first disappointment in the married life of many Americans who spend their honeymoon there."

His own Parisian honeymoon came in 1884, when he married Constance Lloyd. Sons were born in 1885 and 1886, but marital bliss was not to last for long. In 1886, Wilde met a seventeen-year-old Oxford student named Robert Ross and allowed himself to be seduced by the lad. Later Wilde lauded Ross, a devout Catholic, as "St. Robert...Lover and Martyr—a saint known in *Hagiographia* for his extraordinary power, not in resisting, but in supplying temptations to others. This he did in the solitude of great cities."

Soon Wilde was living a double life, keeping his wife and his respectable friends completely in the dark while entertaining a widening circle of available young men.

For Wilde, 1891 was an auspicious year that saw both the publication and stunning success of his novel *The Picture of Dorian Gray* and his introduction to Lord Alfred Douglas, an enthusiastic young fan who claimed to have read *Dorian Gray* nine times. Wilde was stunned by the beauty of this twenty-one-year-old. By the spring of 1892 the two were lovers, and Wilde was confiding to Ross, in a note packed with erotic encodings: "Bosie [Douglas's nickname] has insisted on stopping here for sandwiches. He is quite like a narcissus—so white and gold...he lies like a hyacinth on the sofa, and I worship him."

Douglas was charming, brilliant, reckless, and, according to the parodist Max Beerbohm, "obviously mad (like all his family, I believe)." Wilde was completely in love.

Their passion never aspired to monogamy, and Douglas introduced Wilde to the pleasures of young men who could be had for a few pounds and the promise of dinner: "feasting with panthers," Wilde later called the practice. That it was an extremely risky practice goes without saying, and Wilde was leaving himself vulnerable to blackmail. One of Douglas's boys, Albert Wood, got hold of some of Wilde's letters to Douglas, and Wilde was forced to pay for their return. Unfortunately, a few of the letters, including the famous "Hyacinth" letter (in which Wilde enthuses to Douglas, "Your slim gilt soul walks between passion and poetry. I know Hyacinthus, whom Apollo loved so madly, was you in Greek days") found their way to Douglas's father, the Marquis of Queensberry.

Queensberry was outraged by this confirmation of his suspicions about his son, and he left his card at Wilde's hotel with the scrawled insult, "To Oscar Wilde posing Somdomite [sic]." Egged on by Douglas, who hated his father, Wilde immediately sued Queensberry for criminal libel. When, as required by English law, Queensberry produced evidence of his accusation—a list of twelve young men who were prepared to testify that Wilde had solicited them to commit sodomy—Wilde was advised by friends to drop the case and leave the country. But he persisted in his suit, proclaiming, when the trial finally opened, "I am prosecutor in this case." The tables, however, had been turned, and Wilde found not Queensberry but himself on trial. Wilde's lawyer had to assent to the judgment that Queensberry was justified in calling Wilde a sodomite in the public interest. Within minutes of Queensberry's acquittal, a letter was sent to the director of prosecutions detailing the evidence that Wilde had committed sodomy, and a warrant was issued for his arrest.

The trial took place in April 1895. Wilde's performance on the witness stand was brilliant and to no avail. When asked by the prosecution, "What is the 'love that dare not speak its name'?" (a reference to a line in one of Douglas's published poems), Wilde waxed eloquent:

> The "love that dare not speak its name" in this century is such a great affection of an elder for a younger man as there was between DAVID AND JONATHAN [40], such as Plato made the very basis of his philosophy, and such as you find in the sonnets of MICHELANGELO [12] and SHAKESPEARE. [20]. It is that deep, spiritual affection that is as pure as it is perfect. It dictates and pervades great works of art like those of Shakespeare and Michelangelo.... It is in this century misunderstood, so much misunderstood that it may be described as the "love that dare not speak its name," and on account of it I am placed where I am now. It is beautiful, it is fine, it is the noblest form of affection. There is nothing unnatural about it. It is intellectual, and it repeatedly exists between an elder and a younger man, when the elder man has intellect, and the younger man has all the joy, hope, and glamour of life before him. That it should be so the world does not understand. The world mocks at it and sometimes puts one in the pillory for it.

When the jury announced itself unable to reach a verdict, the judge ordered a new trial, and on May 25, 1895, Oscar Wilde was sentenced to be imprisoned and kept at hard labor for two years—the severest sentence allowed by law. "In my judgment," declared the magistrate, "it is totally inadequate for such a case as this."

In May 1897, Wilde was released from Reading Gaol. Bankrupt and physically broken, he left England for France, where he was reunited with Douglas (who, along with Robert Ross, had fled the country during the trial). On November 30, 1900, at the age of forty-six, Oscar Wilde died in exile in Paris.

Almost all of Wilde's important work belongs to a brief five years at the beginning of the 1890s: in addition to *The Picture of Dorian Gray* he published the symbolist drama *Salomé* (1893); immensely influential essays such as "The Decay of Lying" (with its famous dictum: "Nature imitates Art"), "The Soul of Man Under Socialism," and "The Critic as Artist" ("All bad poetry comes from genuine feeling"); the brilliantly successful comedies *Lady Windermere's Fan* (1892), *A Woman of No Importance* (1893), *An Ideal Husband* (1895), and *The Importance of Being Earnest* (1895), with its titular pun on "uranist," a nineteenth-century term for homosexual. In prison he produced the anguished *De Profundis*, a long letter to Douglas. His long poem *The Ballad of Reading Gaol* ("Yet each man kills the thing he loves... The coward does it with a kiss,/ The brave man with a sword!") was the only work he finished after his release from prison.

Although Wilde liked to claim that his talent went into his work and his genius into his life, both the life and the work have had enormous influence in the twentieth century. In his figure—ironic, witty, self-conscious, "artificial"—he radically revised our notions of the self and laid the groundwork for a modern sensibility. Without Wilde, authors like James Joyce, W. B. Yeats, and Ezra Pound would not have been possible. The tragic arc of his career—a hugely successful and popular playwright brought low by scandal—created an indelible impression on the public mind, making the trial of Oscar Wilde as important in defining our times as the trial of Socrates was for the ancient Greeks. Certainly no one has ever been so thoroughly and widely identified as homosexual or had his identity and sexuality so completely implicated in one another. It is for precisely that reason that Wilde is so modern. In fact, it is perhaps not too outrageous to claim that Oscar Wilde was *the* first modern homosexual on the planet. Poised at the moment in cultural history where the specific kind of organization of sexual identity into homosexual/heterosexual was first possible, Wilde took the revolutionary step of seizing and articulating that homosexual identity. If his trial had the short-term effect of sending a chill through the secret homosexual communities of his time, in the long run the self he brought to trial crystallized gay identity in ways we are still living with. After the brilliant catastrophe of Oscar Wilde neither the public discourse of homosexuality nor the private course of our identity could ever be the same again.

4

Magnus Hirschfeld

1868–1935

Many readers may not be familiar with the name of Dr. Magnus Hirschfeld, but without his pioneering and courageous campaign for gay rights in Germany, our lives might be very different today. His German Gay Emancipation Movement, though doomed to complete annihilation by the Nazis, nevertheless was the prototype of modern gay civil rights movements around the world.

Magnus Hirschfeld was born on May 14, 1868, in Kolbey, Prussia. He studied language and philosophy at Breslau and Strasbourg, then medicine at Munich and Berlin. After some time spent traveling in the United States and Africa, he settled in Berlin to practice medicine.

In 1896 he published, under the pseudonym Th. Ramien, *Sappho und Sokrates*, in which he argued that homosexuality is part of human sexuality and should be studied scientifically rather than criminalized. Laws against homosexuality, he wrote, should be changed.

Strongly influenced by the work of KARL HEINRICH ULRICHS [8], in 1897 Hirschfeld formed the Scientific Humanitarian Committee, the first gay rights organization. The Committee had three goals: to abolish Paragraph 175 of the Prussian penal code that outlawed homosexual relations between men (women were not mentioned in this code); to enlighten public attitudes about homosexuality and homosexuals; and to interest homosexuals in the struggle for their rights. To aid in the first of these goals, Hirschfeld's organization introduced a petition against Paragraph 175 that garnered signatures from more than six thousand prominent figures, including Albert Einstein, Leo Tolstoy, Emile Zola, Hermann Hesse, and Thomas Mann.

Other activities of the Committee included the 1903 distribution of a survey on gay behavior—the first ever—and publication of the *Yearbook for Intermediate Sexual Types*. Beginning in 1899, and continuing for the next twenty-three years until the Weimar Republic's failing economy forced it to shut down, the *Yearbook* published scientific and cultural studies of homosexuality.

In 1907, at the height of the Committee's petition movement, two thousand people turned out for a debate on the pros and cons of Paragraph 175. That same year a scandal (known as the Moltke-Harden-Eulenberg Affair) broke involving prominent gays around Kaiser Wilhelm II. All too predictably, public panic and its attendant backlash against the fledgling homosexual movement set in.

In 1910 a harsh new penal code was instituted that criminalized lesbian as well as gay male behavior. Soon after, World War I further stifled Hirschfeld's campaign. In 1919, after Germany's defeat, Hirschfeld took advantage of the more liberal climate of the Weimar Republic and founded the Institute for Sexual Science in Berlin. Under its auspices, the petition drive resumed and some victories were won. The tenor of the movement can be seen in a 1921 appeal issued by the Scientific Humanitarian Committee. "Homosexuals," it declared. "...in the last analysis, justice for you will be the fruit only of your own efforts. The liberation of homosexuals can only be the work of homosexuals themselves." On March 18, 1922—twenty-five years after Hirschfeld had first inaugurated the petition—it was presented to the Reichstag. And there, due to increasing political chaos in the Weimar Republic, it remained.

In 1919, Hirschfeld produced what was probably the first gay film: *Anders als die Andern (Different From the Others)*. Directed by Richard Oswald and starring Conrad Veidt, the film told the story of a famous but homosexual violinist ruined by a blackmailer. At its premiere on May 24, 1919, Hirschfeld addressed the audience, saying, "The matter to be put before your eyes and soul today is one of severe importance and difficulty. Difficult, because the degree of ignorance and prejudice to be disposed of is extremely high. Important, because we must free not only these people from undeserved disgrace but also the public from a judicial error that can be compared to such atrocities in history as the persecution of witches, atheists and heretics. Besides this, the number of people who are born 'different from the others' is much larger than most parents care to realize... The film you are about to see for the first time today will help to terminate the lack of enlightenment, and soon the day will come when science will win a victory over error, justice a victory over injustice and human love a victory over human hatred and ignorance." Only fragments of the film survive today.

Hirschfeld and his followers paid heavily for their work for human rights. In 1920 right wing agitators attacked a meeting while the police stood by and did nothing. In 1921, Hirschfeld was attacked by thugs, who fractured his skull and left him for dead in a Munich street. In 1923, at a homophile rally in Vienna, Nazi youth opened fire, wounding many, though Hirschfeld himself escaped unhurt.

At its peak in 1923, the World League for Sexual Reform claimed 130,000 members. Throughout the 1920s Hirschfeld continued to lecture and campaign, though the mood in Germany was darkening. In March of 1933, Adolf Hitler was elected chancellor. On May 6, 1933, Berlin's libraries were ordered cleansed of "un-German" books, beginning with the library of the Institute for Sexual Science. Ten thousand books from the Institute's library were burned, and Hirschfeld was placed under protective custody. Upon his release, he fled to France, where he attempted to rebuild the Institute. But his health was destroyed, and his death on his sixty-seventh birthday in 1935 spared him from witnessing the horrors inflicted on gays by the Third Reich.

Despite his many positive accomplishments, Hirschfeld was not without his dark side. There are indications that he was the source of accusations of homosexuality against the industrialist Friederich Alfred Krupp appearing in a Berlin newspaper that led the munitions maker to commit suicide in 1902. Hirschfeld tried to blackmail some of the individuals who, in filling out his surveys, had entrusted him with incriminating information about themselves. His various lapses in professional ethics provoked some of his followers, led by Benedict Friedländer, to break with him and form a rival group called The Community of the Special.

Nevertheless, Hirschfeld's work was impressive. Although his "scientific" positions, especially with regard to gays as the "third sex," now seem dated, his ability to organize and institutionalize a campaign for gay civil rights, in the face of severe cultural stigma and hostility, provided the basis for gay rights movements to resurrect themselves after the cataclysms of World War II had irrevocably altered the social and political terrain of much of humanity.

5

The Patrons of the
Stonewall Inn

June 28, 1969

The patrons of the Stonewall Inn had almost certainly never heard of DR. MAGNUS HIRSCHFELD [4], but they were nonetheless taking his legacy, now over a half century old, one dramatic step further. In this entry I pay homage to the incalculable influence these gay men and lesbians—most of them working-class, third-world, effeminate men and butch lesbians, and most of them anonymous to history—have had on the lives of all gay men and lesbians.

The night that has gone down in history as the beginning of

gay liberation actually began shortly before midnight on Friday, June 27, 1969, when police from Manhattan's Sixth Precinct undertook a routine raid on the Stonewall Inn, a gay bar on Christopher Street in the heart of New York's Greenwich Village. Such raids had been common procedure throughout the 1960s Gay bars, often operating without a liquor license, would be shut down, the patrons roughed up, sometimes arrested, their names printed in the newspapers, lives and careers casually ruined. It was simply another of the risks of being gay, and patrons put up with it because, clearly, they had no other recourse if they wanted to socialize.

In June 1969, New York City was in the midst of a mayoral campaign, and the incumbent, John Lindsay, having recently lost his party's primary, was looking for ways to bolster his image as a politician tough on "vice." The Stonewall Inn was the third gay bar to be raided that week. Armed with a search warrant (the bar had no liquor license), the police made their entrance, questioned the patrons, and released them one by one. But instead of fleeing into the night, about two hundred bar patrons, including Puerto Rican drag queens, street kids, and a few butch lesbians, lingered outside the bar. When the police escorted the bartender, bouncer, and three drag queens to the paddy wagon, the crowd responded with jeers. The last patron to be hauled out, a butch lesbian, resisted the police who were trying to take her to a patrol car. All of a sudden, the scene exploded. The crowd hurled cobblestones, bottles, coins, and garbage at the police. When the police retreated back into the bar, the crowd tore a parking meter from the sidewalk and used it as a battering ram on the door. Flames appeared inside. Police reinforcements managed to rescue the beleaguered police, though four were injured. Rioting continued late into the night, with large crowds charging the police, then dispersing into side streets and alleyways to regroup later.

By the next morning, graffiti had blossomed throughout the neighborhood. SUPPORT GAY POWER was emblazoned on the boarded-up window of the Stonewall Inn. That evening the riots resumed, with fires breaking out all over the neighborhood, and over two thousand gay men and lesbians battling four hundred club-wielding riot police. It was, as historian John D'Emilio writes, "the first gay riot in history." Or as the gay Mattachine Society newsletter campily described it: "The Hairpin Drop Heard Round the World."

Lesbian historian Lillian Faderman puts what became known as the Stonewall Rebellion in context by observing, "The complaints of blacks, students, and poor people, which had been raging through much of the 1960s, had finally ignited masses of homosexuals to articulate their own complaints. It is unlikely that a gay and lesbian riot could have occurred at any previous time in history. But if by chance it had occurred earlier, it is unlikely that it would have come to have as much significance as it did in 1969. The gay liberation movement was an idea whose time had come. The Stonewall Rebellion was crucial because it sounded the rally for that movement. It became an emblem of gay and lesbian power. By calling on the dramatic tactic of violent protest that was being used by other oppressed groups, the events at Stonewall implied that homosexuals had as much reason to be disaffected as they. It reminded homosexuals at just the right moment, during this era of general rebellion, that now their voices might be heard among the cries for liberation."

The Stonewall Rebellion had no identifiable "leaders." Rather, it was the collective action of a community of individuals driven by years of oppression to finally take a stand of overt resistance to that oppression. Within a month after Stonewall, the Gay Liberation Front was established—a group as militant and bold as the old Mattachine Society (founded by HARRY HAY [22]) had been cautious and politic. Within a year, dozens of gay liberation groups had formed across the nation. The revolution had begun. The lives of gay men and lesbians would never be the same.

6

Walt Whitman

1819–1892

Walt Whitman was born on May 31, 1819, in West Hills, Long Island. His father was a carpenter who, failing in a farming attempt on Long Island, moved the family to Brooklyn in 1823. From 1825 to 1830, Whitman received his only formal schooling. After that he apprenticed himself to the printing trade for four years. The succession of odd jobs he held over the next twenty years reads like a catalog from one of his poems: teacher, editor of several newspapers, printer, carpenter, real estate speculator, stationery-store owner. In his spare time he read widely and was a passionate theater- and operagoer. He also walked, endlessly, the streets of Manhattan and Brooklyn, encountering young men and meticulously cataloging their names and attributes in his notebooks. In these same notebooks he recorded other observations that gradually coalesced into a book of poems, which he published in 1855 as *Leaves of Grass*. The rest of his life would be spent revising and expanding this work through eight editions, till the vast final version was published in 1892. In his preface to the first edition of the poems he indicated the scope of his intentions by declaring: "The Americans of all nations at any time upon the earth have probably the fullest poetical nature. The United States themselves are essentially the greatest poem."

Although Ralph Waldo Emerson called the first edition of *Leaves of Grass* "the most extraordinary piece of wit and wisdom" America had yet produced, Whitman had to wait years before widespread public recognition came.

The first edition of *Leaves of Grass* celebrated the body and sex as beautiful: in the third edition, published in 1860, Whitman grouped poems of overtly homosexual desire in a section called "Calamus." The following is characteristic of the luminous eroticism of these poems.

A Glimpse

A glimpse through an interstice caught,
Of a crowd of workmen and drivers in a bar-room around the stove late of a
    winter night, and I remark'd seated in a corner,
Of a youth who loves me, and whom I love, silently approaching and seating
    himself near, that he may hold me by the hand,
A long while amid the noises of coming and going, of drinking and oath and
    smutty jest,
There we two, content, happy in being together, speaking little, perhaps not
    a word.

As Whitman admits elsewhere in the "Calamus" section of *Leaves of Grass:*

Here the frailest leaves of me and yet my strongest lasting,
Here I shade and hide my thoughts, I myself do not expose them,
And yet they expose me more than all my other poems.

During the Civil War, Whitman worked as a volunteer nurse in army hospitals in Washington, D. C. The war's profound effect on Whitman is achingly evoked in the "Drumtaps" poems from *Leaves of Grass,* and his grief over the assassination of President Abraham Lincoln led to the great elegy "When Lilacs Last in the Dooryard Bloom'd."

Having come to public attention for his hospital work, Whitman was made a clerk in the Indian Department in 1865, but was dismissed from his job six months later by Secretary of the Interior James Harlan, who had read Whitman's poems and considered them indecent. Shortly afterward, Whitman met an eighteen-year-old Irish Southerner named Peter Doyle. An ex-prisoner of war, Doyle worked as a horse-car conductor in Washington. In later years he recalled their first encounter: "Walt had his blanket—it was thrown around his shoulder—he seemed like an old sea captain. He was the only passenger, it was a lonely night, so I thought I would go in and talk with him. Something in me made me do it and something in him drew me that way. He used to say there was something in me had the same effect on him. Anyway, I went in the car. We were familiar at once—I put my hand on his knee—we understood. He did not get out at the end of the trip—in fact went all the way back with me....From that time on we were the biggest sort of friends."

Whitman's private take on the relationship was more tortured: in his notebooks he referred to his "incessant abnormal perturbation" about Doyle. Under the rubric of the contemporary phrenological term for male love—*adhesiveness*—he admonished himself: "Depress the adhesive nature   It is in excess—making life a torment   All this diseased, feverish disproportionate *adhesiveness.*"

In 1873, Whitman had a stroke that partially paralyzed him. Leaving Doyle behind, he moved to Camden, New Jersey, to recover at his brother's house. In a Camden print shop he met an eighteen-year-old boy named Harry Stafford, who took Whitman to meet his parents. Soon Whitman was living with the Staffords, often for weeks at a time, and afterward claimed that he owed not only his recovery from the effects of his stroke but his very life to Harry. He bought the boy clothes, gave him what amounted to a wedding ring, and when the two took a trip to Esopus, New York, to visit the naturalist John Burroughs, Whitman wrote ahead to explain, "My nephew and I when travelling always share the same room together and the same bed." Burroughs later complained in his journal, "Can't get them up to breakfast in time."

Their relationship foundered, however. Biographer Phillip Callow writes, "[Harry] could never figure out what Whitman wanted of him, whether the man was a father or mother, a steadfast pal, or a potential husband dreaming of marriage. In fact, Whitman was all these and more, reinventing a social bond that Christianity had lost, dodging in and out of identities, forever concealed, always on the point of revealing himself." Frustrated, Harry wrote Whitman: "If I go up to my room I always come down feeling worse than I do when I go up, for the first thing I see is your picture, and when I come down in the sitting room there hangs the same, and whenever I do anything, or say anything, the picture seems to me is always looking at me."

Whitman, ever wary of adhesiveness, slowly disengaged himself from the boy.

By 1879, his health had recovered to the extent that he was able to make a trip to the American West. In 1884 the financial success of the Philadelphia edition of *Leaves of Grass* enabled the poet to purchase a house of his own in Camden. Another stroke came in 1888, though Whitman continued to revise *Leaves of Grass:* "garrulous," as he said, "to the very last."

He died on March 26, 1892, in Camden, New Jersey.

One of the greatest American poets, Whitman's open treatment of homoerotic desire exercised a profound influence on such pioneering gay writers of his own time as EDWARD CARPENTER [9] and J.A. SYMONDS [10] (who wrote *Whitman: A Study* the year after Whitman's death). Carpenter visited Whitman in 1877, and Symonds and Whitman corresponded, though when Symonds asked Whitman about the homosexual imagery in the "Calamus" poems, Whitman wrote back—perhaps disingenuously—that such questions "quite daze me" and disavowed the possibility in them of what he termed "morbid inferences."

Whatever Whitman may have thought was going on in his "Calamus" poems, they were nonetheless indelibly construed as anthems in the developing gay self-awareness in the late nineteenth and early twentieth century. By 1922, Carpenter could make the bold claim : "In the case of Whitman—united as he was by most intimate ties to one or more men-friends—we see already the emergence of a new organic inspiration and a new power of life. His poems radiate this power in all directions. Thousands of people date from their first reading of them *a new era in their lives....* How *far* this process may go we hardly yet know, but that it is one of the factors of future evolution we hardly doubt. I mean that the loves of men towards each other—and similarly the loves of women for each other—may become factors of future human evolution just as necessary and well-recognized as the ordinary loves which lead to the...propagation of the race."

Whitman was an enormously influential figure for the early homosexual rights movement. His poems galvanized a latent gay sensibility into the beginnings of an identity, and his persona projected a robust and compelling sexual presence. He was, in a sense, our first modern gay author—that is, someone read by an audience of homosexuals who felt that they were being addressed by his work, and that they were entering into a kind of community in the process of reading him. Whitman created a language of gay desire, he gave voice to the love that dare not speak its name even if he did not go so far as to name it himself. That his influence continues to our own day can be seen in the debt owed him by such important twentieth century gay poets as Hart Crane, Federico Garcia Lorca and ALLEN GINSBERG [67], whose vibrantly melancholy "Walt Whitman in the Supermarket" is one of the most often anthologized modern American poems.

7

Gertrude Stein

1874–1946

Gertrude Stein was born on February 3, 1874, in Allegheny, Pennsylvania. After spending her infancy in Vienna and Paris, she grew up in Oakland, California, where her father made a fortune in street railways and real estate. At Radcliffe College, she studied psychology with the philosopher William James. After graduating in 1897, she attended Johns Hopkins University in Baltimore, Maryland, in order to study medicine, but soon decided that her interests lay with literature instead. While at Hopkins, an affair with a woman named May Bookstaver became the inspiration for Stein's novel *Q.E.D.*, her only explicit treatment of lesbian themes. It was a book she never allowed to be published in her lifetime.

In 1903, Stein and her brother Leo moved to Paris, where they shared an apartment until 1912. Leo Stein became an art critic of some note, and together he and his sister collected important works of cubist art, as well as cubist artists. Their apartment became a gathering place for painters like Pablo Picasso, Henri Matisse, and Georges Braque. Stein was the grande dame of this celebrated salon, and her remarks carried enormous weight. Reputations were said to be made or broken on the basis of her offhand comments. The concerns and techniques of the painters she befriended influenced Stein's own writing, especially its use of repetition, fragmentation, and stark simplicity folded over onto itself into concatenations of great complexity. Her first book, *Three Lives*, a study of three working-class women, was published in 1909.

In 1905, an old friend from Baltimore named Etta Cone visited Paris and began an affair with Stein. In the course of their relationship, she came to share the Steins' enthusiasm for modern art, and when she returned to the United States, she and her sister Claribel relied on the Steins' advice to build one of the most important early collections of modern art in America.

In 1907, Stein met Alice B. Toklas (1877–1967), who would become her lifetime companion, and with whom she lived after 1912. Their apartment at 27 rue de Fleurus became the site of the most famous literary salon in Paris and attracted such expatriate American writers as Sherwood Anderson, F. Scott Fitzgerald, and Ernest Hemingway, writers about whom Stein coined her famous phrase "the lost generation."

By the late 1920s, Stein and Toklas were dividing their time between Paris and a country house in Bilignin. The 1930s saw Stein's collaboration with homosexual composer Virgil Thompson on the opera *Four Saints in Three Acts*, based on the life of SUSAN B. ANTHONY [12]. The work's stage success paved the way for a triumphant American lecture tour in 1934–35. The resulting publicity made Stein one of the most famous, if least read, writers in the United States.

Stein and Toklas survived the German occupation of France during World War II at their country house. After the war, Stein befriended many young American soldiers and wrote about them in *Brewsie and Willie* (1949). She died of cancer in Paris on July 27, 1946.

Stein's work was always controversial. Though *The Auto-*

biography of Alice B. Toklas (1933) was written in an accessible style, much of her major work, like *Tender Buttons* (1914) and *The Making of Americans* (1906–8, published 1925), is difficult. Some critics saw in her work a linguistic equivalent of cubism; others saw charlatanism. The Hearst Press once asked in exasperation, "Is Gertrude Stein not Gertrude Stein but somebody else living and talking in the same body?" More recent commentators have seen in her elliptical language—especially in pieces like "Lifting Belly" and *Tender Buttons*— the desire to unleash a lesbian tongue.

Stein is influential not so much for her work or even for her regal Paris salon—though these were certainly influential—as for her uncompromising lesbian persona. At a time when most lesbian lives were still cloaked in silence and secrecy, Gertrude Stein and Alice B. Toklas were the most famous lesbian couple in the world. Theirs was the quintessential butch-femme relationship, Stein the husband and Toklas the wife. Toklas cooked and maintained the household while Stein wrote. As Stein has Toklas say in *The Autobiography of Alice B. Toklas*, "The geniuses came and talked to Gertrude Stein and the wives sat with me." The delicious "Love Song of Alice B." from "A Sonatina Followed by Another" (1921) wonderfully catches the musicality of Stein's language, as well as something of the tone and texture of this radiant and long-lived lesbian relationship.

> I caught sight of a splendid Misses. She had handkerchiefs and kisses. She had eyes and yellow shoes she had everything to choose and she chose me. In passing through France she wore a Chinese hat and so did I. In looking at the sun she read a map. And so did I. In eating fish and pork she just grew fat. And so did I. In loving a blue sea she had a pain. And so did I. In loving me she of necessity thought first. And so did I. How prettily we swim. Not in water. Not on land. But in love. How often do we need trees and hills. Not often. And how often do we need birds. Not often. And how often do we need wishes. Not often. And how often do we need glasses not often. We drink wine and we make, well we have not made it yet. How often do we need 'a kiss. Very often and we add when tenderness overwhelms us we speedily eat veal. And what else, ham and a little pork and raw artichokes and ripe olives and

chester cheese and cakes and caramels and all the melon. We still have a great deal of it left. I wonder where it is. Conserved melon. Let me offer it to you.

Gertrude Stein's prominent place in this ranking reflects my sense that no one else has personified lesbian identity so clearly as she. When asked to name a famous lesbian, Stein's is the name that invariably comes to people's minds. Though few have read her work or know much about her personal life besides the fact of Alice B. Toklas, Gertrude Stein nonetheless occupies a central and singular place in our imaginations—the grande dame of lesbianism in our century.

8

Karl Heinrich Ulrichs

1825–1895

Karl Heinrich Ulrichs was born on August 28, 1825, in Aurich, in the kingdom of Hanover. His father was a civil architect, and his mother came from a family of Lutheran ministers. From 1844 to 1847 he studied law, first at the University of Göttingen and then at the University of Berlin, and afterward became a junior attorney in the Hanoverian civil service. He left that position, however, in 1854, to work as a freelance journalist and, a few years later, a private secretary for a representative to the German Confederation in Frankfurt am Main. For the remainder of his life he earned his living from his writing.

The sexologist Henry Havelock Ellis, writing at the turn of the century, characterized Ulrichs as "a man of most brilliant ability...his knowledge is said to have been of almost universal extent; he was not only well versed in his own special subjects of jurisprudence and theology, but in many branches of natural science, as well as archaeology; he was also regarded by many as the best Latinist of his time."

Beginning in 1864, under the pseudonym Numa Numantius, Ulrichs wrote a series of five booklets called "Researches into the Riddle of Love Between Men" in which he began to develop a theory of homosexuality. Men who love men, he argued, consist of a female soul trapped in a male body. They are neither male nor female in the conventional sense, but rather a third sex, which he called urning—or uranian—after the famous myth in Plato's *Symposium* in which Pausanias calls love between men "the beautiful love, the Heavenly love, the love belonging to the Heavenly Muse Urania."

Summarizing Ulrichs's theories in his 1908 book, *The Intermediate Sex*, EDWARD CARPENTER [9] characterized the male uranian as "a man who, while possessing thoroughly masculine powers of mind and body, combines with them the tenderer and more emotional soul-nature of the woman—and sometimes to a remarkable degree....[E]motionally they are extremely complex, tender, sensitive, pitiful and loving, 'full of storm and stress, of ferment and fluctuation' of the heart; the logical faculty may or may not, in their case, be well-developed, but intuition is always strong; like women they read characters at a glance, and know, without knowing how, what is passing in the minds of others; for nursing and waiting on the needs of others they have often a peculiar gift; at the bottom lies the artist-nature, with the artist's sensibility and perception. Such an one is often a dreamer, of brooding, reserved habits, often a musician, or a man of culture, courted in society, which nevertheless does not understand him."

As for the female uranian, "the inner nature is to a great extent masculine; a temperament active, brave, originative, somewhat decisive, not too emotional; fond of outdoor life, of games and sports, of science, politics, or even business; good at organization, and well-pleased with positions of responsibility, sometimes making an excellent and generous leader. Such a woman, it is easily seen, from her special combination of qualities, is often fitted for remarkable work, in professional life, or as manageress of institutions, or even as ruler of a country....Many a Santa Clara, or abbess-founder of religious houses, has probably been a woman of this type; and in all times such women—not being bound to men by the ordinary ties—have been able to work the more freely for the interests of their sex, a cause to which their own temperament impels them to devote themselves *con amore*."

According to Ulrichs, uranianism was congenital: hence, uranians should be considered neither unnatural nor criminal.

In 1865, in a burst of optimism, Ulrichs founded the Uranian Union to advance the cause of uranians—but the next year Prussia invaded, and he was jailed until 1867. On his release, he fled to Munich, where on August 28, 1867, at a Congress of German Jurists, he did what no one had ever done before. Speaking as a self-acknowledged homosexual—a uranian—he urged the repeal of antihomosexual laws. His speech was greeted with instant hostility, and he was shouted down by outraged jurists. Even had they been receptive, it would have made little difference because with German unification in 1871 the harsh Prussian antihomosexual statute known as Paragraph 175 was extended by the Reichstag to cover the whole of Germany.

Ulrichs exiled himself to Italy in 1880, settling first in Naples, and later at Aquila in the Abruzzi, where he published a Latin journal. JOHN ADDINGTON SYMONDS [10], who visited Ulrichs in 1891, wrote of him, "Ulrichs is *chrysostomos* to the last degree, sweet, noble, a true gentleman and man of genius. He must have been at one time a man of singular personal distinction, so finely cut are his features, and so grand the lines of his skull."

Karl Heinrich Ulrichs died in Aquila on July 4, 1895.

In the latter part of the nineteenth century, Ulrichs's theories were overshadowed by the work of the sexologist Richard von Krafft-Ebing, whose 1886 *Psychopathia Sexualis* outlined a degeneration theory of homosexuality that would greatly influence Sigmund Freud, among others. Whereas Ulrichs's model had posited the naturalness of the "third sex" in the scheme of things, Krafft-Ebing's work marked the homosexual as pathological in nature, though Krafft-Ebing was not without sympathy for the individual homosexual. Ulrichs's work was revived by MAGNUS HIRSCHFELD [4], who found in Ulrichs's "third sex" a way to argue for the decriminalization of homosexuality.

This notion of the third sex may strike us as impossibly quaint, even bizarre, but historically it was an important way of conceptualizing homosexuals in that it allowed an argument to be made that homosexual traits were innate and inborn, that gay identity was as fixed and "normal" as heterosexual identity. If this could be agreed on, then there could be no justification for criminalizing homosexuality. Ulrichs's work provided a very important first step in the long road toward the acceptance of gay existence. He has been called, justifiably, "the grandfather of the gay liberation movement," and it is as such that he earns his place high in this ranking.

9

Edward Carpenter

1844–1929

Edward Carpenter was born on August 29, 1844, in Brighton, Sussex, England. He entered Cambridge divinity school in 1864 and in that same year had his first homosexual experiences, with other students there. He was elected fellow in 1868, and in 1870 he was ordained. Three years later, however, having lost his faith, he resigned from the Church of England to become a traveling lecturer in the industrial towns of northern England. There he promoted the newly established university extension movement, whose purpose was to serve people unable to attend regular university. His experiences in this movement shifted his political views toward socialism, and he became an advocate of William

Morris's anti-industrial arts-and-crafts movement.

Carpenter's reading of the poems of WALT WHITMAN [6], with their passionate evocations of love between men, changed his life, and in 1874 he wrote the first of many letters to Whitman: "Yesterday there came (to mend my door) a young workman with the old divine light in his eyes…and perhaps, more than all, he has made me write to you. Because you have, as it were, given me a ground for the love of men I thank you continually in my heart. (—And others thank you though they do not say so.) For you have made men to be not ashamed of the noblest instinct of their nature. Women are beautiful; but, to some, there is that which passes the love of women."

In 1877 and again in 1884, Carpenter visited the United States and met with Whitman, who was impressed by this young man: "a thoroughly wholesome man," Whitman averred, "alive, clean, from head to foot." Later Whitman would tell a friend, "The best of Carpenter is in his humanity: he manages to stay with people: he was a university man, yet managed to save himself in time."

Carpenter's long poem *Democracy* (1883; expanded in 1905) was greatly influenced by the language and ideals of Whitman's poetry and won him a following. He became a leading advocate of the New Thought, an amalgam of Whitman, William Morris, Tolstoy, and Hinduism (spurred on by a visit to India and Ceylon in 1890). The New Thought explicitly rejected Victorian commercialism, the futility of its social conventions and the hypocrisy of its religion, its denial of the human body and stultifying class divisions, its "cruel barring of women from every natural and useful expression of their lives."

With some inheritance money, Carpenter bought a farm in Millthorpe, near Sheffield, in 1883, where he lived with his working-class lover Albert Fearnehough and Fearnehough's wife. The relationship had a utopian agenda: Carpenter firmly believed that romancing across class lines could break down the class barriers that plagued England and lead to a society animated by the spirit of cooperation rather than competition. Carpenter lived simply, abstaining from meat and alcohol, dressing casually (he popularized the wearing of sandals), raising vegetables in his market garden, undertaking what he called an "exfoliation"—the shedding of conventional customs in order to create a space for the New Life.

Fearnehough was later replaced by a succession of young working-class friends until 1891, when a chance meeting in a railway carriage with a young man from the slums of Sheffield named George Merrill resulted in a relationship that lasted until Merrill's death in 1928. During those thirty years, the house at Millthorpe became a place of pilgrimage for homosexuals such as E. M. FORSTER [58], who came seeking guidance from Carpenter.

Carpenter wrote copiously on a variety of subjects, and his books, widely translated in their time, include *England's Ideal* (1887), *Civilization: Its Cause and Cure* (1889), *Days With Walt Whitman* (1906), and his autobiography, *My Days and Dreams* (1916). He also composed music, including the famous labor song "England, Arise."

Carpenter's most influential work was on the subject of homosexuality, especially *Love's Coming-of-Age* (1896) and *The Intermediate Sex* (1908). This latter volume introduced the notion of what Carpenter called "homogenic love" (he preferred that term to the barbarous Greek-Latin mutant *homosexual*). Influenced by the urning theories of KARL HEINRICH ULRICHS [8], as well as by the figures of the berdache and shaman from Native American cultures (see WE'WHA [53]), Carpenter believed that people of the intermediate sex, because of their doubleness, "have a special work to do as reconcilers and interpreters of the two sexes to each other." Homogenic love, as Carpenter celebrated it, was a spiritualized and altruistic comrade attachment that owed much in conception to ancient Greek platonic love, with its sublimation of passion into finer emotions, as well as to Whitman's "fervid comradeship."

In his more visionary moments, Carpenter saw the intermediate sex as a further stage in human evolution. "Before the facts of Nature," he wrote, "we have to preserve a certain humility and reverence.... Though these gradations of human type have always, and among all peoples, been more or less known and recognized, yet their frequency today...may be the indication of some important change actually in progress. We do *not* know, in fact, what possible evolutions are to come, or what new forms, of permanent place and value, are being already differentiated from the surrounding mass of humanity. It may be that, as at some past period of evolution the worker-bee was without doubt differentiated from the two ordinary bee-sexes, so at the present time certain new types of human kind may be emerging, which will have an important part to play in the societies of the future—even though for the moment their appearance is attended by a good deal of confusion and misapprehension."

Carpenter's writings greatly influenced the sexologist Henry Havelock Ellis and the novelist D. H. Lawrence, among others.

In 1902, to encourage a positive sense of gay self-identity in the aftermath of the trial of OSCAR WILDE [3], Carpenter edited *Ioläus*, probably the first anthology of gay writing in English: "The bugger's bible," as one critic derisively anointed it.

A man of great physical beauty, Carpenter's personality was, by all accounts, magnetic. His early biographer, Edward Lewis, writing in 1915, waxed rhapsodic in ways that tell us much about early notions of the intermediate sex: "Carpenter is a holy man, a natural saint. He has all the inward immovableness and courage of his type, arrayed in a rare and loveable gentleness. I do not think I am mistaken in saying that he himself is one of the children of Uranus....Masculinity and femininity are at equipoise in him. He might be said to be a man-woman consciousness....He gives me the impression of a delicately-balanced organism in a state of perfect equilibrium....He has the broad intellectual sweep of the masculine mind, and yet is a woman in his sense of the details. He has the man's profound appreciation of order, and that barbaric elemental soul-quality which is characteristically the woman's."

Edward Carpenter died on June 28, 1929, at Guildford, Surrey.

A visionary, Carpenter transcended the limitations of his culture to imagine remarkable possibilities in the world for gay men and lesbians—as knowers, healers, pioneers. His work, though almost a hundred years old now, still seems bracingly modern, and should be more widely read. He lived his life with a grace and integrity that irrevocably changed the lives of men like J.A. SYMONDS [10] and E.M. FORSTER [58] who came in contact with him. On the basis of his pathbreaking writings and his charismatic personality, I rank him as one of the most influential early pioneers of the homosexual rights movement.

10

John Addington Symonds

1840–1893

John Addington Symonds was born on October 5, 1840, in Clifton near Bristol, Gloucestershire, England. His father was one of the most eminent physicians of his day. His mother died when he was four, and he was thereafter raised by his sisters and aunts. From a very early age he realized that he was homosexual: one of his recurrent childhood dreams found him in a room surrounded by naked sailors.

In 1854 he entered the prestigious Harrow School, where he was revolted by the rampant homosexual behavior of the boys around him. As he wrote in his extraordinary *Memoirs*, which were suppressed by his literary executor and unpublished until 1984, "every boy of good looks had a female name, and was recognized either as a public prostitute or as some bigger fellow's 'bitch.' *Bitch* was the word in common usage to indicate a boy who yielded his person to a lover. The talk in the dormitories and the studies was incredibly obscene. Here and there one could not avoid seeing acts of onanism, mutual masturbation, the sports of naked boys in bed together. There was no refinement, no sentiment, no passion; nothing but animal lust in these occurrences." Symonds got his peculiar revenge, however. In 1858 he discovered that Dr. Vaughn, the headmaster, had begun an affair with one of the boys. With the aid of his father, Symonds made public the accusation and succeeded in getting Vaughn dismissed. The act appalled Symonds's friends, who broke off their relations with him, and the memory of the despicable episode troubled Symonds for the rest of his life.

His last year at Harrow, Symonds fell deeply in love with Willie Dyer, a choirboy three years younger than himself. It was from moment of their first meeting, on April 10, 1858, that Symonds dated the birth of his real self. When his father discovered the nature of his affection for Dyer, he advised Symonds to withdraw from the intimacy. Recognizing that his love did indeed resemble that of the ruined Dr. Vaughn, Symonds ended the relationship, at least publicly. The two continued to see one another in secret for some time thereafter.

In the fall of 1858, Symonds entered Balliol College, Oxford, where he fell in love with another choirboy, Alfred Brooke, whom he loved from afar and to whom he addressed much bad poetry. After graduating with a first-class in litterae humaniores in 1862, he was elected to an open fellowship at Magdalen College ("I had long wished to enter that establishment on the foundation— attracted by its medieval beauty, its solemn chapel and the choiring voices of singing boys. These were not perhaps the best reasons..."). While at Magdalen, Symonds suffered various symptoms of "neurosis," and in 1863 he traveled to Switzerland for a cure. There he met Catherine North, whom he married the following year in the hopes that he could be cured of his homosexual tendencies: "I thought that by honest endeavor I could divert my passions from the burning channel in which they flowed for Alfred Brooke, and lead them gently to follow a normal course toward women. I neglected the fact that poetry and power of expression and the visionary pomp of dreams awoke in me only beneath the touch of the male genius." Symonds and North nevertheless had three daughters.

Symonds's ill-health continued, as did his passion for the

male genius. By 1869, we find him writing in his journal about one Norman, a boy in the sixth form at Clifton College, where Symonds was lecturing: "As he read, I leaned on his shoulder, and his ear tip touched my forehead, and I felt his voice vibrate in his lungs, and I could see the subtle smile upon his lips....O Love, why hast thou brought me to this barren shore again?" Symonds' *Memoirs* record in achingly lyric detail the exquisite course of the relationship.

In 1877, a severe lung hemorrhage sent Symonds to Davos in Switzerland, and in 1880 he settled there permanently in order to treat his tuberculosis. There he produced the great work for which he was chiefly known during the nineteenth century, a seven-volume aesthetic and cultural history called *The Renaissance in Italy*. He also wrote studies of Shelley (1879), Ben Jonson (1886), MICHELANGELO [17] (1893), and WALT WHITMAN [6] (1893), with whom he corresponded. He also published the first English translation of *The Sonnets of Michael Angelo Buonarroti and Tommaso Camparrella* (1878).

For our purposes, Symonds's most important contributions were his pamphlets *A Problem in Greek Ethics* (1871, one hundred copies privately printed in 1883) and *A Problem in Modern Ethics* (privately printed in 1891). The first of these essays surveyed the instances of homosexuality in ancient Greek literature, while the second looked at the repression of homosexuality in the Christian era. Symonds exposed the limitations of current "scientific" degeneracy theories of homosexuality by confronting them with the observation that, far from being a disease caused by "hereditary neuropathy complicated with onanism" (as the nineteenth-century sexologists thought), "what the Greeks called *paiderastia*, or boy-love, was a phenomenon of one of the most highly organized and nobly active nations." He also challenged the confusion of male homosexuality with effeminacy, and the notion that homosexuals "recruit" or "prey on" youth.

"What has to be faced," Symonds argued, "is that a certain type of passion flourished under the light of day and bore good fruits for society in Hellas; that the same type of passion flourishes in the shade and is the source of misery and shame in Europe. The passion has not altered; but the way of regarding it morally and legally is changed." This argument was a vital step in refocusing the study of homosexuality away from the narrow consideration of the so-called pathological individual toward the broader issue of the social construction of sexuality.

During the last years of his life, Symonds spent considerable time and energy lobbying doctors, lawyers, and politicians to overturn the Labouchere Amendment of 1885, which stipulated two years of hard labor for "acts of public indecency between males" (the law under which OSCAR WILDE [3] would be charged and convicted). He also assembled, with the sexologist Havelock Ellis, a large number of homosexual case histories, including his own, for the volume *Sexual Inversion*. When the work appeared in 1897, after Symonds's death, his alarmed literary executor bought up all the copies he could and persuaded Ellis to drop Symonds's name from the title of any subsequent edition.

Symonds's final years at Davos were marked by an increasing self-acceptance of his homosexuality, and by the therapeutic pleasure that he took in young Swiss peasants like Christian Buol, and in Angelo Fusato and the other gondoliers of Venice, a city he visited often. His wife gamely put up with his "temperament," though she didn't always like the young men who were to be found about the house. As Symonds noted in his own case study for *Sexual Inversion*, "when A. had once begun to indulge his inborn homosexual instincts, he rapidly recovered his health. The neurotic disturbances subsided; the phthisis—which had progressed as far as profuse hemorrhage and formation of cavity—was arrested."

John Addington Symonds died on April 19, 1893, in Rome.

Along with the previous entry, EDWARD CARPENTER [9], J. A. Symonds stood at the forefront of the early British homosexual rights movement. He was one of the first to ask, who are we, where have we come from, what is our history? His privately circulated essays on homosexuality dispelled misguided notions, provided a historical and cultural context for the discussion of the subject and greatly influenced pioneering sexologists such as Havelock Ellis and MAGNUS HIRSCHFELD [4]. An indefatigable correspondent (see, for example, his letters to WALT WHITMAN [6]), Symonds helped establish a fledgling international network of intellectuals who were interested in addressing homosexual issues—the first tentative steps toward gay/lesbian political organization. John Addington Symonds's invaluable role as a formative figure in the development of modern homosexual consciousness leads me to rank him at number ten in terms of his overall influence on our history.

11

Mary Wollstonecraft

1759–1797

In the standard encyclopedias, Mary Wollstonecraft's biography runs something like this. She was born on April 27, 1759, near London. Her mother came from a respectable Irish family. Her father was a weaver who used his modest inheritance to set himself up as a gentleman farmer. His ensuing economic ruin led him to fits of drunkenness and rage, and Wollstonecraft remembered standing watch "whole nights at their chamber door" to protect her mother from her father's abuse.

To help support the family, Wollstonecraft was forced to work at an early age as a schoolteacher and governess. Beginning in 1787 she worked in London for the publisher James Johnson, first as a translator and reader, then later as a reviewer and editorial assistant. The 1787 publication, by Johnson, of her *Thoughts on the Education of Daughters* gained her entry into that group of radical thinkers who met at Johnson's home, including the social philosopher William Godwin, the American revolutionary Thomas Paine, and the poets William Blake and, after 1793, William Wordsworth.

In 1790, in answer to Edmund Burke's conservative *Reflections on the Revolution in France*, she wrote *Vindication of the Rights of Man*, in which she affirmed her belief in liberty and political rights. Her major work appeared in 1792: *A Vindication of the Rights of Woman*. In this pioneering document in the history of women's rights, Wollstonecraft decried the present, degraded state of women. "Women," she wrote, "are not allowed to have sufficient strength of mind to acquire what really deserves the name of virtue." She went on to argue that "till women are more rationally educated, the progress of virtue and improvement in knowledge must receive continual checks." The purpose of this rational education would be "to enable the individual to attain such habits of virtues as will render it independent." In addition to education, Wollstonecraft called for increased opportunities for women in such professions as law and medicine—"why may not women be doctors as well as nurses?" she asked—and also in the political arena. "Women ought," she wrote, articulating a hope that seemed inconceivable in its day, "to have representatives, instead of being arbitrarily governed without having any direct share allowed them in the deliberations of government." Her critique of the status quo was insightful and far-reaching.

In 1792 she traveled to Paris to observe firsthand the French Revolution. After a failed attempt at a relationship with Henry Fuseli, who was married, Wollstonecraft began a liaison with an American adventurer named Gilbert Imlay, who registered her at the U.S. embassy as his wife to protect her, and whose child she bore. When the relationship fell apart in 1793, she attempted suicide. After she returned to London, Johnson published her *An Historical and Moral View of the Origin and Progress of the French Revolution* (1794). In 1796 she began a liaison with William Godwin, whom she had known for years through Johnson's radical circle, and though they both were averse to marriage, they nonetheless undertook that ceremony on March 29, 1797. Wollstonecraft was pregnant at the time, and the following

August bore Godwin a daughter named Mary. Because of the incompetence of the physician in attendance, placenta that remained in her body for several days became gangrenous, and Mary Wollstonecraft died eleven days later, on September 10, 1797. Her daughter Mary grew up to marry the poet Percy Bysshe Shelley and, more important, to write *Frankenstein*.

Such accounts of Wollstonecraft's life manage to conceal (as do the mainstream accounts of so many individuals in this ranking) the primary relationship in her life. In his fascinating *Memoirs of Mary Wollstonecraft* (1798), William Godwin gives a remarkably clear-eyed account of what took place in 1775, when Mary was sixteen: "A connection more memorable originated about this time, between Mary and a person of her own sex, for whom she contracted a friendship so fervent, as for years to have constituted the ruling passion of her mind. The name of this person was Fanny Blood; she was two years older than Mary.... The situation in which Mary was introduced to her, bore a resemblance to the first interview of Werter with Charlotte [alluding to Goethe's romantic novel of tragic love].... Before the interview was concluded, she had taken, in her heart, the vows of an eternal friendship."

In 1782, after the death of her mother (whom she had nursed through her last illness), Wollstonecraft moved in with Blood's family. Financial troubles abounded there, and Wollstonecraft struggled for two years to help alleviate the family's impoverishment. She also spent much effort trying to find a way for her and Fanny to set up house together. As historian Lillian Faderman writes, "Correspondence and memoirs of the period indicate that it was the ambition of many romantic friends to set up households together. Those households would differ from ordinary heterosexual arrangements in that the two women would be always inseparable, always devoted; their relationship would be truly intimate, based on no consideration other than their love for each other." (Faderman adds evidence that this was not the first household with another woman Wollstonecraft had endeavored to set up.)

When Wollstonecraft finally managed to find a place for the two to move to, Blood was reluctant. Wollstonecraft kept wooing her and in 1783 managed to convince Blood to open a school with her. Their first school attempt at Islington failed, but a second attempt at Newington Green succeeded, at least for a while. By this time, however, Blood was sick with tuberculosis, and Wollstonecraft, disillusioned by what Godwin describes as a "morbid softness of temper" in her friend, advised her to accept the marriage proposal of one Hugh Skeys and move to Portugal with him for the good of her health.

In 1785, Wollstonecraft journeyed to Portugal to assist Blood in the birth of her first child. As Godwin records, "her residence in Lisbon was not long. She arrived but a short time before her friend was prematurely delivered, and the event was fatal to both mother and child. Fanny Blood, hitherto the chosen object of Mary's attachment, died on the twenty-ninth of November, 1785."

As if to stress the nature of Wollstonecraft's relationship with Fanny Blood, in later parts of his memoir Godwin couches Wollstonecraft's heterosexual liaison with Imlay in the same terms he used to describe the friendship between the two women: Imlay becomes "the object of her attachment," and Wollstonecraft is, once again, "the female Werter," the unhappy lover in the relationship. Wollstonecraft names her first child Frances, "in remembrance," as Godwin puts it, "of the dear friend of her youth, whose image could never be erased from memory." Indeed, Godwin ruefully locates Wollstonecraft's constitutional unhappiness in "her first youthful passion, her friendship for Fanny, [which] had encountered many disappointments, and, in fine, a melancholy and premature catastrophe." Her aversion to marriage, he understood, came from her desire to hold the memory of Fanny Blood dear.

Wollstonecraft's reputation suffered from the publication of Godwin's memoir, especially from its revelations concerning her affair with Imlay. One contemporary magazine index, under the heading "Prostitution," went so far as to suggest "See Mary Wollstonecraft"! Mid-nineteenth-century feminists avoided her work, but by the end of the century her writings had been rehabilitated. In 1889, when SUSAN B. ANTHONY [12] and Elizabeth Cady Stanton published the first three volumes of their *History of Woman Suffrage*, Wollstonecraft's name stood first in the ranks of earlier feminists to whom they dedicated their work. Today she is regarded as one of the earliest prophets of the movement for women's rights.

Was Mary Wollstonecraft a lesbian in the 1780s? The answer is no; she would almost certainly not have understood what the term meant. No one was a lesbian in those days. She was, however, in a time before modern or present-day lesbians existed, a woman who fervently desired to live with another woman, whose primary emotional relationship was with another woman, and who critiqued with great insight and passion the unjust domination of heterosexual males over women. I have ranked her very high on this list because I believe that women like Mary Wollstonecraft influenced, in powerful and profound ways, the gradual evolution of social conditions that made it possible for lesbians as we know them in the twentieth century—as well as modern women in general—to come into existence. About the sexuality of eighteenth-century women like Mary Wollstonecraft we can never know for certain, though the work of lesbian historians such as Lillian Faderman (whose name will appear with some frequency in these pages) is gradually reclaiming them from the shadows and silence of history.

Who, then, were the lesbians of the eighteenth century? Very probably women a lot like, if not exactly like, Mary Wollstonecraft.

12

Susan B. Anthony

1820–1906

Susan Brownell Anthony was born on February 15, 1820, in Adams, Massachusetts. The daughter of Quaker abolitionist parents, she grew up in a tightly knit household informed by a crusading moral spirit. By the age of three she was able to read and write. When she was six, her family moved to Battensville, New York, where her father opened a cotton mill. She attended first a district school, later a school set up by her father, and finished her education at a boarding school near Philadelphia.

Taking up what was virtually the only profession open to women at the time, she became a teacher at Eunice Kenyon's Quaker academy in New Rochelle, New York. Her life was thrown into anguish and confusion around this time when her sister Guelma decided to marry. Her biographer Kathleen Barry writes: "Susan's loyalty to her sister was a part of her fuller emotional world, which was based on networks of women: her mother, sisters, cousins, and friends. Disrupting any of these relationships would risk emotional havoc for her."

In 1846, Anthony moved to Rochester, New York, to be headmistress of the female department at the Canajoharie Academy. Seeking a wider field for her talents than simply teaching, she became involved in the temperance movement. She was also beginning to formulate her views on the inequality of the sexes. At that time in the United States, there were no legal procedures allowing women the right to own, manage, or inherit property, or to obtain the custody of their children. Indeed, the tenor of the law still echoed the influential English jurist Blackstone, who, writing in the 1760s, had opined that "the very being or legal existence of the woman is suspended during marriage, or at least is incorporated and consolidated into that of the husband." By her early thirties, Anthony had come to the conclusion that until women had equal rights, there could be no hope for social betterment in the United States.

In 1851, Anthony made the acquaintance of Elizabeth Cady Stanton, the women's rights campaigner from nearby Seneca Falls who would become the major influence on Anthony's life, and with whom she would enter into a fifty-year-long personal and political partnership. Barry writes: "Theirs was a friendship of profound loyalty and egalitarian love that neither had known with anyone else and that when mixed with their political visions and daring actions, ultimately made them one of the great couples of nineteenth century America." Stanton herself described their working relationship thus: "In writing we did better work together than either could alone. While she is slow and analytical in composition, I am rapid and synthetic. I am the better writer, she the better critic. She supplied the facts and statistics, I the philosophy and rhetoric, and together we have made arguments that have stood unshaken by the storms of thirty long years; arguments that no man has answered." Anthony called their relationship "a natural union of head and heart."

Barry speculates, "Because she was unmarried, Anthony had a particular vantage point from which to consider sexuality and its role in the exploitation of women. She first began to comprehend the power of sexual surrender in the subordination of women when her married sisters turned away from her and rejected her sisterly society. Stanton had transcended this domination politically and theoretically, but not personally—at least not enough to keep her marriage from standing in the way of her love for Susan....As Anthony was neither a masochist nor unlovable, she would never have chosen to live without sex if she had believed that she could experience it as fulfillment instead of degradation. What we do not know is to what extent she may have wanted to experience this human fulfillment in sexual relations with Stanton, who being tied to her husband made it a living impossibility for Susan."

Joining with Stanton and Amelia Bloomer in their campaign for women's rights, for a time Anthony wore what was known as the bloomer costume—a skirt and loose trousers—to protest restrictive women's clothing.

Finding herself rebuffed by male temperance leaders, Anthony formed, in 1852, the Women's State Temperance Society of New York. Stanton became its first president. After 1854, Anthony became increasingly active in the cause of abolition, though she alienated some of her abolitionist allies by asserting the rights of black people to equal citizenship (many abolitionists at the time favored freeing the slaves in order to send them back to Africa). The Civil War put the struggle for women's rights on hold, but once the war was over, Anthony resumed her campaign, first in New York, then across the country, for the right of women to control their own property, to have guardianship of their children, and to divorce. When the Fourteenth Amendment in 1868 guaranteed the right of all males to vote, she led an unsuccessful attempt to include women.

From 1868 to 1870, she and Stanton published *The Revolution*, a New York weekly devoted to the cause of woman suffrage.

During all this time, Stanton was struggling with her marriage and family (she had borne eight children in all), and Anthony was feeling the familiar old pangs of betrayal. When two of her closest associates in the women's rights movement, Lucy Stone and Antoinette Brown, two women who had been roommates and possibly lovers at Oberlin College, both eventually got

married, Anthony was furious. "I have *very weak* moments," she
confided to Stanton, "and long to lay my weary head somewhere
and nestle my full soul close to that of another in full sympathy. I
sometimes fear that I too shall faint by the wayside, and drop out
of the ranks of the faithful few."

Some bit of full sympathy may have come her way in 1868,
when she met Anna Dickinson, a popular lecturer for women's
rights some twenty years her junior. Characterizing the relationship as "intense, loving, erotically suffused," historian Jonathan
Katz quotes the following intriguing bit from among four letters
from Anthony to Dickinson that have survived:

My Dicky Darling,

... Now when are you coming to New York—Do
let it be soon—then do let me see the child—I have
plain quarters—at 44 Bond St—*double bed*—and big
enough & good enough to take you *in*—So come &
see me—or let me know & I'll meet you...any place
you shall say—and let me see you—I do so long for
the scolding & pinched ears & every thing I know
awaits me—

I have a budget full to say to you—what worlds
of experience since I last snuggled the wee child in
my long arms—Well let me know when & where I am
to see you—In an awful hurry—Your loving Friend

Susan

In 1872, Anthony registered and voted in Rochester to test
the legality of women's exclusion from suffrage. When arrested,
tried, and fined, she refused to pay on moral grounds. The trial
garnered much publicity for her cause. From 1892 to 1900 she
served as president of the North American Woman Suffrage
Association. She helped organize the New York Working Women's
Association, which fought for equal pay for women. Between 1881
and 1900 she helped compile, along with Stanton and Matilda
Joslyn Gage, the first four volumes of a *History of Woman Suffrage*
(which was dedicated to, first among the rest, MARY
WOLLSTONECRAFT [11]).

Stanton's death in 1902 left Anthony bereft, and she wrote
numerous articles for magazines and newspapers in which she

extolled Stanton's contributions to the public good. Susan B. Anthony herself died on March 13, 1906, in Rochester, New York. Fourteen years after her death, in 1920, the Nineteenth Amendment to the Constitution—the so-called Anthony Amendment—granted women full suffrage.

Susan B. Anthony was one of the great pioneers of women's rights in the United States. It is impossible to overestimate the influence her work has had on all our lives. One of the important consequences of the political and economic enfranchisement of women that Anthony fought to bring about was the increasing ability of women to choose their own lives, a situation that made the modern lesbian economically and socially possible. In her own life and times, Susan B. Anthony embodied as a revolutionary act the autonomy and independence that we tend to take for granted.

13

Virginia Woolf

1882–1941

Virginia Adeline Woolf (née Stephen) was born on January 25, 1882, in London, England. Her father was the eminent Victorian writer and critic Sir Leslie Stephen, and a moving portrait of both her parents may be found in the characters of Mr. and Mrs. Ramsey in Woolf's 1927 masterpiece, *To the Lighthouse*. The death of her mother in 1895 shattered the thirteen-year-old, and she suffered a mental breakdown. She was thereafter educated at home by her father and given "the free run of a large and unexpurgated library." Unlike her brothers, she did not attend university. When her father died in 1904, Virginia moved with her older sister, Vanessa, and brothers Adrian and Thoby from the fashionable Kensington district where they had grown up to a house in Gordon Square in Bloomsbury, a bohemian section of London. By 1905, she was doing regular review work for the *Times Literary Supplement*. The death of her brother Thoby in 1906 came as a devastating blow and would later provide the wound at the center of her novel *The Waves*.

In 1907, after Vanessa married the art critic Clive Bell, Virginia and Adrian moved to Fitzroy Square, also in Bloomsbury. It was here that the so-called Bloomsbury Group began meeting. A loose collection of like-minded individuals, most of whom were homosexual, the Group had originally begun with friendships Thoby had started at Cambridge. Influenced by the philosopher G. E. Moore, they held that the ideals of friendship, love, and affection were paramount, and that these could only flourish where frankness and freedom from prudery prevailed. Social convention was to be replaced by the rigors of personal morality and responsibility. The Group regarded communication as the supreme goal—in the words of the novelist E. M. FORSTER [58], "Only connect." In addition to Forster, the Group included economist John Maynard Keynes, biographer and essayist Lytton Strachey, painter Duncan Grant, and art critics Roger Fry and Clive Bell.

In 1912, after having warned him that she found the idea of sex with a man distasteful, Virginia married Leonard Woolf, a Cambridge graduate recently returned from a judgeship in Ceylon. Theirs was a marriage of mutual respect and emotional support in which sexual relations were minimal. Together they established the Hogarth Press, which in addition to publishing Virginia Woolf's novels also published important writers such as Forster, T. S. Eliot, and Katherine Mansfield.

Work on her first novel, *The Voyage Out*, led Woolf to another serious nervous breakdown and a suicide attempt in 1915. She recovered, however, and in 1919 published a second novel, *Night and Day*. Both of these were fairly conventional works, but with her next novel, *Jacob's Room* (1922), she began to experiment with narrative in radical ways. This fertile experimentation continued in her three masterpieces: *Mrs. Dalloway* (1925), *To the Lighthouse* (1927), and *The Waves* (1931). Highly innovative in their deployment of temporal subjectivity, interiorized landscape, and multiple consciousness, they are among the greatest works in the canon of literary high modernism.

Virginia Woolf's strongest emotional ties had always been with women: first, her sister, Vanessa (whom she loved to the point of "thought-incest"), later Madge Vaughn (the daughter of J. A. SYMONDS [10], and inspiration for the character of Mrs. Dalloway), Violet Dickinson, and the ever-troublesome ETHEL SMYTH [94]. In 1922, Woolf met and fell in love with VITA SACKVILLE-WEST [64]. After a tentative start, they began an affair that lasted through most of the 1920s. In 1928, Woolf presented Vita with *Orlando*, a fantastical romp of a biography in which the eponymous hero's life spans three centuries and both genders. It has been called by Nigel Nicolson, Vita Sackville-West's son, "the longest and most charming love letter in literature."

Woolf was a tireless writer, producing in addition to her novels several books of criticism, including *The Common Reader* (1925), *The Common Reader: Second Series* (1932), and *The Death of the Moth* (1942), as well as thousands of letters and some five hundred thousand words of diaries. Her ambitious 1937 novel, *The Years*, which like all her novels cost her much in psychic terms, is generally considered a valiant failure, though her last work, *Between the Acts* (1941), shows her embarking on bold new paths.

After their home was destroyed by German bombs in the London blitz, Virginia and Leonard Woolf moved to Rodmell in Sussex. Severely depressed by the war and exhausted by the composition of *Between the Acts*, Woolf again began to hear the birds singing in Greek that had presaged her 1915 breakdown. Wishing to spare Leonard the pain of another bout with madness, she drowned herself in the River Ouse on March 28, 1941.

Virginia Woolf's great influence is twofold. First, her gorgeously innovative novels dramatically changed the landscape of modern fiction. As one of this century's preeminent fiction writers, she has been a role model for countless women struggling to find their own voice and talent in the face of a patriarchy that, like Charles Tansley in *To the Lighthouse*, is constantly reminding them, "Women can't write." Second, her essays *A Room of One's Own* (1929) and *Three Guineas* (1938) have become the cornerstones of much contemporary feminist thought. Perhaps thinking of her own failure to attend university, Woolf asks the great question in *A Room of One's Own:* "What would have happened had Shakespeare had a wonderfully gifted sister?" The answer is haunting.

She was as adventurous, as imaginative, as agog to see the world as he was. But she was not sent to school. She had no chance of learning grammar and logic, let alone of reading Horace and Virgil. She picked up a book now and then, one of her brother's perhaps, and read a few pages. But then her parents came in and told her to mend the stockings or mind the stew and not moon about with books and papers.... Perhaps she scribbled some pages up in an apple loft on the sly, but was careful to hide them or set fire to them. Soon, however, before she was out of her teens, she was betrothed to the son of a neighboring wool-stapler. She cried out that marriage was hateful to her, and for that she was severely beaten by her father.... The force of her gift alone drove her to it. She made up a small parcel of her belongings, let herself down by a rope one summer's night and took the road to London. She was not seventeen. The birds that sang in the hedge were not more musical than she was. She had the quickest fancy, a gift like her brother's, for the tune of words. Like him, she had a taste for the theatre. She stood at the stage door; she wanted to act, she said. Men laughed in her face.... At last Nick Greene the actor-manager took pity on her; she found herself with child by that gentleman and so—who shall measure the heat and violence of the poet's heart when caught and tangled in a woman's body?—killed herself one winter's night....

Time will only serve to enhance Virginia Woolf's stature as a germinal figure in the evolution of the modern lesbian. Through the questions she asked, the visions she had, the stories she told, she helped create an intellectual space in which women could begin to imagine those rooms of their own that they would require in order to fully explore the myriad possibilities so long denied them. Although GERTRUDE STEIN [7] is more present as a lesbian in the common imagination, Woolf's work—at once gossamer as a butterfly's wing and fierce as a steel trap—is likely, in the long run, to prove the more durable of the two in its contribution to lesbian identity.

14

Alexander the Great

356–323 B.C.

Alexander was born in the Macedonian capital of Pella in 356 B.C. His father was Philip II of Macedonia, who had created out of his conquest of Greece a federation of city-states with himself at the head. He had also organized a first-rate army. Both of these accomplishments would prove important assets to his son Alexander.

When Philip was assassinated by a disgruntled relative at a theater in Aigai in 336 B.C., Alexander was twenty years old. His first act upon ascending the throne was to swiftly put down the opportunistic uprisings that erupted in Thrace and Ilyria in the wake of Philip's death. Then he turned his attention to fulfilling his father's dream: the conquest of Greece's age-old enemy Persia, which for the last two hundred years had held vast sway over all the lands from the Mediterranean to India. In 334 B.C., Alexander started east with a comparatively small army of thirty-five thousand to attack the much superior Persian forces. Moving with relative ease through Asia Minor—only the mountain city of Termessos managed to hold out against him, and he simply bypassed it—he met and defeated the full fury of the Persian army at Grancius in 334 and Issus in 333. The cities of Tyre and Gaza fell before him, and in 332 he entered Egypt without a fight. There he rested for a while, founded Alexandria in honor of himself, was crowned pharaoh and declared by the Egyptian priests to be a god.

Venturing into Mesopotamia the next year, he soundly defeated the Persian king Darius III at the battle of Gaugamela, clearing the way for his advance on Babylon, and the Persian capitals at Susa and Persepolis. From there, he continued ever eastward, through the far reaches of the now defunct Persian empire and into present-day Afghanistan. In 326 B.C. his army entered the Hindu Kush in northern India, but by then the men were exhausted, far from home, their supply routes stretched dangerously thin, and they refused to press on any farther. Bitterly disappointed, Alexander began the long march back through the desert, reaching Susa in 324 B.C. He spent the next year consolidating his territories, reorganizing his army, and planning new conquests—the Arabian peninsula, the lands north of the old Persian empire, perhaps even another try at India. But in June of 323, Alexander was suddenly taken ill with a fever in Babylon and died ten days later. He was thirty-three years old.

Alexander was a military genius who, in eleven years of warfare, never lost a battle. In part his leadership was based on his personal courage and charisma. Often in the pitch of battle he would lead decisive cavalry attacks himself and was frequently—and sometimes seriously—wounded.

Despite the range of his conquests, at his death Alexander left no named successor, and in the ensuing power struggle between his generals, Alexander's mother, wives, and children all were killed and his short-lived empire completely dismembered.

His legacy, however, was not so much territorial as cultural. Educated to believe that Hellenistic culture was superior to all others (Aristotle had been his tutor), Alexander came to appreciate the splendor and complexity of Persian civilization. It was even said that the farther east he traveled, the more Eastern he became, donning Persian dress and customs. Perhaps his greatest achievement was his bringing together these two cultures, his insistence that they could learn from one another. To symbolize this, not only did he marry the daughter of Darius III (as well as another Asian princess), but he organized the Wedding of East and West, an immense feast in which he married thousands of his Macedonian troops to Persian wives.

Alexander's marriages were invariably political alliances; he spent almost no time with his wives. His primary love seems to have been reserved for his companion from boyhood, the brilliant Hephaestion. According to Plutarch, when Alexander came to the site of ancient Troy, he laid a wreath on Achilles' tomb, and Hephaestion laid one on the tomb of Patroclus: a clear and public avowal of their relationship, given that the ancients commonly supposed Achilles and Patroclus to have been lovers. When Alexander and Hephaestion visited the Persian queen mother after Darius's defeat, she mistook Hephaestion—who was the taller of the two men—for Alexander and prostrated herself before him. Alexander raised her up saying, "Never mind, Mother. You made no mistake. He too is Alexander." When Hephaestion died, Alexander was so distraught that he ordered the physician who failed to save him crucified. Hephaestion's funeral has been called by MARY RENAULT [80] "the most spectacular funeral known to history."

Ancient sources such as Plutarch, Curtius, and Athenaeus also record Alexander's love for the eunuch Bagoas, whom he acquired from the entourage of the defeated Darius, and who remained a lifelong companion. The ancient commentators regarded Bagoas as Alexander's "little eccentricity"—not because he was a boy, but because he was a "barbarian." Alexander's ideal of a single human race was not shared by many of his contemporaries; they equated his penchant for a Persian boy with his adoption of Persian attire. MARY RENAULT [80] brilliantly chronicles Alexander's love of Bagoas in her 1972 novel *The Persian Boy*.

Alexander was more than simply a military leader: although his empire evaporated after his death, the results of his conquests—the wedding of West and East—changed the course of civilization. For our purposes here, not the least of his influence stems from the ancient and widely disseminated tradition of his love for Hephaestion. Alexander has been one of the most commonly cited homosexuals in history—one of those beacons by which gay people have been able to locate themselves in the world. Furthermore, his example has always offered a persuasive rebuttal to the stereotyped equation of male homosexuality and effeminacy. Because he has been so well-known to history as a fighting man who loved men, Alexander takes his place in *The Gay 100* in lieu of other well-documented figures such as Julius Caesar, Trajan, Frederick the Great, or Lawrence of Arabia, the fame of whose military exploits obscures—at least in the popular imagination—the glory of their love for their own sex.

15

Hadrian

A. D. 76–138

Publius Aelius Hadrianus was born on January 24, A.D. 76, in Italica, in the Roman province of Baetica in what is present-day southern Spain. His forebears were Italian army veterans who had settled the area some two hundred years previously: hence his name Hadrian, from *Adriatic*. When his father died in A.D. 85, Hadrian was entrusted to the care of his father's cousin Trajan, with whose fortunes he would be closely linked. Of Hadrian's boyhood years we know little, except that he undertook military training, spent some time in Rome, and was an enthusiast of the hunt. His early career was typical of someone destined for the Roman Senate: he served as military tribune with different legions—posted to the province of Upper Moesia on the Danube River with the Legion II Adjutrix in 95, to Lower Moesia with the Fifth Macedonica in 96.

In A.D. 97, Trajan was adopted by the aging emperor Nerva and in the following year succeeded him as emperor. Hadrian suddenly found himself in the inner circles of imperial power. He was favored both by Lucius Licinius Sura, Trajan's most powerful political backer, and by Trajan's wife, Plotina. In A.D. 100 he further secured his position by marrying Vibia Sabina, Trajan's grandniece. His career moved along at startling speed over the next few years. By 107 he was governor of the province of Lower Pannonia, and in 108, the year of Sura's death, he became consulate. But then for the next ten years his career seems to have stalled, and there is speculation that in those years voices opposed to Sura and his protégé Hadrian may have had Trajan's ear. Probably most important for Hadrian's development during that time was his being named archon (or magistrate) at Athens. Hadrian fell in love with the city, and with Greek culture, to the extent that his enemies in Rome derided him as "the Greekling."

As emperor, Trajan pursued aggressive military campaigns. In 117, Hadrian accompanied him against the Parthians. Trajan left Hadrian behind as the commander of the crucial backup army in Syria as he proceeded east. But the campaign did not fare well, and the emperor was stricken with illness. He began to make his way back to Rome. On August 9, 117, Hadrian learned that Trajan had adopted him, meaning he was to be Trajan's successor. On August 11, word arrived that the emperor was dead. The rapid succession of events disconcerted some, and there were rumors of a conspiracy on the part Hadrian and Plotina, especially after the only witness besides Plotina to Trajan's adoption of Hadrian died suddenly. Nevertheless, in charge of the Syrian army, Hadrian was in a position of strength. The quick execution of four senators for conspiracy against him stabilized the situation.

Hadrian was one of the greatest of the Roman emperors—indeed, many historians think that the Roman Empire reached its full height under his rule. He reversed Trajan's aggressive military policies, ending the war with Parthia and even returning conquered lands. Concentrating on building up frontier defenses, such as the massive Hadrian's Wall in Great Britain, he also undertook extensive public works projects, building innumerable roads, bridges, harbors, and aqueducts. During his reign, he made two extensive tours of the Empire, traveling to the western provinces in 121–23, and to the east in 123–26. Perhaps because of his Spanish origins, he was the first emperor to conceive of the Empire not just as Italy but as all the provinces, west and east together.

With the exception of a Jewish revolt in Palestine in 132, which he crushed in 135, Hadrian's twenty-year reign was peaceful.

An administrator of genius, he built up a permanent and powerful bureaucracy, codified Roman law, and established the imperial post to facilitate communication. He founded numerous cities, including Hadrianopolis (present-day Edirne in Turkey). As a talented architect, he restored the Pantheon in Rome and finished the great Temple of the Olympian Zeus in Athens, which had stood unfinished for five hundred years. Perhaps his greatest architectural achievement was the villa he had built for himself at Tivoli, outside Rome, where he collected and displayed artifacts from his travels. His monumental tomb for himself in Rome still stands, known today as the Castel Sant' Angelo.

An aesthete who wrote capable poetry, some of which survives, Hadrian was famous for having climbed Mt. Etna in Sicily and Jabal Agra' in Syria simply to watch the sunrise. His revolutionary fashion of wearing a beard set the trend for generations of Roman emperors.

In 123, while traveling in the province of Bithynia in northwestern Asia Minor, Hadrian met a languid, moody boy named Antinous. Little is known of him, except that he was probably born in 110. But for the next seven years, he and the emperor were inseparable. Then in 130, while the two were in Egypt, Antinous drowned in the Nile River. The circumstances were mysterious and have given rise to endless speculation: he was murdered by those jealous of his influence, or he committed suicide because of the "immoral" nature of his relations with the emperor, or because he was outgrowing the age prescribed for pederastic relations between the *erastes* (the older male lover) and the *eromenos* (the beloved boy), or he deliberately threw himself in the river as part of some sacred sacrifice to protect the emperor's fortunes, perhaps to cure the emperor of an illness. We will never know. What we do know is that Hadrian was devastated. He wept publicly. He ordered Antinous deified and in his honor founded the city of Antinoöpolis, where every year special games were held in the young god's honor. Cults of Antinous sprang up all over the empire; he was the last god of the ancient world and much vilified by the early Christians. Countless statues celebrated his sensuous, melancholy beauty—over five hundred still survive. Together they represent the last great original creation of the classicizing style of Greek sculpture, and they have haunted observers ever since. Writing in the eighteenth century, JOHANN JOACHIM WINCKELMANN [21] called the graven image of Antinous "the glory and crown of art in this age as well as in all others," while the nineteenth-century poet Alfred, Lord Tennyson, was said to have remarked, gazing at a statue of Antinous in the British Museum, "The inscrutable Bithynian....If we knew what he knew, we should understand the ancient world."

After three suicide attempts, Hadrian died, painfully, of some unknown and incurable ailment, at the seaside resort of Baia, near Naples, on July 10, 138. He penned for himself an epitaph whose characteristically elusive wordplay nearly defies translation:

Animula, blandula, vagula,	Little soul, gentle, wandering,
Hospes comesque corporis,	Guest and friend of the body
Quae nunc abibis in loca	In what place will you now abide,
Pallidula, rigida, nudula,	Pale, stark, bare,
Nec ut soles dabis iocos?	Unable, as you used, to play?

At the urging of his successor, Antoninus Pius, the Roman senate—which had never liked Hadrian much since he had had four of their number executed at his accession—grudgingly deified him.

Many of the Roman emperors could have been included in this book for the simple reason that the Romans made little fuss about the sex of whomever one fell in love with. In *The Decline and Fall of the Roman Empire,* the eighteenth-century historian Gibbon noted that, of the Julio-Claudian emperors, only Claudius was "correct" in his sexual tastes. I have chosen Hadrian for this ranking not only because he was one of the greatest of the Roman emperors, but because he and Antinous were one of the great pairs of lovers in the history of the world. Technically speaking, they are the only gods in this ranking. The early Christians hated them for their "unnatural lusts," but in others the story of their love inspired reverence and awe. That their story continues to inspire is evidenced by Marguerite Yourcenar's brilliant novel *The Memoirs of Hadrian* (1951).

Few rulers in history have so influenced the course of empire as Hadrian. Few beauties in history have so influenced the course of art as Antinous.

16

St. Augustine

354–430

Augustine was born on November 13, 354, in Tagaste, Numidia (present-day Souk-Ahras, Algeria). His father, Patricius, was a Roman official and a pagan. His mother, Monica, was a Christian. As a child, Augustine was not baptized nor did he receive a Christian education; instead, he was sent at age eleven to school in Madauros, a center of pagan culture and learning. It was at Madauros that he acquired his extensive knowledge of Latin literature.

He returned home in 369 and spent a year in idleness, though his reading of Cicero's *Hortensius* during this time awakened his interest in philosophy. The next year he moved to Carthage, where he encountered and partook of urban pleasures of the flesh, including, apparently, homosexuality. As he wrote later in his *Confessions,* "I came to Carthage and all around me hissed a cauldron of illicit loves. As yet I had never been in love and I longed to love.... To me it was sweet to love and be loved, the more so if I could also enjoy the body of the beloved. I therefore polluted the spring water of friendship with the filth of concupiscence. I muddied its clear stream by the hell of lust, and yet, though foul and immoral, in my excessive vanity, I used to carry on in the manner of an elegant man-about-town. I rushed headlong into love, by which I was longing to be captured." He converted to Manichaeanism, an Eastern blend of Christianity and other religions that taught the dualism between good and evil, the transmigration of souls, and the possibility of salvation. Historian John Boswell writes, in *Christianity, Social Tolerance and Homosexuality,* "Most Manicheans opposed all forms of sexuality equally.... But [homosexual pleasures] were seen by many as less serious than heterosexual acts since (a) they did not partake of the false aura of sanctity which marital sexuality used to seduce the unwary into lives of self-indulgence, and (b) they did not entrap souls in matter, as heterosexual intercourse did when children resulted."

It was during this time that Augustine renewed his friendship with a young Christian man from his childhood and lured him astray. The relationship, lasting barely a year, was "sweet to me beyond all the sweetness of life that I had experienced." Writing years later in the *Confessions,* Augustine praised the beneficent hand of God for causing the young man to fall ill with a fever—for without Augustine's knowing it, the young man's family had him baptized on his sickbed, and "he was snatched away from my lunacy, so that he might be preserved with you for my consolation. After a few days, while I was absent, the fever returned, and he died."

Unable at the time to see the wonder of God's mysterious ways, the young Augustine was devastated: "All that I had shared with him was without him transformed into a cruel torment.... I was surprised that any other mortals were alive, since he whom I had loved as if he would never die was dead. I was even more surprised that when he was dead I was still alive, for he was my 'other self.' Someone has well said of his friend, 'He was half my soul.' I had felt that my soul and his soul were 'one soul in two bodies.' So my life was to me a horror. I did not wish to live with only half of myself, and perhaps the reason why I so feared death was that then the whole of my much loved friend would have died."

Boswell writes, "This type of relationship—passionate or 'erotic' friendship between males...borrowed heavily from the language of sexual relations and often deliberately imitated the homosexual literature of antiquity....It would be inaccurate to suggest any exact parallel between such relationships and modern phenomena—as it is to compare medieval marriage with its modern counterpart. But to suggest that this difference is due simply to changing concepts of friendship and not related to the status of homosexuality is to beg the question: the erotic content of 'friendship' in antiquity was due in no small measure to the fact that homosexuality was conventional in many ancient societies and could have been part of the relationship: friends of the same sex borrowed from the standard vocabulary of homosexual love to express their feelings in erotic terms....Saint Augustine himself, writing in these terms, expressed the love he felt for a friend of his youth....Unlike many of his Christian contemporaries, Augustine bitterly regretted the sexual aspect of such passions...and rejected as an adult the possibility of licit homosexual relationships."

During these years Augustine also took on a mistress, who in 371 bore him a son named Adeolatus. Between 374 and 383, Augustine conducted a school of rhetoric in Carthage; then he moved to Rome, where he continued to teach rhetoric. He came under the influence of Ambrose, who was preaching in Rome, and eventually rejected the doctrines of Manichaeanism. On Easter Sunday, April 25, 387, Augustine and his son Adeolatus were baptized into the Christian faith.

Summarily dismissing his mistress, Augustine returned to Africa in 388. He sold his patrimony, distributed the money among the poor, and converted his house into a monastic community. Adeolatus joined him in the monastery until his premature death at the age of eighteen. Augustine was ordained in Hippo (present-day Annaba, Algeria), and in 395–96 was consecrated auxiliary bishop. Soon thereafter he succeeded to the bishopric. During the next thirty years he composed his most important works, including the *Confessions* (397-401), *On the Trinity* (400–416), and *The City of God* (413–426).

In August 430, Vandals seized Carthage and lay siege to Hippo. On August 28, 430, in the midst of the siege, Augustine died. The story goes that, soon thereafter, the Vandals looted and burned everything in Hippo except for Augustine's monastery.

Augustine is regarded as one of the greatest fathers of the Roman Catholic Church, a thinker who changed the course of Western civilization. He adumbrated notions of sin, perversion, and the relationship between good and evil that have so permeated our thought that it is impossible, for better or worse, to conceive of our world without them. It is not an exaggeration to claim that Augustine is in large measure responsible for nothing less than our sense of the subjective self. He was also influential in introducing an ascetic strain into Christianity that would have far-reaching implications. Building on the teachings of Paul, Augustine condemned most sexual acts, even those performed by married couples. Sex for procreation was, for Augustine, the only moral sexual act—and even that was distasteful. "There is nothing," he wrote in the *Soliloquia*, "which degrades the manly spirit more than the attractiveness of females and contact with their bodies." Homosexual behavior was, of course, also proscribed. A thoroughgoing misogynist, Augustine was particularly disgusted by men who allowed their bodies to be used "as that of a woman," since, as he wrote in *Contra mendacium*, "the body of a man is as superior to that of a woman as the soul is to the body." More than anyone else, Augustine furthered Christianity's long attempt to suppress any physical expressions of love except those that resulted in children.

The presence of Augustine on this list will no doubt provoke some protest. What I am claiming here is that Augustine appears to have indulged, in his early life, in pleasures of the flesh, both with males and females. In this he was probably very little different from many denizens of the late Roman Empire who did not recognize our modern distinction between homosexual and heterosexual. His later disgust at his younger self has had, and continues to have, enormous consequences for all of us. Had I not chosen Augustine for this list, I might have included the apostle Paul, whom a recent and controversial book by the Episcopal bishop John Spong has characterized as a "self-loathing and repressed gay male." In Spong's words: "Nothing else, in my opinion, could account for Paul's self-judging rhetoric, his negative feeling toward his own body, and his sense of being controlled by something he had no power to change." Much as we may decry the centuries of repression and persecution these men helped impose on gays and lesbians, we must nonetheless acknowledge their powerful influence on Western civilization.

17

Michelangelo Buonarroti

1475–1564

Michelangelo Buonarroti was born on March 6, 1475, in the Tuscan village of Caprese, of which his father was mayor. His mother died when he was an infant, and he was raised by a family of stonemasons in nearby Settigano. When his father remarried in 1485, Michelangelo joined him in Florence. In that city of great artistic ferment, the boy befriended art students and spent much of his time copying the work of masters like Donatello, Giotto, Masaccio, and Botticelli. Over his father's strenuous objections, he apprenticed himself in 1488 to the muralist Ghirlandaio and in 1498 began studying at the art school of Lorenzo de' Medici under the tutelage of the sculptor Bertoldo, who had been a pupil of Donatello's. For the next three years Michelangelo lived in the Medici palace, where he was deeply influenced by the Neoplatonism that was the intellectual currency of the court.

When Lorenzo died in 1492, the austere reformer Savonarola incited the public to rise up and expel the Medicis from Florence. In the ensuing civil strife, Michelangelo fled first to Venice and then to Rome. During the next five years in Rome he did his first major work, including the sculptures *Bacchus* (1496–98) and the much acclaimed St. Peter's *Pietà* (1498–1500). In the meantime Florentine opinion had turned against Savonarola, and the citizenry burned him at the stake in 1498. In 1500, at the invitation of the city of Florence, Michelangelo returned in triumph. Shortly thereafter he was commissioned to carve a thirteen-foot-tall block of marble that had thwarted two previous sculptors. Working for the next three years in secrecy, he stirred much anticipation, and when his monumental nude statue of *David* was unveiled in 1504, the public was in awe.

Everyone wanted Michelangelo's service. In 1505, the powerful and worldly Pope Julius II ordered him back to Rome and commissioned a funerary monument for himself. This project, the most frustrating of Michelangelo's career, marked the beginning of his long and turbulent relationship with the Medici popes. He spent a year working on a gigantic bronze statue for the monument, only to see it melted down to make cannons shortly after its completion.

Between 1508 and 1512, he was engaged in the execution of another of Julius's immense projects, the painting of the ceiling of the Sistine Chapel. The heroic tale of the artist lying on his back on the hard scaffolding while paint dripped in his face has become the stuff of legend. After Julius died in 1513, his heirs contracted for another attempt at a tomb for their predecessor—the resulting labor, accompanied by protracted litigation, would occupy Michelangelo for the next forty years. "I have lost all my youth chained to this tomb," he would write. In the end, he was forced to abandon his plan for the tomb in St. Peter's. The colossal marble statue *Moses* and the statues known as *The Slaves* remain as impressive parts of the never completed whole.

In 1516, Pope Leo X (Julius's successor and the son of Lorenzo de' Medici) ordered Michelangelo back to Florence to design a chapel for the Medici family. Work on this continued under Leo's successor, another Medici named Clement VII. When troops of the Holy Roman Empire sacked Rome in 1527, Clement marched on Florence, angry with the city for having failed to come to his aid. Michelangelo was put in charge of the Florentine defenses against his old patron, and the city held out for nine months. But in 1530 a traitor opened the gate and Clement's forces entered Florence. Michelangelo was forced to spend several weeks hiding in a belfry before being pardoned and told to continue his work on the Medici chapel.

In 1534, the chapel complete, Michelangelo left Florence for the last time and moved to Rome. He was nearly sixty by then. Pope Paul III commissioned him to paint a Last Judgment on the wall of the Sistine Chapel, which occupied him for the next fifteen years. In 1547 he was made chief architect of St. Peter's Basilica in Rome and designed the great dome there—it remains one of the great architectural masterpieces of all time.

Michelangelo died in Rome on February 18, 1564, three weeks before his eighty-ninth birthday.

Contemporary accounts report that Michelangelo was a reclusive and introverted man, liable to outbursts of fiery temper. He lived frugally, eating and drinking little, sleeping hardly at all. Unlike other artists of his day such as LEONARDO [18] and Raphael, he eschewed fashionable clothing in favor of simple workman's clothes and boots. It was said he even slept in them.

Though he thought of himself mainly as a sculptor, Michelangelo's splendid genius was evident in everything he did, whether sculpture or painting or architecture or poetry. He wrote over three hundred sonnets, many of them to young men such as Gherardo Perini and Febo di Poggio.

In 1532, when he was fifty-seven, Michelangelo met a beautiful young nobleman named Tommaso de' Cavalieri, to whom he devoted the rest of his life. He wrote numerous love sonnets to him and sent him drawings, including one showing himself as Zeus in the guise of an eagle snatching up into the skies Cavalieri as the shepherd boy Ganymede. It appears that in real life their relationship was platonic, with Michelangelo playing the part of the adoring older man, and Cavalieri the unattainable youth. Nevertheless, their friendship lasted for thirty-two years, and Michelangelo died in Cavalieri's arms. When the poems to Cavalieri were posthumously published in 1623, Michelangelo's nephew saw fit to change the pronouns, indicating that his contemporaries understood and were embarrassed by the homo-sexual implications of the sonnets.

During his lifetime, Michelangelo's sexuality was interpreted in two ways. Aretino accused him of sodomitical relations with Perini and Cavalieri, writing, "Even if you are divine, you don't disdain male consorts." Others, like Vasari, claimed that Michelangelo was "married to his art."

Particularly intriguing and suggestive are a group of fifty sonnets Michelangelo composed in 1544 on the death at age fifteen of Francesco (Cecchino) di Zanobi Bracci, the favorite nephew of Luigi del Riccio. "I was only given over to you an hour," he wrote of the boy, "I am given over to death forever." Michelangelo (who was sixty-eight when he knew Cecchino) seems to have been uncommonly frank about his feelings in his correspondence with the boy's uncle. In a 1542 letter to Luigi, for example, Michelangelo writes of what may well have been a homoerotic dream about Cecchino. His tone suggests a certain knowing complicity between himself and his correspondent. "I sent this [madrigal] a short while ago to Florence. Now that I have reworked it more fittingly, I send it to you, so that you may give it, if it please you, to the flame, that is, to the one who consumes me. I should like even another favor from you, and that is that you should clear up a certain perplexity which has laid hold of me since last night; when greeting our idol in a dream, it appeared to me that he was laughing and threatening me; and I not knowing which of the two things I am to believe in, I beg you to find out from him, and there when we see each other tomorrow, you may clear it up."

Michelangelo was perhaps the greatest visual artist of all time, excelling in every medium in which he worked. A man who loved men, his sexual orientation was central to his work. The male body fascinated him—even the women in his paintings, some have claimed, seem to possess male bodies. It is through his heroic conceptualization and representation of the male body that he has exercised incalculable influence not only on the gay imagination but on our collective cultural imagination. Every once in a while an ideal image of human beauty seizes our collective imagination: such was the case with Antinous, the beloved of HADRIAN [15], whose beautiful features obsessed late classical art. The image of Michelangelo's *David*—confident yet tentative, poised yet relaxed, youthful yet powerfully muscled—

introduced into history a new type of masculine beauty that remains with us to this day. Every time you walk past another gym-buffed body in Chelsea or the Castro or West Hollywood or Key West, you're walking past a gay man paying unconscious homage to a way of thinking about male beauty that Michelangelo bequeathed to us five hundred years ago. His influence permeates the way we see ourselves. His sculptor's hands continue to shape our world.

18

Leonardo da Vinci

1452–1519

Leonardo da Vinci was born in 1452 in Vinci, in the province of Tuscany in Italy. The illegitimate son of a Florentine notary and a peasant girl, he was brought up by his paternal grandparents. Leonardo's precocious talent was recognized by the painter Andrea del Verrocchio, and Leonardo became his apprentice at the age of fourteen. Ten years later, while still living with Verrocchio, Leonardo and three others were accused of having committed "godless acts" with a seventeen-year-old model named Jacopo Saltarelli. They were issued a reprimand.

In 1482, Leonardo moved to Milan and the court of Ludovico Sforza, where he composed the famous *Notebooks* and painted such masterpieces as the *Madonna of the Rocks* (1483–86) and the now-much-deteriorated *Last Supper* fresco (1495–98) in the church of Santa Maria delle Grazie. When the French invaded in 1499, Leonardo returned to Florence where he served as a military engineer for Cesare Borgia. His great fresco to commemorate Borgia's victory over the French (1503–5) was never completed—Leonardo's unceasing interest in new and experimental fresco techniques continually cost him. While in Florence he also painted the celebrated *Mona Lisa* (1503).

In 1507 he entered the service of the French King Louis XII, first in Milan and then in Rome, where he was able to pursue his many scientific interests in such fields as geology, botany, and mechanics. In 1515, Francis I of France invited him to settle in the castle of Cloux and pursue his researches.

Leonardo was a very private man with a penchant for secrecy—his notebooks, for example, were all composed in a mirror script. We thus know little of his private life, except that he was devoted to an array of beautiful young men whom he made his assistants: Cesare de Sesto, Boltraffio, Andrea Salaino, and a young aristocrat named Francesco Melzi, whom Leonardo adopted and made his heir. He also took in a pretty ten-year-old boy named Caprotti, whom he called "the little Satan" because the boy repeatedly stole from him, thefts that Leonardo meticulously—and indulgently—recorded in his notebooks. His many drawings and paintings of the boy cover a period of twenty years.

Leonardo worked slowly and found it difficult to finish projects (the unfinished *Mona Lisa* took four years). Many of his contemporaries thought he frittered his time and talent away, and he is reported by the historian Vasari to have reproached himself on his deathbed for having offended God and man by his failure to do his duty in his art.

Leonardo died at Cloux in 1519, with Francesco Melzi by his side. The quintessential universal genius, Leonardo was an artist of great originality and power, a versatile thinker, and a far-ranging innovator and scientist. He left over eight thousand pages of notebooks containing scientific projects, inventions, architectural designs, and sketches.

It is through Sigmund Freud's famous essay "Leonardo da Vinci and a Memory of His Childhood" (1910) that the Renaissance master has had the most influence on the modern gay psyche, for it was in this essay—written at a time when Freud was analyzing his feelings about his former intimate friend Wilhelm Fliess—that Freud first developed his theories about the causes of homosexuality. Freud's essay addresses a childhood memory recorded by Leonardo in his notebooks: "I recall as one of my very earliest memories that while I was in my cradle a vulture came down to me and opened my mouth with its tail, and struck me many times with its tail against my lips." This memory, Freud argued, was not a memory at all, but a later fantasy of fellatio transposed onto memory. Fellatio, Freud went on to point out, "only repeats in a different form a situation in which we all once felt comfortable—when we were still in our suckling days and took our mother's nipple into our mouth and sucked it."

From this he deduced, in an argument at once brilliant and highly dubious, that "the boy represses his love for his mother: he puts himself in her place, identifies himself with her, and takes his own person as a model in whose likeness he chooses the new objects of his love. In this way he has become a homosexual. What he has in fact done is to slip back into auto-eroticism: for the boys whom he now loves as he grows up are after all only substitutive figures and revivals of himself in childhood—boys whom he loves in the way his mother loved *him* when he was a child. He finds the object of his love along the path of *narcissism*, as we say."

Freud goes on to argue that "by repressing his love for his mother, [the homosexual] preserves it in his unconscious and from now on remains faithful to her. While he seems to pursue boys and to be their lover, he is in reality running away from the other women, who might cause him to be unfaithful....[T]he man who gives the appearance of being susceptible only to the charms of men is in fact attracted by women in the same way as a normal man; but on each occasion he hastens to transfer the excitation he has received from women onto a male object, and in this manner he repeats over and over again the mechanism by which he acquired his homosexuality."

In all this convolution of desire, according to Freud, lies the secret of the *Mona Lisa*'s enigmatic smile.

It is difficult to underestimate—for better or, more likely, for worse—the influence Freud's powerful but questionable reading of Leonardo has had on the lives of countless gay men who have undergone therapy of one kind or another. Freud's interpretation of the "mechanism" by which homosexuality is acquired (though based in part on a mistranslation of the word *vulture*) has been at the root of much of the medical and psychoanalytic thinking about homosexuality in this century, and we are only now beginning to move beyond it. As the vehicle of Freud's analysis, Leonardo continues to exercise great influence on gay men and lesbians today. But Leonardo is influential in his own right as well—as a man of unabashed creative energy and insight whose gayness is commonly perceived as integral to his genius. If Leonardo was gay, what could possibly be wrong with being gay? The power of such an argument has always been difficult to dismiss.

19

Christopher Marlowe

1564–1593

The son of a Canterbury shoemaker, Christopher Marlowe was baptized on February 26, 1564. In 1579 he entered the King's School in Canterbury and from there proceeded, in 1581, to Corpus Christi College, Cambridge, where he earned a BA in 1584. After that, he continued his education at Cambridge, studying for an MA. His mysterious absences from the college during that time led the Privy Council, in 1587, to issue a letter on Marlowe's behalf, letting it be known that he had performed valuable services for the government, including several trips abroad. Marlowe, the letter stated, should not be defamed "by those who are ignorant in the affairs he went about." Indications are that Marlowe had been recruited by the secret service, and records exist of a "Marley" or "Marlin" (spelling was blissfully inexact in those days) sent as a messenger to the Continent.

After Cambridge, Marlowe went to London, where he began writing for the theater. Information on his next few years is scarce, though we find him in various kinds of legal trouble from time to time: in 1589, for instance, he spent some time in Newgate prison after being implicated in a squabble in which one William Bradley was killed. And in May 1592 it is recorded that he was picked up by the constables in Shoreditch for disturbing the peace.

In 1593 the playwright Thomas Kyd was arrested for libeling Flemish Protestant refugees in London. His lodgings were searched, and certain heretical papers found in his possession. Under torture, he claimed these papers actually belonged to Marlowe, who had already gained a reputation among his contemporaries for "atheism," a term that, in Elizabethan times, could mean many different kinds of unorthodoxy. Marlowe, Kyd accused, authored "vile and heretical conceits denying the deity of Jesus Christ." The spy Richard Baines corroborated some of Kyd's testimony against Marlowe in a "note containing the opinion of one Christopher Marly concerning his damnable judgement of religion and scorn of God's word." Among Marlowe's assertions, according to Baines, was "that St. John the Evangelist was bedfellow to Christ and leaned always in his bosom; that he used him as the sinners of Sodoma." Perhaps even more shockingly, Marlowe was said to maintain "that all they that love not tobacco and boys were fools."

On May 18, 1593, the Privy Council ordered Marlowe's arrest, though two days later they told him only to remain in the neighborhood. On May 30, after spending the day at a tavern in Deptford with Nicholas Skeres, Robert Poley, and Ingram Frizer, Marlowe was killed by Frizer. According to Frizer, there had been a quarrel over the bill. Marlowe grabbed Frizer's knife from his belt and attempted to cut him, whereupon, in self-defense, Frizer wrestled the knife from Marlowe and stabbed him above the right eye, lodging the knife blade deeply in Marlowe's skull and killing him instantly. Marlowe was buried in Deptford on June 1. On June 28, Ingrim Frizer was pardoned.

Was Marlowe killed in self-defense, or was he assassinated? We will never know. What we do know is that Skeres and Poley were both secret agents, and that Poley was in fact a double agent.

Given Marlowe's own mysterious services to the government, and his controversial reputation, the circumstances of his death are suspicious at best.

It is of course Marlowe's plays that ensure his place in history. He was the first great playwright of the Elizabethan age, and his innovations changed the course of English drama. His sensibility tended toward the dark, the complex, the ambiguous. He introduced blank verse, what Ben Jonson called Marlowe's "mighty line," as the medium for Elizabethan drama, thus paving the way for the plays of WILLIAM SHAKESPEARE [20]. It is always tempting to imagine what might have been: by age twenty-nine, the time of his death, Marlowe had produced such masterpieces as *Tamburlaine the Great* (c. 1587), *The Tragicall History of Doctor Faustus* (1588), *The Jew of Malta* (1589), and *The Troublesome Raigne and Lamentable Death of Edward the Second* (c. 1592). His contemporary Shakespeare, in contrast, had by that young age written nothing at all of import.

I have ranked Marlowe higher than Shakespeare, not only because of Marlowe's immense influence on English drama, including Shakespeare, but also because his remarkable and unflinching investigation of the complexities of homosexual desire in *Edward II* makes that work one of the first "modern" queer texts. Marlowe's outspoken homosexuality and atheism, his courageous and rebellious unorthodoxy that both exhilarated and discomfited the Elizabethans even as it brought about his own destruction, mark Marlowe as a larger-than-life figure whose example has resonated down through the ages—as evidenced in the recent and lavish film *Edward II* by DEREK JARMAN [82], in which the British director celebrates the figure from Marlowe's play as "Our Queer Edward."

In words that capture something of the spirit of the man and his work, fellow poet and contemporary Michael Drayton eulogized Christopher Marlowe:

> Neat Marlowe, bathed in the Thespian springs,
> Had in him those brave translunary things
> That your first poets had; his raptures were
> All air and fire, which made his verses clear:
> For that fine madness still he did retain
> Which rightly should possess a poet's brain.

20

William Shakespeare

1564–1616

The biographical facts concerning William Shakespeare are few. We do not know when he was born, but parish records show he was baptized in the Holy Trinity Church in Stratford-upon-Avon, Warwickshire, England, on April 26, 1564. His father, John Shakespeare, was a prominent businessman who became mayor of Stratford in 1568. His mother, Mary, was the daughter of a wealthy landowner. We know little of Shakespeare's schooling, except that according to his contemporary Ben Jonson he knew "little Latin and less Greek." He did not attend university.

Two legends regarding the young Shakespeare record that he was apprenticed to a butcher, and that he left Stratford because he had been caught poaching a deer in the park of Sir Thomas Lucy of Charlecote. What can be verified is that on November 27, 1582, the eighteen-year-old Shakespeare applied for a marriage license. His bride-to-be, Anne Hathaway, must already have been pregnant, since on May 26, 1583, the parish register records the christening of a daughter, Susanna. The inscription on Anne Hathaway's tombstone—stating that she died in 1623 at the age of sixty-seven—indicates that she was eight years older than Shakespeare. Records from 1585 attest to the birth of twins, Hamnet and Judith.

There is no evidence of Shakespeare's whereabouts during the next seven or eight years, until he is mentioned in a 1592 pamphlet by London playwright Robert Greene, who warns his friends of an actor who has had the audacity to write plays: "an upstart crow, beautified with our feathers, that with his *Tiger's heart wrapped in a player's hide,* supposes he is as well able to bombast out a blank verse as the best of you; and being an absolute *Johannes fac totum* is in his own conceit the only Shake-scene in a country."

By 1595, Shakespeare is mentioned as a leading member and stockholder in The Lord Chamberlain's Men (later, under James I, The King's Men). No record remains of which parts Shakespeare may have played as an actor, though it is thought he may have played supporting roles like the ghost in *Hamlet;* what we do know is that, between the 1590–91 and 1612–13 seasons, he contributed thirty-eight plays, a substantial part of the company's repertoire. In 1599 he became part owner of the Globe Theatre and in 1608 part owner of Blackfriars Theatre.

In 1612 or 1613 he retired to Stratford and the house he had purchased with his theater earnings in 1597. He died on April 23, 1616.

During Shakespeare's twenty years in London, Anne Hathaway remained in Stratford. In his will he left her his "second best bed" and on his tomb had a curse inscribed that effectively prevented his wife from being interred next to him.

Shakespeare's plays offer only the most tantalizing evidence of homosexual concerns: various cross-dressing, gender-confusion episodes such as the one in *As You Like It* between Orlando and Rosalind (disguised as Ganymede, a name with clear homo-

sexual connotations in the Renaissance), and between Viola and
Orsino in *Twelfth Night*. It is in the sonnets, probably written
sometime in the 1590s and published without Shakespeare's
permission in 1609, that the clearest indications exist. The 154
sonnets are, in their unauthorized printing, dedicated "To the
only begettor: Mr. W. H." Numerous identities for Mr. W.H. have
been proposed down through the years, ranging from Henry
Wriothesley, Earl of Southampton, to William Herbert, Earl of
Pembroke, to Oscar Wilde's nomination of one Willie Hughes, a
boy actor in Shakespeare's company, to the possibility that W.H. is
simply a misprint for the initials of William Shakespeare himself.

The sonnets fall into two distinct groups: the first 126 are
addressed to a young man of great charm and beauty, whom the
poet in sonnet 20 provocatively calls "the master-mistress of my
passion"; the last 28 to a "dark lady." The two groups seem to
intersect in sonnets 40–42 and 133–136, where an intrigue
between the young man and the dark lady causes both to be
untrue to the poet. Sonnet 144 is perhaps clearest in its delinea-
tion of the "plot" of the sequence:

> Two loves have I, of comfort and despair,
> Which like two spirits do suggest me still;
> The better angel is a man fair right,
> The worser spirit a woman colored ill.
> To win me soon to hell, my female evil
> Tempteth my better angel from my side,
> And would corrupt my saint to be a devil,
> Wooing his purity with her foul pride.
> And whether that my angel be turned fiend
> Suspect I may, yet not directly tell;
> But being both from me, both to each friend,
> I guess one angel in another's hell.
>   Yet this shall I ne'er know, but live in doubt,
>   Till my bad angel fire my good one out.

(The last line apparently refers to the syphilis the poet fears
his young man may contract from the dark lady.)

Since early editions of the sonnets changed some of the
pronouns and scrambled the order, it was not until the late
eighteenth century that some of the poems were perceived as
homosexual in content. In 1780, George Steevens, in editing the

poems, attacked sonnet 20 with its apostrophe to "the master-mistress of my passion," claiming, "It is impossible to read this fulsome panegyrick, addressed to a male object, without an equal mixture of disgust and indignation." And in the nineteenth century, the father of the gay poet Gerard Manley Hopkins complained that Shakespeare's "mysterious sonnets present the startling peculiarity of transferring every epithet of womanly endearment to a masculine friend,—his master-mistress, as he calls him by a compound epithet, harsh as it is disagreeable."

Whatever one's take on the sexual politics of the sequence, the sonnets remain works of honeyed, haunting beauty. This is, of course, not the place to gauge Shakespeare's general influence. He is, by most accounts, the greatest writer in the English language, perhaps in any language. His influence on the English language is equaled only by that of the King James Bible, to the extent that people unconsciously quote Shakespeare in their everyday speech.

For the purposes of this particular ranking, however, Shakespeare's influence falls behind that of, say, CHRISTOPHER MAR-LOWE [19]. In part this is because the issue of the sonnets will almost certainly never be resolved. Gay writers like W. H. Auden and A. L. Rowse have concluded that Shakespeare was not, in fact, gay at all. Others, like Joseph Pequigney in his recent scholarly study, have painstakingly "proved" the opposite. In the end, the fact that Shakespeare's sonnets have been read as homosexual texts by a not insubstantial number of readers through the years merits his ranking at number twenty on this list.

21

Johann Joachim Winckelmann

1717–1768

Johann Joachim Winckelmann, the son of a shoemaker, was born on December 9, 1717, in Stendal, Prussia. From an early age he was fascinated by the ancient Greeks, especially Homer, whom he first read in Alexander Pope's English translation. Beginning in 1738 he studied theology at the University of Halle, and later medicine at the University of Jena. In 1742 he began tutoring a handsome young man named F. W. Peter Lamprecht, with whom he fell in love. When he moved to Seehausen a year later, Lamprecht followed him, and the two lived together until 1746, when Lamprecht broke off the relationship. Winckelmann was beside himself: "I renounce all," he wrote to Lamprecht, "honor and pleasure, peace and contentment, unless I can see you and enjoy you....My eyes cry for you alone....I shall love you as long as I live."

In 1748, Winckelmann became librarian to Count von Bünau at Nöthnitz near Dresden. It was here that he began to undertake an extensive study of classical Greek art which led, in 1755, to his seminal essay "Reflections on the Imitation of Greek Works in Painting and Sculpture." In this essay Winckelmann articulated his famous paradox: "The only way for us to become great and, if possible, inimitable, lies in the imitation of the Greeks." His exhortation electrified the European intellectual community, and the essay was translated into several languages.

In the meantime, Winckelmann had converted to Roman Catholicism and moved to Rome, where he eventually became librarian to the Vatican, president of Antiquities, and secretary to Cardinal Albino—a position that gave him access to the cardinal's stupendous private collection of classical art.

Life in Rome agreed with Winckelmann, and we find him writing, in a 1756 letter to a friend, "I can be satisfied with my life. I have no worries other than my work, and have even found someone with whom I can speak of love: a good-looking, blond young Roman of sixteen, half a head taller than I am; but I only see him once a week, when he dines with me on Sunday evening."

In 1764, Winckelmann published his *History of the Art of Antiquity*. Its thesis was that Greek art evolved organically from an archaic mode to the sublime style of such masters as Phidias in the fifth century B.C. and Praxiteles in the fourth century. This evolution, Winckelmann argued, was a result of the personal liberty afforded by the ancient Greek state: a utopian society, as Winckelmann saw it, organized in such a way that its citizens had been able to express to the fullest their artistic gifts.

At the heart of Winckelmann's passionate appreciation of Greek art, its "noble simplicity and quiet grandeur," was a frank celebration of the idealized male body, whose attributes he cataloged with painstaking precision: "In facial structure, the so-called Greek *profile* is the foremost characteristic of high beauty. This profile consists of an almost straight or a slightly depressed line formed by forehead and nose...In ideal heads, the *eyes* are invariably set deeper than in nature, a fact that accentuates the upper edge of the socket....The *chin*, whose beauty lies in the rounded fullness of its arched form, is not bisected by a dimple...which, occurring as it does in nature only individually and by accident, was not deemed by Greek artists...to be a prerequisite of pure and universal beauty. A wide and deeply arched *chest* was regarded as a universal mark of beauty in male figures...the *abdomen* is like that of a person who enjoys a good rest and sound digestion, that is, without belly...the *sex organs*, too, have a beauty of their own. Of the testicles, the left is always larger, as is the case in nature, just as they say that the left eye sees better than the right."

Artistic beauty, for Winckelmann, was a moral force. Standing in front of the Apollo Belvedere, he wrote, "I forget all else over the sight of this miraculous work of art, and assume a more exalted position myself in order to be worthy of this sight." In ancient Greece, body and soul were inextricably intertwined. "The gymnasia," he enthused, "were the school of artists, where the young, otherwise clothed in accordance with public decency, did their exercises naked. There they went, the philosopher and the artist: SOCRATES [1] in order to teach...Phidias in order to enrich his art through [the contemplation of] these beautiful creatures."

Taking into its account of artistic production everything from available technology to cultural context to the weather, the *History of the Art of Antiquity* created, in a single stroke, the discipline of art history as we know it today. Similarly, Winckelmann's visits to Pompeii and Herculaneum and his "open letters" uncovering the scandalous ineptitude of the early excavations have earned him the approbation "father of modern archaeology."

Winckelmann never made it to Greece, though friends from time to time tempted him with the possibility of what was in those days an arduous journey. Greece remained for him a thing of the mind, not so much an actual place as a state of being. In this respect, Winckelmann's idealized Greece became enormously influential in the nineteenth century, not only for the burgeoning neoclassical movement in the arts but also, in its evocation of a classical world in which male beauty was enshrined, for the gay imagination. Winckelmann's work was a touchstone for such important nineteenth century gay writers as Walter Pater (*The Renaissance*) and J.A. SYMONDS [10] (*A Problem in Greek Ethics*).

In 1768, Winckelmann returned to Dresden for the first time since moving to Italy over a decade before. On June 8, on his way back to Rome, he was murdered in Trieste by a young man named Francesco Arcangeli, whose acquaintance he had made the day before.

About Winckelmann's particular genius Goethe wrote, "While the characters of many men, and especially scholars, tend to disappear from view as we look at their achievements, the opposite is true of Winckelmann: everything that he produces is great and remarkable because it reveals his character." Winckelmann was perhaps the most significant figure in the eighteenth-century rediscovery of the classical world, and much of his significance lay in his ability to reanimate the past, to breathe his own particular vision of life into the ruined and partial figures of antiquity. His work made Greek homoerotic ideals accessible to the gay imagination at a crucial historical moment when gay people were becoming conscious of a sensibility as well a history they could begin to claim as their own. More than anyone else of his age, Winckelmann articulated that sensibility in ways that were both deeply personal and resonant on the larger stage of an evolving cultural identity.

22

Harry Hay

1912–

Harry Hay was born on April 7, 1912, in Worthing, England. His father, a former manager of Witwatersrand Deep (the South African mine responsible for producing half the world's gold), had recently been posted to the Gold Coast of Africa to supervise the opening of mines there. Since the Gold Coast lacked any medical facilities, Hay's mother was sent back to England to give birth. She and her child stayed there for three years, then joined her husband at his new job with a copper mine in South America. A serious injury soon forced him to move to southern California for medical treatment, and it was there that Harry Hay grew up.

After graduating from high school in 1929, he worked for a year in a Los Angeles law office. By this time he was regularly having sex with men whom he met on the streets of downtown Los Angeles. Enrolling at Stanford University in 1930 to study drama, he soon found himself part of San Francisco's community of gay actors, artists, and writers.

After Stanford he returned to Los Angeles, and in 1933, unable to find regular work as an actor during the Depression, he joined a left-wing agitprop theater group that performed at strikes and demonstrations. This experience served to increase Hay's political awareness, and the next year he joined the Communist Party. Party work would consume him for the next fifteen years and have an immense effect on his private life. In 1938, after revealing his homosexuality to fellow Party members, he was advised to repress that "degenerate" side of his personality. He obeyed faithfully and in that same year married Party member Anita Platky, whom he fully advised of his predicament. Such may seem an odd move for the man who would become the father of the American gay rights movement, but as his friend James Kepner observed, "in the forties, for many gays who wanted to be socially productive, marriage was a necessity. It was inescapable." Marriage—and the adoption of children—did not, however, entirely stifle Hay. He continued to meet men from time to time, and at one point his seven-month-long affair with a young architect named Bill Alexander threatened to wreck the marriage.

After working briefly as a union organizer during World War II, Hay became involved in 1945 with the People's Education Center in Los Angeles, a workers' education project. In 1948, during the presidential bid of Henry Wallace, a chance attendance at a party where all the guests were gay men started Hay thinking: he proposed a Bachelors for Wallace group, but no one was interested. Two years later, in November 1950, five men—Hay, Bob Hull, Chuck Rowland, Dale Jennings, and "R."—met in secret at Hay's home to discuss the formation of a homosexual rights organization. From those initial discussions came the Mattachine Society, so-named for the Matachinos, court jesters of the Italian Renaissance who, behind their masks, were free to speak the truth.

The Mattachine Society was informed by the Marxist intellectual orientation of its members. In their discussions, they came to the understanding that homosexuals as a group represented an oppressed minority, even though homosexuals as individuals were in general unaware of their status as an oppressed minority. Most homosexuals were trapped by false consciousness, seeing themselves as aberrant individuals rather than as a collective force. The structure of the Society, with its secretive cells, owed much to Communist organizing tactics.

In April 1951 the Society quietly circulated a one-page manifesto. The first meetings took place in an atmosphere of fear: participants were not sure whether it was legal for such meetings to take place, even behind closed doors and in private residences. Gradually, however, the sense of fear was replaced by a collective sense of mutual support. By May 1953 the Mattachine Society could claim over two thousand members, with one hundred separate discussion groups. The Society's newsletter, *One*, distributed two thousand copies a month.

Meanwhile, conscious of the Communist line on homosexuality, Hay had left the Party. But his past would come back to haunt him. The year 1953 saw rising anticommunist sentiment throughout the country, fueled by Sen. Joseph McCarthy and his aide ROY COHN [84]. Afraid that his former ties to the Communist Party might damage the Mattachine Society, Hay decided to step down as an officer of the society.

The move left Hay nearly suicidal. His marriage had broken up as well, and he found himself in a demanding relationship with his querulous young Danish lover, Jorn Kamgren. Alimony payments caused him to be chronically strapped for cash. During this difficult time, Hay threw himself into an intensive study of homosexuality and became particularly interested in the berdache, the shamanic men-women of the Native American cultures (see WE'WHA [53]). Over the next twenty years Hay would be at work on this enormous undertaking, his study of "the contribution of gay consciousness to humankind." Ironically, his contributions to gay studies would be derided in later years by scholars whose very existence had been made possible by events Hay had started in the first place.

In May 1955, Hay was called to testify before the dread House Un-American Activities Committee, with the result that the Mattachine Society distanced itself even further from its founder.

The 1960s saw Hay's continued activity in the struggle for

gay rights: he helped organize the first gay pride parade in Los Angeles (and perhaps in the nation) and in 1966 was chair of the LA Committee to Fight the Exclusion of Homosexuals from the Armed Forces (though as the war deepened, the pacifist Hay would become a draft counselor). Perhaps as a sign of the times he opened a kaleidoscope factory with his lover John Burnside, whom he had met in 1963 and with whom he formed The Circle of Loving Companions. When the STONEWALL RIOTS [5] broke out in New York City in 1969, Hay was not particularly impressed—"because of all the open gay projects we had done throughout the sixties in Los Angeles. As far as we were concerned, Stonewall meant that the East Coast was finally catching up." Nevertheless, he got caught up in the excitement soon enough. By December 1969, he was serving as the first elected chair of the Southern California Gay Liberation Front, one of many such groups that sprang up in the heady days following Stonewall. Among the GLF's activities: holding a one-day "Gay-In" in the face of police warnings against gay gatherings and sponsoring "funky dances," despite the questionable legality of same-sex dances under California law at the time.

In 1970, Hay, Burnside, and their mail-order kaleidoscope factory moved to New Mexico, a part of the country that had enchanted Hay ever since he had traveled there in the 1950s in an unsuccessful quest to interview a living berdache. Perhaps it was the still-haunted air of New Mexico, but in the late seventies and early eighties, Hay became increasingly concerned with spiritual issues. He formed the Radical Faeries, a movement devoted to ecology, spiritual truth, and gay-centeredness. The first gathering of Radical Faeries took place in the Arizona desert in 1978, with over two hundred gay men in attendance. Hay urged them, "Throw off the ugly green frogskin of hetero-imitation to find the shining Faerie prince below." He imagined a network of sanctuaries where gay men could be healed and nurtured, and spent time and energy attempting to buy land for a Radical Faerie community. Hay's relationship with the Faeries soon became problematic, however, and in a replay of events in the Mattachine Society thirty years earlier, he found himself ousted from the Faeries' leadership.

Harry Hay's long and extraordinary life has been, in many ways, a barometer of gay life in the United States during this century. His influential achievement was that he seemed to find

himself always on the forefront of changes, always anticipating
the historical forces continually shaping our culture. Although
the Mattachine Society came under much attack for its political
timidity during the 1960s, the fact remains that it was an essential
and exceedingly courageous first step in the long battle for gay
rights in America. Those who criticize it do so from a position
made secure by the accomplishments of a movement begun by
the first tentative steps of the Mattachine Society. For that reason,
the shadow Harry Hay casts is a long and distinguished one.

23

Harvey Milk

1930–1978

Harvey Milk was born on May 22, 1930, in Woodmere, Long Island. At Bayshore High School he was a mediocre student, playing on the football and basketball teams and on the weekends taking the train in to Manhattan. There he attended the opera and theater, to which he had become passionately devoted. He had also, since the age of fourteen, been passionately devoted to having sex with men and took the opportunity of his jaunts to Manhattan to go cruising in Central Park. When he was seventeen, he was arrested for indecent exposure in the park (he had his shirt off, but that was enough in those days). The police issued him a warning and let him go.

In 1951, Milk graduated from the New York State College for

Teachers in Albany, where he had majored in mathematics and
been sports editor for the school newspaper. Three months later,
concerned with stopping the Communists in Korea, he signed up
for the Navy. Rising rapidly through the ranks, he eventually
became chief petty officer on the aircraft carrier USS *Kittiwake*,
stationed in the Pacific. Although he would later claim to have
been dishonorably discharged from the Navy for his homosexuality, this appears not to have been the case. He left the Navy in
August 1955, after three years and eleven months—with the last
month off for good behavior.

Returning to Long Island in July 1956 to teach high school,
at Riis Beach he met handsome Joe Campbell. The two became
lovers and settled into a safe, middle-class marriage in Manhattan, where Milk began working first as an actuarial statistician
with the Great American Insurance Company, then later with a
Wall Street investment firm. When the relationship with Campbell ended in 1962, Milk moved on to a young radical named
Craig Rodwell, who attempted to politicize his conservative
boyfriend. But Milk would have none of it: in 1964 he did
volunteer work for Barry Goldwater's presidential campaign. In
the late 1960s, though, Milk's social and political conservatism
finally began to change. Through his new lover, the suicidal Jack
McKinley, he became friendly with New York's theater world,
especially Tom O'Horgan, the successful producer of such musi-
cals as *Hair* and *Jesus Christ Superstar*. Milk dropped out of Wall
Street, grew his hair long, adopted hippie attire, burned his Bank
of America card to protest the Vietnam War. Moving to San
Francisco in 1972, he and his latest lover, Scott Smith, opened a
camera store on Castro Street, in a neighborhood that was
quickly becoming a haven for gays. Milk explained the location's
attraction: "I like to sit at the window and watch the cute boys
walk by."

Angered by the mendacity of the Senate Watergate hearings,
Milk made a quixotic run for San Francisco supervisor in 1973.
Man of La Mancha, with its injunction to dream the impossible
dream, had always been his favorite musical, and this campaign,
he thought, looked impossible. An openly gay candidate, he
ruffled the feathers of older, more cautious gays, and his hippie
appearance put off many voters. Nonetheless, he came in tenth in
a field of thirty-two candidates, garnering an impressive 17,000
votes.

He decided to get serious about his political image: he cut his hair, stopped smoking marijuana, and swore never to be seen in a San Francisco bathhouse again. In 1974 he established the Castro Village Association, an organization of local merchants, and also founded the Castro Street Fair. Two years after its inception, the yearly event was attracting crowds of one hundred thousand people. Before long Milk became known as the Mayor of Castro, holding court in his financially strapped camera store that by this point was little more than a front for his political activities.

With strong support from the labor unions, whom he had impressed with his work on the Coors-beer boycott, he ran again for supervisor in 1975 and came in seventh. The next year, in recognition of the growing political clout of gays in the city, Mayor George Moscone appointed Milk to the Board of Permit Appeals, making Milk the first openly gay city commissioner in the country. But Milk was never good at playing by the rules; he quickly ran afoul of the Democratic machine by announcing his candidacy for a vacant State Assembly seat that Moscone had discreetly promised someone else. Fired from the Board, he also lost the election—by 3,600 of 33,000 votes cast. The months of feverish campaigning had taken their toll: Milk's neglected camera business was nearly in financial ruin, and his lover Scott Smith had moved out. The established gay politicians found much to rejoice over in Milk's defeat: clearly this upstart candidate was finished for good. But he confounded them. In November 1977, campaigning on a broad platform that, in addition to a gay rights ordinance, included expanded child care, free municipal transportation, low-rent housing, and a civilian police-review board, he won election as supervisor from San Francisco's District Five. Among sixteen candidates, he received 30 percent of the vote. It was the first time an openly gay candidate had been elected in any big city in the United States, and Harvey's supporters were delirious. "This is not my victory," he proclaimed, "it's yours and yours and yours. If a gay can win, it means that there *is* hope that the system can work for all minorities if we fight. We've given them hope."

A week after he won, he tape-recorded a will in which, with chilling prescience, he expressed the dark desire "If a bullet should enter my brain, let that bullet destroy every closet door."

As city supervisor, he fought against downtown corporations

and real estate developers and campaigned hard for the rights of senior citizens. His sense of theatricality and political expedience served him well in introducing such popular measures as a bill requiring owners to clean up after their pets. Under his urging, the city council passed a gay rights ordinance, nine to one, with the lone dissenting vote by Supervisor Dan White.

Tragedy struck in August 1978. According to author Randy Shilts, "Harvey had always had a penchant for young waifs with substance-abuse problems." His latest lover, a young Mexican American named Jack Lira, was no exception. One day he hanged himself in Milk's apartment.

Much of Milk's energy during 1978 went into the fight against Proposition 6, an initiative sponsored by state senator John Briggs that would require the state of California to fire any teacher found guilty of "public homosexual conduct," which the law broadly defined as "advocating, imposing, encouraging or promoting of private or public homosexual activity directed at, or likely to come to the attention of school children and/or other [school] employees." Due in large part to Milk's tireless campaigning against the measure, it was resoundingly defeated by California voters in November.

Three weeks after the election, on November 27, 1978, Harvey Milk and Mayor Moscone were assassinated by Supervisor Dan White, a defender of "family values" who had long clashed with Milk over gay issues. White had impetuously resigned from the city council and wanted his job back, but Moscone, at Milk's urging, had refused the request and was preparing to appoint White's successor the morning of the assassination. A former police officer, White climbed in a back window at City Hall, proceeded to the mayor's office, and after a brief argument, shot the mayor four times. He reloaded and went to Milk's office, where he fired four bullets into Milk. Then he knelt beside the body and fired a last bullet, at point-blank range, into Milk's brain.

In the ensuing trial, White's lawyers argued the infamous "Twinkies" defense—that White had become disoriented after consuming too much junk food. The jury declared him guilty of voluntary manslaughter—the verdict the defense had asked for—and he was sentenced to seven years, eight months for the two murders. The verdicts outraged gay San Franciscans, and thousands of angry demonstrators converged on City Hall. The resulting riots became known as the White Nights.

In assessing Harvey Milk's legacy, Wayne Dynes has written: "Later mythology has portrayed Harvey Milk as a radical leftist, but more careful scrutiny shows that he retained elements of his conservative background to the very end. At bottom he held an almost Jeffersonian concept of the autonomy of small neighborhoods, prospering through small businesses and local attention to community problems.... Milk anticipated the later strategy of the 'rainbow coalition,' but because of his personal gifts, and the time and place in which he lived, he was able to make it work more effectively for gay and lesbian politics than any other single individual has done before or since."

Milk always insisted, "I have never considered myself a candidate. I have always considered myself part of a movement, part of a candidacy." And he was right: his election was the result of a historic convergence of social and political forces. It was his genius—for timing, for theater, for a sense of people's needs—that enabled him to embody those forces. As the first openly gay official elected in the U.S., Milk's influence on the course of American history was profound. On a practical level, his courageous example paved the way for later openly gay politicians like BARNEY FRANK [56]. On a more tangible plane, however, Milk's candidacy gave gays and lesbians, perhaps for the first time in their history, a visible, articulate, persuasive leader. Harvey Milk was the Martin Luther King, Jr. of the movement for gay and lesbian civil rights, and if his martyrdom was a painful reminder of how long and difficult the journey to freedom would be, the tireless example of his heroic life was an empowering spur to action. The cry "Remember Harvey Milk!"—shouted in such grief and anger during the White Night riots of 1979—echoes to this day as a call to justice for gay men and lesbians everywhere.

24

Queen Christina
of Sweden

1626–1689

Christina, daughter of King Gustavus II Adolphus of Sweden and Maria Eleonora of Brandenburg, was born December 8, 1626. Her intellectual brilliance and strong will were evident early in childhood, and she was educated as a prince. At the age of six, she became queen-elect upon the death of her father at the battle of Lützen. Until 1644 she ruled under a regency headed by Count Axel Gustafsson Oxenstierna, who had been her father's chancellor. Oxenstierna instructed Christina in politics, and at the age of fourteen she began attending council meetings. Upon assuming the throne, Queen Christina was instrumental in gaining the peace of Westphalia, which effectively put an end to the Thirty Years' War, which had devastated Europe and left

Sweden financially ruined. Her interest in state affairs, however, was surpassed by her enthusiasm for learning. She attracted to her court musicians, poets, and scholars and became known as the Minerva of the North. She would rise at five in the morning and read. The great philosopher René Descartes himself would teach her philosophy. She invariably dressed in men's clothes.

Then, on June 6, 1654, Christina shocked Europe by abdicating the throne. Pleading that she was ill, and that ruling a nation was too heavy a burden for a woman, she named her cousin, Charles X, as her successor. It was generally known, however, that the heavy burden this brilliant queen purported to be unable to bear had to do not at all with governing, but with the persistent expectation that she should marry and produce an heir.

After her abdication, she left Sweden and traveled leisurely southward. Stopping at Innsbruck, she dropped another bombshell by publicly renouncing her Lutheran faith and announcing her conversion to Roman Catholicism. In staunchly Lutheran Sweden, such a conversion was against the law. Christina's announcement was a brilliant coup for the pope in Rome and a shattering blow to European Protestants. In December 1655, Pope Alexander VII received his new convert with open arms at the Vatican. According to EDWARD CARPENTER [9], "it is said that she shook the pope's hand, on seeing him, so heartily that the doctor had to attend to it afterwards!"

Soon, however, the propaganda-hungry pope became disillusioned by Christina's insistence that matters of faith were private. Furthermore, her personality and manner created a sensation in Rome. Almost immediately after establishing herself there, she began to scheme with the French foreign minister to seize the city of Naples, then under Spanish control, and rule as queen, leaving the throne at her death to a French prince. In 1657, however, this scheme collapsed while she was visiting Fountainbleau in France. Sensing that one of her closest advisers, the Marchere Gian Riccardo Monaldeschi, had betrayed her, she summarily ordered his execution. Some commentators believe Monaldeschi was murdered because he was about to reveal Christina's homosexuality. Whatever the cause, her unilateral action, swift and vengeful, shocked the French court. Pope Alexander, in the meantime, made it clear she was not welcome back in Rome.

She returned to Rome, however, and with characteristic energy set about establishing herself in her magnificent palace—the Riario—where, as in Stockholm, she surrounded herself with artists, intellectuals, and musicians. Her choirmaster was Alessandro Scarlatti. Arcangelo Corelli (who was gay) directed her orchestra. The sculptor Bernini considered himself eternally in her debt for her help during various difficulties. She was, without a doubt, one of the most influential figures of her time. Friend to four popes, splendid and generous patroness even though she herself was usually in financial difficulties, she founded the Arcadia Academy in Rome (an institution that flourishes to this day), campaigned for the first public opera house in Rome, and militantly championed the cause of personal freedoms. She was particularly known as the protectoress of Jews in Rome.

After the death of Charles X she returned to Sweden in 1660 and again in 1667 in attempts to regain the throne, but met with an unenthusiastic response both times. So she settled for the splendors of her Italian court.

Rumors about her personal life abounded. Historian Lillian Faderman reports that such contemporaries as Count Palatine, the Duke de Guise, and Mlle. de Montpensier all recorded her advances to women. Particularly intriguing are her passionate letters written to one Ebba Sparre during her travels: "If you remember the power you have over me, you will also remember that I have been in possession of your love for twelve years; I belong to you so utterly, that it will never be possible for you to lose me; and only when I die shall I cease loving you." Although such was often the language of romantic friendship in those days, many commentators saw a conscious and insistent sexual element in her relations with women—a perception that persisted. In 1719, thirty years after Christina's death, the memoirist Princess Palatine, mother of the regent of Orléans, remembered that Christina once tried to "force" Mme. de Bregny, "who was almost unable to defend herself."

In the words of nineteenth-century sexologist Havelock Ellis, her "very marked masculine traits and high intelligence seem to have been combined with a definitely homosexual or bisexual temperament." In her later years she was associated with Decio Cardinal Azzolini, the leader of a group of cardinals known as the *squadrone volante,* and it was rumored that she and the cardinal were lovers. When she died—on April 19, 1689—

Cardinal Azzolini was left heir.

Queen Christina is buried in St. Peter's Basilica in Rome.

Flamboyant, powerful, compelling both to her allies and her enemies, Queen Christina is an extraordinary presence on the stage of history, a woman of unabashed sexuality and great courage who insisted on reshaping the world for her own aims time and again. She is ranked here with EDWARD II [25] as one of history's best-known gay monarchs. Other queens—and here I do actually mean women—contending for a position on the list include Russia's Catherine II (1729–1796), and England's Queen Anne (1665–1714).

That Christina's influence has continued to our own day is evidenced by the famous 1933 film *Queen Christina* in which Greta Garbo plays the title role with requisite and alluring sexual ambiguity.

25

Edward II

1284–1327

Edward II was born on April 25, 1284, at Caernarvon Castle, Wales. The only surviving son of Edward I ("The Hammer of the Scots") and Eleanor of Castile, Edward was a great disappointment to his warlike father because of his distaste for martial activities. When Edward I invited Piers Gaveston to tutor his son in the arts of war, Gaveston and Edward fell in love, and the king, who rather liked Gaveston but disapproved of the relationship, had him exiled. Upon Edward II's accession to the throne on July 8, 1307, he immediately recalled his lover from exile and conferred on him the earldom of Cornwall. He also imprisoned his father's chief minister and began reversing most of his father's policies, especially the avid prosecution of a long-standing war with Scotland. In 1308, Edward married Isabella of France, the daughter of Philip IV, and they produced four children.

Uninterested in the affairs of government, Edward left much of the management of the country to Gaveston, who, though capable, nevertheless managed to alienate many of the powerful barons who had already been restless under Edward's predecessor. They allied to force Edward, in 1310, to accept a council of "lords ordainers." This twenty-one-member council issued a document known as the Ordinances, which banished Gaveston and curtailed much of Edward's monarchical authority. Gaveston didn't stay banished for long, but soon rejoined Edward, whereupon the infuriated barons had the king's lover hunted down and killed in June 1312. This savage act split the government of the Ordainers, though only briefly: Edward's disastrous 1314 defeat by the Scottish Robert I the Bruce at the battle of Bannockburn reunited the barons against him. In the wake of their victory, the Scots invaded much of northern England and Ireland, and chaos and famine set in. By 1321, England was in the midst of civil war, provoked in part by the barons' hatred of Edward's new favorite, Hugh le Despenser the Younger. Hugh and his father were exiled in August 1321, but feuding among the king's opponents gave Edward the opportunity to counterattack, and in March 1322 the leader of the opposition, Edward's cousin Thomas, Earl of Lancaster, was captured and executed.

Hugh le Despenser returned to the king's side, and Edward instituted a reign of terror, revoking the Ordinances, executing scores of opponents and dispossessing their families. On September 24, 1326, Edward's estranged wife, Isabella, accompanied by her lover, Robert Mortimer, an old baronial enemy of Edward's, landed with troops at Harwich. Her armies met no resistance, and the city of London welcomed her. Edward found himself deserted by his allies. Hugh was caught by Isabella's forces: according to the medieval chronicler Jean Froissart, Isabella ("the she-wolf of France") ordered that Hugh's genitals be cut off and burned in front of his eyes before he was decapitated.

No wonder CHRISTOPHER MARLOWE [19] thought this was good material for a play.

Edward fled to the Despenser stronghold at Glamorgan in Wales, where he was captured on November 16, 1326. Threatened with the dispossession of his dynasty, he abdicated in favor of his heir, Edward III, who ascended the throne on January 25, 1327. Imprisoned at Berkeley Castle in Gloucestershire, Edward escaped only to be recaptured and, on September 21, 1327, was murdered by the insertion of a red-hot iron poker into his anus. This rather horrifying method of execution may have been as much an attempt to conceal the crime as to punish the king for his homosexuality. After the murder, Edward's body was exhibited bearing no apparent wounds. If this was meant to placate the onlookers, however, no one was fooled since Edward's shrieks had been heard throughout the castle.

Historian John Boswell writes, "Although there is no way to assess how the populace in general felt about their gay monarch, there can be little doubt that his erotic preferences were widely known and generally regarded as the cause of his downfall. The most restrained of all his biographers [in *Vita Edwardi Secundi*] noted that Edward's love for Gaveston, like DAVID'S for JONATHAN [40], went "beyond the love of women." The *Chronicle of Melsa* tersely observed that "Edward in fact delighted inordinately in the vice of sodomy and seemed to lack fortune and grace throughout his life." Ralph Higden [in *Polychronion*] eloquently linked Edward's affections to his troubles. "He was ardently in love with one of his friends, whom he exalted, enriched, advanced, and honored extravagantly. From this cause came shame to the lover, hatred to the beloved, scandal to the people, and harm to the kingdom." In attempting to moderate this judgment, Boswell suggests that "the inordinateness of the favors Edward bestowed on Gaveston has been exaggerated by historians, both medieval and modern, as a mask for disgust at the nature of the relationship."

Likewise, gay scholar A. L. Rowse, in his *Homosexuals in History*, presents us with an appealing rehabilitation of this vilified king: "He had no love of fighting, or even of the mock-war of tournaments: this made him unpopular with fighting fools, especially the barons. His tastes were banausic [i.e., inclined to things mechanical], distinctly lower class: he liked hedging and ditching, building and trenching. A tall, handsome, easy-going fellow, he liked country (and other) sports, racing and hunting, gaming and dicing. He was good at mechanical arts—very unsuitable for a king—blacksmith work, for example; he enjoyed the gay and unrepressed company of jolly workmen, grooms, sailors, rowing men.... It was particularly offensive that, apart from a few intimates among the courtiers, he did not care for the company of his own class. His great defect was that he had no head for politics and found the ways of politicians unbearably boring. This was fatal in his job, which he neglected or attended to by fits and starts."

Other gay kings have sat on the throne of England, among them William II, Richard I "the Lionhearted," James I, William III, and possibly George III. I have chosen Edward II because of the ongoing influence he has had on the gay imagination from CHRISTOPHER MARLOWE [19] in the sixteenth century to DEREK JARMAN [82] in our own time. This fascination is due in part to the hideous nature of Edward's death, but not entirely: his loyalty to Piers Gaveston gives us an appealing glimpse of gay devotion and affection through history's usually obscuring veils.

26

Jane Addams

1860–1935

Jane Addams was born on September 6, 1860, in Cedarville, Illinois. Resisting her family's attempts to fashion her as a debutante and marry her to her stepbrother, she attended Rockland College in Illinois and graduated in 1881. After that she entered the Women's Medical College in Philadelphia, but her health failed, and she was invalided for two years. Between 1883 and 1885, and again in 1887–88, she traveled extensively in Europe with her companion, Ellen Gates Starr, whom she had met in college. While in England the two paid a visit to the Toynbee Hall settlement house in the Whitechapel industrial district of London. The settlement house was a place where upper-class young women with a social conscience could live among the poor, study conditions, and then go about working for reforms. Toynbee Hall greatly impressed Addams and Starr, and they returned home determined to create something similar on

American soil: a place where, as Jane Addams wrote, young women could "learn of life from life itself."

In a working-class district in Chicago, the two women found and purchased a large vacant house that had been built in 1856 by Charles Hull. On September 18, 1889, they moved into the newly christened Hull House.

The mission of Hull House was twofold: to provide services and cultural opportunities for the working-class population of the neighborhood, and to train young social workers in a real-life setting. Among the services provided were playground facilities, a day nursery, a gymnasium, a community kitchen, and a boarding club for working girls. College courses were offered, as well as training in music and the arts. The settlement eventually grew to include thirteen buildings and a camp near Lake Geneva, Wisconsin. Hull House also sponsored one of the first community theater groups in America, the Hull House Players.

Over the years, many prominent social workers and reformers came to live and work at Hull House, including Julia Lathrop, Grace and Edith Abbott, and Florence Kelly. One young lady who came in 1890 and stayed was Mary Rozet Smith: she became Addams's companion for the next forty years. They shared the same bed, and when they traveled, Addams always wired ahead to make sure the hotel would have a double bed for them. As for Ellen Starr, she continued to work at Hull House, but it was now Mary Smith who accompanied Addams on her frequent lecture tours. The two thought of themselves as wedded and in 1904 bought a house together in Maine.

About their relationship historian Lillian Faderman writes, "It would seem that Jane and Mary, who became 'lovers' near the turn of the century, did not fear they had much to hide—they could even allow strange hotel keepers to know that they preferred to sleep in a double bed together. They understood (regardless of the sexual nature of their relationship) that they could rely on the protective coloring of pearls and ladylike appearance and of romantic friendship, which was not yet dead in America.... It is only in the last few years that we can acknowledge, without diminishing her stature, that Jane Addams— whether or not she knew to use the term about herself—was what our day would consider lesbian. She devoted her entire emotional life to women, she considered herself married to a woman, and she believed that she was 'delivered' by their shared love."

Addams's public causes were many. She campaigned tirelessly for the first juvenile-court law in America, the eight-hour working day for women, the regulation of tenement houses and inspection of factories, workers' compensation, women's suffrage, and pacifism. She was an eloquent champion of equal justice for blacks and immigrants and proposed research into the causes of poverty and crime. For this she was branded a radical by some of her wealthy patrons, who withdrew support from Hull House.

In 1910, Addams became the first woman president of the National Conference of Social Work, and in 1915 she was chairwoman of the International Congress of Women at The Hague, Netherlands, a gathering that led to the formation in 1919 of the Women's International League for Peace and Freedom, of which Addams served as president until 1935. A committed pacifist who considered war to be the supreme social evil, Addams found herself vilified by many politicians and the press when she opposed U.S. participation in World War I. The venerable Daughters of the American Revolution went so far as to expel her from its ranks.

In 1920, Addams helped found the American Civil Liberties Union. For her work in social reforms and as leader of the international women's peace movement, she was awarded the 1931 Nobel Peace Prize. This was the first time an American woman had ever won a Nobel Prize.

Jane Addams died on May 21, 1935, in Chicago. Her numerous books include *Democracy and Social Ethics* (1902), *Newer Ideals of Peace* (1907), *The Spirit of Youth and the City Streets* (1909), *Twenty Years at Hull House* (1910), and *The Second Twenty Years at Hull House* (1930).

As a pioneering social reformer, Jane Addams contributed much to twentieth-century social progress. As a lesbian, she helped create an identity within which talented, independent women could come together and work to create a world in their own collective image. Lillian Faderman characterizes these women as "cultural feminists, fueled by the belief that male values created the tragedies connected with industrialization, war, and mindless urbanization and that it was the responsibility of women, with their superior abilities, to straighten the world out again. Their love of women was at least in part the result of their moral chauvinism." It would not be without warrant to suggest that the role Hillary Rodham Clinton plays today on the stage of health-care reform owes itself in large part to the example of Jane Addams and her kind. Addams's high ranking in *The Gay 100* reflects my sense of her lasting contribution not only to our century's noblest ideals of social progress, but to the enhanced roles in the public sphere available to capable women whether lesbian or straight. It was, to a large extent, her lesbianism that freed her from the demands conventionally made upon women, and that enabled her to work for her ideals. For the purposes of this ranking, I see Jane Addams as following in the footsteps of such liberators as MARY WOLLSTONECRAFT [11] and SUSAN B. ANTHONY [12].

27

Emily Dickinson

1830–1886

Emily Dickinson was born on December 19, 1830, in Amherst, Massachusetts. Her wealthy grandfather had founded Amherst College in 1810, and her father served as its treasurer from 1835 to 1870. After graduating from Amherst Academy, Dickinson studied at Mount Holyoke Female Seminary (later to become Mount Holyoke College) for a year in 1847–48. Religious instruction was an important part of the curriculum at both the schools she attended, and considerable social pressure to become a Christian was brought to bear on the young Dickinson. Though she was moved by a religious revival in 1845–46, and again in 1848 while she was at Holyoke, she felt she had no conviction of faith and was therefore unable to publicly testify to that effect in order to join the Congregational Church (the only denomination in town). In 1850 her resistance to the certainties of faith received support from an unexpected quarter: as a Christmas gift, a law student in her father's office named Benjamin Newton gave her a copy of the poems of Ralph Waldo Emerson, the freethinking transcendentalist from Concord, Massachusetts. Emerson became what Dickinson would later call her "validator," and under the influence of his poems she began to write her own.

In 1855, during a stopover in Philadelphia while on a trip to Washington, D.C., Dickinson met Charles Wadsworth, a pastor who became her "dearest earthly friend." When he moved to California in 1862, she suffered an emotional crisis that led to a decline in what had been a prolific output of poetry during the years between 1858 and 1862. In that same year, she showed a Cambridge clergyman named Thomas Wentworth Higginson, with whom she had been corresponding, four of her poems and asked him if her poetry was alive. He assured her that it was indeed, though he advised her against publishing any of it. He also offered her advice on the practice of her craft, none of which—fortunately—she took.

In the years after 1862, she produced fewer poems, but much of her greatest work dates from this later period of her life. In language stripped to the bone, with familiar words made remarkable by their placement in unfamiliar contexts, with syntax and rhythm incessantly teased into new-sounding musics, her poetry confronted with unsparing honesty the nether regions of the soul, its agonies of doubt and blasts of ecstasy. She collected her poems together—often with variant versions—in little booklets that she sewed together by hand and stored in her bureau. She resisted the attempts of friends to have her work published, and within her lifetime only seven of her poems appeared in print.

Persistent eye trouble led her to Cambridge for extended periods of treatment in 1864 and 1865. After the late 1860s, she never left the family property. Around town she was known as "the nun of Amherst." She lived quietly in her upstairs room, her privacy assiduously guarded by her unmarried younger sister, Lavinia, who cooked and cleaned in order to give Dickinson the time to write. Her brother Austin and his wife, Dickinson's close friend Susan Gilbert, lived next door. Dickinson read voluminously and gardened (a talented horticulturalist, she grew pomegranates and calla lilies in the family greenhouse) and corresponded with various close friends: Wadsworth, Higginson, Judge Otis Lord, Kate Anthon, Helen Hunt Jackson, and Mrs. Josiah Holland, wife of the editor of the *Springfield Republican*.

Emily Dickinson died on May 15, 1886. Her bureau was found to contain over one thousand poems. In all she wrote nearly eighteen hundred poems. Higginson, who had always considered Dickinson "partially cracked," edited and "corrected" a selection of these, which he published in 1890. It was not until 1955 that Dickinson's complete poems were published as she wrote them.

So much energy has been poured into attempts either to picture Dickinson as a quaint, asexual spinster or to uncover a conventionally heterosexual if sublimated love life from the inner fire of her poems that it is difficult to see past the cloying, sentimental myths that have accrued around her. About her intense woman-to-woman relationships, an important aspect of her life, virtual silence has long been the rule.

Recent thinking has painted a richer, more provocative picture for us. Of such revisionist work, educator Toni McNaron has written, "I am not waiting to turn Emily Dickinson into a practicing lesbian.... What I do want is a lesbian-feminist reading of her poetry and her life as the most accurate way to handle that otherwise confusing constellation of myth and fact surrounding her."

In an important and influential 1975 essay, "Vesuvius at Home: The Power of Emily Dickinson," the poet ADRIENNE RICH [47] attempts to refute some of the clichés by which we have presumed to know Dickinson. She takes her cue from an incident narrated by Dickinson's cousin Martha, in which "she told of visiting her in her corner bedroom on the second floor at 280 Main Street, Amherst, and of how Emily Dickinson made as if to lock the door with an imaginary key, turned, and said: 'Matty: here's freedom.'"

The stakes for someone like Dickinson were high. As Rich observes, "the terms she had been handed by society—Calvinist Protestantism, Romanticism, the nineteenth century corsetting of women's bodies, choices, and sexuality—could spell insanity to a woman of genius. What this one had to do was retranslate her own unorthodox, subversive, sometimes volcanic propensities into a dialect called metaphor: her native language. 'Tell the Truth—but tell it Slant—.' It is always what is under pressure in us, especially under the pressure of concealment—that explodes in poetry."

Stressing that Dickinson's life was "no hermetic retreat, but a seclusion that included a wide range of people, of reading and correspondence," Rich observes about the poet's relationships: "Obviously, Dickinson was attracted by and interested in men whose minds had something to offer her; she was, it is by now clear, equally attracted by and interested in women whose minds had something to offer. There are many poems to and about women, and some which exist in two versions with alternate sets of pronouns." Dickinson's emotional world was far more complex than our insipid myths have given her credit for. As if to confirm this, it has recently been shown (by historian Lillian Faderman, for instance) that Dickinson's passionate letters to her friend Susan Gilbert were heavily edited for publication by her niece, in order to tone down the ardent protestations of love they contained.

As Rich sees Dickinson's case: "Given her vocation, she was neither eccentric or quaint; she was determined to survive, to use her powers, to practice necessary economies." Emily Dickinson was, in other words, living out precisely the kind of hard-won creative life that VIRGINIA WOOLF [13] would call for in her essay *A Room of One's Own* some fifty years later.

Some will think that the inclusion of Emily Dickinson on this list is completely unwarranted. My position is that we will never know her secrets. What we can know is that this is a woman who had intense and intimate relationships with other women, who was thoroughly heterodox in her religious beliefs, and who was a marriage resister in the most classic sense of the term. In order to create a space in which her courageous sense of self could blossom, she resolutely and without regret abandoned the patriarchy's expectations. While influencing countless women seeking a measure of autonomy in their own emotional and creative lives, Dickinson's life-choices continue to have a particular resonance in the lesbian imagination, as evidenced by recent powerful lesbian/feminist readings of her life and work. If the last hundred years have worked fruitlessly to heterosexualize Emily Dickinson, perhaps the next hundred will be more successful in lesbianizing her.

28

Radclyffe Hall

1880–1943

Radclyffe Hall was born Marguerite Radclyffe-Hall on August 12, 1880, in Bournemouth, Hampshire, England. Hailing from a wealthy though by no means happy family, she was educated at King's College, London, and enjoyed the privileges of wealth: fox hunting, fast cars, travel—and women. With her short haircut and men's clothes, she was known to her friends as John. According to Jane Rule, by age twenty-seven "Radclyffe Hall had probably loved more women than she had read books." It was at twenty-seven that Hall met Mabel Batten, a woman who was over twenty years her senior. The two fell in love and moved in together, and under Batten's influence Hall converted to Roman Catholicism.

In 1915, at a London tea party, Hall and Batten met Una, Lady Troubridge, the wife of an admiral. When Batten died a few months later—she dropped dead of a heart attack in the midst of a spat about Hall's burgeoning relationship with their new friend—Hall and Troubridge began a companionship that would last for the next thirty years. That the relationship was not without a twinge of guilt is suggested by Hall's dedication of all of her books "To the three of us."

Hall had written poetry since earliest childhood, publishing four volumes and even setting some to music. In 1915, a publisher who had seen her short stories suggested she write a novel. The result, *The Unlit Lamp,* was rejected by ten publishers before finally appearing in 1924. Although it treated lesbian themes, it stirred little controversy. Soon thereafter, respectable success seemed upon her. Her novel *Adam's Breed* won the coveted Prix Fémina in 1926, and in 1927 the James Tait Black Memorial Prize for Fiction.

Then in 1928 she ended all that with the publication of *The Well of Loneliness,* the sexual biography of a masculine girl named Stephen Gordon who loves (and loses) women, becomes an ambulance driver during World War I, and ends up with a modicum of peace as a successful writer living in Paris. Although the book seems utterly tame by today's standards—the most explicit the physical relationship between the two women ever gets is the sentence "And that night they were not divided"—London magistrate Chartres Biron was not amused. "The better an obscene book is written," he decreed, "the greater is the public to whom it is likely to appeal. The more palatable the poison, the more insidious it is." Because the book not only asked "decent people" to acknowledge the existence of lesbians, but went so far as to actually suggest that lesbians might be human, he declared the book "obscene libel" and ordered the police to destroy all copies of it.

In the United States, meanwhile, the court disagreed, arguing that discussions of homosexuality were not in and of themselves necessarily obscene. When *The Well of Loneliness* was published to much attention in the United States, it engendered a far-ranging discussion of the forbidden topic and, more than any other document of its time, brought lesbian existence out in the open. The British ban on the book was not repealed until after Hall's death fifteen years later. (It is interesting that VIRGINIA WOOLF [13] published *Orlando,* her whimsical paean to lover VITA SACKVILLE-WEST [64], the same year as *The Well of Loneliness* without provoking similar controversy: perhaps because Woolf and Sackville-West were both married and dressed like women rather than men.)

After the scandal, Hall and Troubridge deemed it prudent to leave England and lived abroad for several years. Though Hall published other novels, including *The Master of the House* (1932) and *The Sixth Beatitude* (1936), she never again touched on the controversial topic that had made her notorious.

She died, after a long struggle with cancer, on October 7, 1943, in London. A devout Roman Catholic to the end, her separation from Troubridge, she was sure, would be brief: they would soon meet in heaven. The manuscript of her final novel-in-progress was destroyed, in accordance with her wishes.

To read *The Well of Loneliness* today is something of a chore. Couched in the old language of "sexual inversion," it seems more quaint than anything else. Nonetheless, it is difficult to overestimate the impact the book had, the vast silences it broke, and the new territory it opened up for countless lesbian and gay authors who came after. For years it was known as "the lesbian bible," and a generation of butch lesbians modeled themselves on Stephen Gordon. Historian John D'Emilio has even suggested that the book, by creating "an almost magical aura around military life through its description of the...women's ambulance corps in World War I," played a part in making the Women's Army Corp during World War II "the almost quintessential lesbian institution."

Be that as it may, Radclyffe Hall is an excellent example of what I mean by "influence": her novel, mediocre at best, has nonetheless had far more influence on the world than many works of much higher quality, and her ranking here above much greater authors such as MARCEL PROUST [31] or JAMES BALDWIN [36] or WILLA CATHER [55] reflects that level of influence.

29

Peter Ilyich
Tchaikovsky

1840–1893

In E. M. FORSTER's [58] classic gay novel, *Maurice,* written in 1913 but not published until 1971, the eponymous and closeted hero runs into his scandalous friend Risley at a concert at which Tchaikovsky's last symphony has been played.

> "*Symphonie Pathique,*" said Risley gaily.
> "*Symphony Pathetic,*" corrected the Philistine.
> "*Symphonie Incestueuse et Pathique.*" And he informed his young friend that Tchaikovsky had fallen in love with his own nephew, and dedicated his masterpiece to him. "I come to see all respectable London flock. Isn't it supreme!"

"Queer things you know," said Maurice stuffily....
But he got a life of Tchaikovsky out of the library at
once. The episode of the composer's marriage conveys
little to the normal reader, who vaguely assumes incom-
patibility, but it thrilled Maurice. He knew what the
disaster meant....Reading on, he made the acquaintance of "Bob," the wonderful nephew to whom
Tchaikovsky turns after the breakdown, and in whom is
his spiritual and musical resurrection. The book blew
off the gathering dust, and he respected it as the one
literary work that had ever helped him.

Peter Ilyich Tchaikovsky was born on May 7, 1840, in
Votkinsk, Russia, where his father was a government superintendent of mines. From an early age, he evinced remarkable musical
abilities, though his parents, fearing that music would un-
necessarily excite their already high-strung child, discouraged
him. In 1848, the family moved first to Moscow, and then to St.
Petersburg, where Tchaikovsky entered the preparatory department of the School of Jurisprudence in 1850. Here he studied
only a little music, but fell in love with the opera, which he
attended as often as possible, and which profoundly influenced
the development of his musical taste. His days at school were not
happy—he was continually derided as provincial—and his fragile psychic world was dealt a devastating blow in 1854 when his
mother died of cholera. In great distress, not only over his
mother's sudden death but also his father's seeming nonchalance,
the fourteen-year-old Tchaikovsky composed his first piece of
music.

He entered the St. Petersburg Conservatory in 1862 and in
1865 was offered a teaching position there. The next year, he
suffered a nervous breakdown during the composition of his
Symphony No. 1 (*Winter Daydreams*). Nevertheless he regrouped
and continued to compose. A brief affair with a woman in the
mid-1870s led to another nervous breakdown.

In 1876 he began a strange and intense correspondence with
a wealthy widow named Nadezhda von Meck. She was an ardent
admirer of his music and eventually granted him an annuity that
allowed him to quit teaching and devote himself full-time to
composing. Theirs was a platonic friendship (often unduly ro-
manticized by commentators desperate for heterosexual love

interests in Tchaikovsky's uncooperative biography), and Tchaikovsky found the various effusions of their relationship increasingly irksome as time went by. When the two correspondents finally met face-to-face, the result was more than happy.

Tormented by his homosexuality, ever conscious of the demands of social propriety, in 1877 Tchaikovsky married one of his students who had become infatuated with him. He was unable, however, to consummate the marriage—and his wife's insistent sexual demands led him to attempt suicide. His rare moments of happiness came during the summers he spent at his sister's house at Kamenka in Ukraine. Only trouble lurked there as well. He fell hopelessly in love with his fourteen-year-old nephew, "Bob" (Vladimir) Davydov, an obsession he detailed in his diaries:

> May 1, 1884: Played duets with my darling, the incomparable, enchanting, ideal Bob, to his immense enjoyment.
> May 22: As soon as I do not work or walk (and that is also work for me) I begin to crave Bob and get lonesome without him. Frightful how I love him.
> May 31: After dinner was inseparable from my wonderful, incomparable Bob; first he was lolling on the balcony, on the little bench, languishing charmingly and chattering about my compositions.
> June 3: A strange thing: I've a terrible wish not to leave here. I think it all has to do with Bob.

There is some evidence to indicate that as Bob grew older, his relationship with the composer became more than platonic. The incomparable, enchanting, ideal Bob committed suicide in 1906 at the age of thirty-five.

In between emotional crises, nervous breakdowns, and bouts of heavy drinking, Tchaikovsky nonetheless managed to compose glorious music at a frenetic pace: six symphonies, a violin concerto and three piano concerti, operas such as *Eugene Onegin* (1879) and *The Queen of Spades* (1890), and enormously popular ballets, including *Swan Lake* (1876), *The Sleeping Beauty* (1889), and *The Nutcracker* (1892).

He completed his last work, the Symphony No. 6 in B Minor (*Pathetique*), in August 1893 and dedicated it to Bob. On October

28 he conducted the first performance. Convinced—and rightly so—that it was his masterpiece, Tchaikovsky was devastated by the public's lack of enthusiasm at its premiere. On November 2, 1893—six days after the premiere—he died. In his will he named Bob his sole heir.

The official story—promulgated by Tchaikovsky's gay brother, Modest—was that the composer inadvertently drank a glass of unboiled water and died of the cholera epidemic that was raging in Moscow at the time. There have always been inconsistencies in that version, however, and early on rumors surfaced that Tchaikovsky had in fact committed suicide. Evidence that has recently come to light indicates that Tchaikovsky may have been forced to poison himself in order to avoid a scandal concerning his sexual relationship with the young nephew of Duke Stenbok-Fermor, who had ties with the imperial family. Such a scandal would, in nineteenth-century Russia, have meant for Tchaikovsky the loss of all his rights, exile to Siberia, and permanent disgrace.

Tchaikovsky was one of the great composers of all time. Although we are now learning that many of the great composers were probably gay—Arcangelo Corelli, George Frideric Handel, Franz Schubert, perhaps even Ludwig van Beethoven, whose strange obsession with his nephew was recently the subject of a film by gay director Paul Morrissey—it is Tchaikovsky who, down through the years, has been the most widely identified in the public imagination as gay. As the incident in Forster's *Maurice* shows, Tchaikovsky's tragic life and immortal music have been indelibly woven into the legend of gay existence, that secret network of knowledge that has sustained us through beleaguered years of silence and secrecy—the whispered and consoling reminder, *He was one of us.*

30

André Gide

1869–1951

Andŕe Gide was born on November 22, 1869, in Paris. His father was a law professor at the University of Paris. His mother came from a wealthy Norman family with extensive estates near Rouen. When Gide was eleven, his father died; his protective mother, concerned for her son's delicate health, withdrew him from school and had him tutored at home in Rouen. His upbringing was strict and uncompromisingly Protestant, and the young Gide—who had learned the Bible by heart— underwent periods of intense religious fervor. It was during these years that he first developed a deep attachment to his cousin Madeleine Rondeaux, whom he would later marry.

After passing his baccalauréat examination in 1889, he

decided to devote himself to writing and travel. In 1891 he published his first work, *The Notebooks of André Walter*, written in the intimate and confessional mode that was to be his literary hallmark throughout his long career. In the same year, he began attending "Tuesday evenings" at the symbolist poet Stéphane Mallarmé's Paris apartment.

In 1893 he visited North Africa with a young painter named Paul Albert Laurens. The experience was a profound one: he felt liberated from the claustrophobic social and sexual strictures of Europe and glimpsed for the first time certain possibilities in himself, including the possibility of his homosexuality.

Back in Paris, though, Gide found it difficult to maintain this euphoric sense of liberation and felt himself slipping back into a slumber of the soul. On a second trip to North Africa the following year, he happened to see on a hotel register in Blida, Algeria, the names of OSCAR WILDE [3] and Lord Alfred Douglas. In a strange panic, Gide fled the hotel, only to turn around, halfway to the station, and head back. As critic John Dollimore writes, "the consequent meeting with Wilde precipitated a transformation in Gide's life and subsequent writing, and through the latter, exerted a far-reaching influence on modern literature." In Algiers, Wilde took Gide to an out-of-the-way cafe that he and Douglas frequented. As Gide described it later, in his autobiography *If It Die...*:

> Lulled by the strange torpor of the place, I was just sinking into a state of semi-somnolence, when in the half-open doorway, there suddenly appeared a marvellous youth. He stood there for a time, leaning with his raised elbow against the door-jamb, and outlined on the dark background of the night. He seemed uncertain as to whether he should come in or not, and I was beginning to be afraid he would go, when he smiled at a sign made him by Wilde and came up and sat down opposite us on a stool.... He took a reed flute out of his Tunisian waistcoat and began to play on it very exquisitely. Wilde told me a little later that he was called Mohammed....[Wilde] said in a whisper, "Dear, would you like the little musician?"
>
> ...I thought my heart would fail me; and what a dreadful effort of courage it needed to answer: "Yes," and with what a choking voice!

...No scruple clouded my pleasure and no remorse followed it. But what name then am I to give the rapture I felt as I clasped in my naked arms that perfect little body, so wild, so ardent, so sombrely lascivious?

For a long time after Mohammed had left me, I remained in a state of passionate jubilation, and though I had already achieved pleasure five times with him, I renewed my ecstasy again and again, and when I got back to my room in the hotel, I prolonged its echoes until morning.

One of the results of Gide's Algerian awakening was *The Fruits of the Earth*, which, though poorly received when first published in 1897, became after the First World War an exceedingly influential book for a new generation of French writers and intellectuals.

Sexually speaking, however, Gide was not out of the woods yet. In a move characteristic of his lifelong struggle to reconcile the conflicting puritan and sensualist within himself, he married his cousin Madeleine Rondeaux in 1895, shortly after his mother's death. It was hardly a realistic marriage—a union more mystic than carnal—and from the beginning there were difficulties, chronicled in fictional guise in the novels *The Immoralist* (1902) and *Strait Is the Gate* (1909). Both novels dramatize the tension between responsibility to convention and the existential imperative to discover and explore one's "authentic" self, no matter what the consequences.

In 1908, Gide helped found and edit the influential *Nouvelle Revue Française*, a progressive literary journal. During World War I he worked for the Red Cross in Paris. His marriage came to a crisis in 1918 when he fell in love with a young man named Marc Allégret—when Madeleine learned of this, she destroyed all Gide's letters to her, an act that affected Gide greatly. It was during this time of crisis that he composed *Corydon,* a defense of homosexuality in the form of four platonic dialogues. The publication, in 1924, of *Corydon* and the autobiography *If It Die...* scandalized Gide's closest friends, and he found himself completely ostracized by them. He in turn felt that he had betrayed not them but himself—by waiting nearly six years to publish *Corydon.* In response, he sold his estates and went to French Equitorial Africa with Allégret. The year spent traveling in the Congo and Chad resulted in *Travels in the Congo* (1925), a bitter condemnation of French colonial rule. In 1926, during Gide's absence from France, his masterpiece, *The Counterfeiters*, was published. It remains one of the most strikingly original and formally innovative novels of its time.

During the 1930s, Gide gradually turned toward Marxism and in 1932 embraced Communism, in part because of Lenin's decriminalization of homosexuality. A trip to the Soviet Union in 1934–35 left him profoundly disillusioned, however. An ardent antifascist, he spent most of World War II in North Africa. In 1947, he was awarded the Nobel Prize for Literature for his "extensive and artistically important authorship in which he exposed the problems and conditions of mankind." His books remained banned by both the Vatican and the Communists.

Gide's search for an inner authenticity is perhaps best expressed in the journals he kept for over sixty years—an intimate record of more than a million words by one of the century's most acute minds.

Gide was influential not only through his works but through his presence: he was a force not so much of literature as of life itself. And like all forces, he was a creature of contradictions: Jean-Paul Sartre saw him as balancing "the risk and the rule...the law of the Protestant and the non-conformity of the homosexual, the proud individualism of the grand bourgeois and the Puritan's taste for social restraint." As if to confirm this assessment of his temperament, when Gide was asked shortly before his death what he had most enjoyed in life, he answered, "*The Arabian Nights*, the Bible, the pleasures of the flesh, and the Kingdom of God."

André Gide died in Paris on February 19, 1951, at the age of eighty-two.

The names of André Gide and OSCAR WILDE [3] are often paired, as much for their differences as for the obvious things they had in common. Gide is commonly seen as espousing what is now known as an essentialist view of sexuality: in other words, his life's work revolved around the quest to know his authentic self, the true core of his being. Wilde, on the other hand, with his interest in masks, role-playing, and artifice, is understood as the epitome of the social-constructionist view of identity, which argues that we are shaped more by the vagaries of culture than by the truths of nature. If I have ranked Gide substantially below Wilde in this ranking, it is not because I wish to throw my weight behind the notions of sexual identity embodied by Wilde's persona. The verdict is still out. Wilde's ranking right near the top of the list merely indicates his enormous visibility in our collective history, whereas Gide, an invaluable foot soldier in the early days of the struggle, is today less well-known. I have ranked Gide with MARCEL PROUST [31], as one of the writers who in the early years of this century courageously dared to speak love's name, and who thereby changed the stakes of the game forever.

31

Marcel Proust

1871–1922

Marcel Proust was born on July 10, 1871, in Auteuil, France. His father was a prominent physician, and his mother hailed from a wealthy Jewish family. Beginning at the age of nine, Proust suffered from severe asthma. His cherished holidays in Illier and Auteuil—towns that would later become the fictional Combray of his masterpiece—came to an end, and henceforth holidays were spent with his grandmother at seaside resorts in Normandy.

From 1882–1889 Proust studied at the lycée Condorcet in Paris. A two-year stint in the military at Orléans was followed by university study at the Ecole des Sciences Politiques, from which he received a degree in law in 1893 and in literature in 1895. Among the teachers who influenced him were the philosophers

Henri Bergson and Paul Desjardins, and the historian Albert Sorrel. After leaving the university, he began to frequent the salons of Paris, making his way up the social ladder from the bourgeois salons of Madames Strauss, Aubernon, and Lemaine to the drawing rooms of nobility such as the flamboyant Robert, Count de Montesquiou-Fezensac.

Proust published his first work, a collection of short stories called *Pleasures and Days*, in 1896. From 1895 to 1899 he was engaged in the composition of *Jean Santeuil*, a novel whose thousand-page manuscript he eventually abandoned. Growing ill health and his involvement in the Dreyfus Affair led to his gradual withdrawal from and disillusionment with high society. The death of his father in 1903 and his mother in 1905 left him grieving but financially independent and ready, at last, to begin his great work. Between 1905 and 1908 he struggled with early versions, but abandoned them. In January 1909, the chance tasting of tea and a rusk biscuit brought on that famous experience of memory that, in the guise of the famous madeleine cake, forms the basis for *In Search of Lost Time*—or, as it was called for so many years in English translations, *Remembrance of Things Past*. In July 1909, Proust began work in earnest and completed a first draft by September of 1912. He showed the manuscript to a number of editors, including ANDRÉ GIDE [30], all of whom rejected it, so he paid for the publication of the first volume, *Swann's Way*, in 1913. At that point he was planning two more volumes, but the advent of World War I, and the death of his secretary/chauffeur/lover Alfred Agnostelli—while piloting an airplane Proust had given him—changed those plans.

In 1914, having reconsidered, Gide offered to bring out Proust's work, and in 1919 the second volume, *Within a Budding Grove*, appeared. When it won the coveted Prix Goncourt later that year, Proust suddenly found himself world famous. Over the next three years, he published three more installments: *The Guermantes Way* and parts one and two of *Sodom and Gomorrah*.

During this time, one of Proust's more memorable undertakings was the financing of a male brothel, to be run by his young friend Albert Le Cuziat and decorated with furniture from Proust's dead parents. Proust was a frequent guest in this establishment, which became the model of Jupien's S/M brothel in *In Search of Lost Time*. Proust's biographer George Painter writes with homophobic condescension: "In this pit of Sodom [Proust] was following his vice, which had begun with love for his equals (Reynaldo [Hahn] and Lucien [Daudet]), progressed through platonic affection for social superiors (Fénelon, Antoine Bibesco, and the rest) to physical affection for social inferiors (Ulrich and Agostinelli), and now ended, disillusioned with all, in a sterile intercourse with professional catamites." Painter believes that the flagellations in chains the Baron de Charlus undergoes in Jupien's fictional brothel are "a mere scapegoat for Proust's own experiences" in Albert Le Cuziat's establishment.

On November 18, 1922, Marcel Proust died of pneumonia in the cork-lined bedroom where he spent most of his later years insulated from the noise and pollution of Paris. The last three volumes of his 3,500-page masterpiece—*The Captive, The Fugitive,* and *Time Regained*—were posthumously published.

It is impossible in this brief entry even to begin to describe that intricate and splendid work in which the various transformed strands of Proust's life are woven into the tapestry of art. *In Search of Lost Time* is probably the greatest novel of the twentieth century, a work about the nature of time, of memory, of being itself. It is also, contrary to rumor, impossible to put down once you get started on it.

At the very heart of the novel, and utterly indispensable to its project, is the subject of homosexuality, which is both enthroned and obscured within its pages. Enthroned because, in Proust's universe, most characters turn homosexual in the end. The second half of the work is dominated by that patron saint of homosexuality, the unforgettable Baron de Charlus (a character based in part on Proust's old friend Montesquiou). Obscured, on the other hand, by what has become famous as "the Albertine Strategy," whereby Proust's real-life male lover Alfred becomes, in the novel, the female Albertine in order to disguise the narrator "Marcel's" sexuality (though in the novel's various complications, Albertine turns out to be lesbian, much to the "heterosexual" Marcel's distress).

Especially important for early twentieth-century discourse on homosexuality were two passages, both at the beginning of *Sodom and Gomorrah.* The first is a grotesque insect-and-flower description of the Baron de Charlus's attraction to Jupien the tailor that takes its cue from the "scientific" model of homosexuality prevalent at the time. The second is more revolutionary: an extended, passionate encomium to the homosexual "race," a race whose history and destiny, according to Proust, bear comparison to that of the Jews:

> A race upon which a curse is laid and which must live in falsehood and perjury because it knows that its desire, that which constitutes life's dearest pleasure, is held to be punishable, shameful, an inadmissible thing....Lovers who are almost precluded from the possibility of that love the hope of which gives them the strength to endure so many risks and so much loneliness....Their honor precarious, their liberty provisional, lasting only until the discovery of their crime; their position unstable, like that of the poet one day feted in every drawing room and applauded in every theatre in London, and the next driven from every lodging, unable to find a pillow upon which to lay his head...a freemasonry far more extensive, more effective and less suspected than that of the Lodges, for it rests upon an identity of tastes, needs, habits, dangers, apprenticeship, knowledge, traffic, vocabulary, and one in which even members who do not wish to know one another recognize one another immediately...a reprobate section of the human collectivity, but an important one, suspected where it does not exist, flaunting itself, insolent and immune, where its existence is never guessed; numbering its adherents everywhere, among the people, in the army, in the church, in prison, on the throne....

Proust was influential because he was the first modern writer to treat homosexuality in literary terms. His complex analysis of his homosexual characters opened up a new kind of discourse on the subject that was removed from the medical models currently in vogue. As a gay man writing about gay existence, Proust created and presented a richer, more detailed portrait of homosexuality than either the doctors or the apologists of the early homosexual rights movement could do. Furthermore, his discussion of homosexuality introduced the subject to a much wider audience and ensured that what had for so long been taboo could no longer be passed over in silence. Along with ANDRÉ GIDE'S, Proust's work centralized the status of homosexuality in the modern literary world.

32

Michel Foucault

1926–1984

Michel Foucault was born on October 15, 1926, in Poitiers, France. His father was an eminent local surgeon who wanted his son to follow in his career footsteps. When the young Foucault proved a moody, introverted child with tendencies toward juvenile delinquency, his father entered him in the college Saint-Stanislas, a Catholic school known for its strict discipline and regimentation. There Foucault blossomed as a student, and after graduating from Saint-Stanislas he entered the prestigious lycée Henri-IV in Paris. In 1946 he was admitted to the Ecole Normale Supérieure as the fourth-highest-ranked student. Studying philosophy with the distinguished Maurice Merleau-Ponty, Foucault emerged as a brilliant young thinker. He received his *licence* in philosophy in 1948, in psychology in 1950, and in 1952 was awarded a diploma in psychopathology.

From 1954 to 1958, Foucault taught French at the University of Uppsala in Sweden, then spent a year at the University of Warsaw followed by a year at the University of Hamburg. In 1960, the year he returned to France as the head of the philosophy department at the University of Clermont-Ferrard, he published his landmark work *Madness and Civilization*. In this he argued that "madness" as we know it, and the scrupulous and troubled distinctions we make between it and "sanity," is a hallmark invention of the age of reason. The book won him a *doctorat d'état*.

In that same year, Foucault met Daniel Defert, a philosophy student ten years his junior. Defert's political activism would exercise a major influence on Foucault's development. About their relationship, Foucault said in a 1981 interview, "I have lived for eighteen years in a state of passion toward someone. At some moments, this passion has taken the form of love. But in truth, it is a matter of a state of passion between the two of us."

Foucault's second major work, *The Order of Things,* a comparative study of the development of economics, the natural sciences, and linguistics in the eighteenth and nineteenth centuries, appeared in 1966. A surprise bestseller in France, it made Foucault a household name—at least in intellectual circles. Especially notorious and much quoted was his prediction, at the book's end, that "man," a recent discursive formation made possible only by fundamental changes in the arrangement of knowledge during the last 150 years, is nearing his end: soon he will be "erased, like a face drawn in sand at the edge of the sea." If Foucault's intellectual forebear Friedrich Nietzsche had proclaimed the death of God, Foucault had proclaimed the death of man.

When Daniel Defert went to Tunisia to fulfill his volunteer-service requirements, Foucault followed him and spent 1966–68 teaching there (and smoking hashish). The two returned to Paris—Foucault to head up the philosophy department at the University of Paris–VIII at Vincennes, Defert to teach sociology—just as the student revolts of May 1968 unleashed their fury. Foucault was profoundly affected by the unrest. In that year he joined with other intellectuals in forming GIP, the Prison Information Group, an organization that sought to provide prisoners with a way to talk about prison concerns.

His study *Archaeology of Knowledge* appeared in 1969. In 1970 he was elected to the College de France, the country's most eminent institution of research and learning, as professor of the history of systems of thought. In 1975 he published *Discipline and Punish: The Origin of the Prison,* perhaps his most influential book. During the last decade of his life he devoted himself to *The History of Sexuality,* a monumental but unfinished project. *Volume I: An Introduction* appeared to much controversy in 1976, and the second and third volumes—*The Uses of Pleasure* and *The Care of the Self*—came out shortly before his death in 1984.

Foucault's experience in San Francisco during 1975, when he was teaching at the University of California at Berkeley, was a watershed in his development. He was thrilled by the liberated gay sexuality he found there, especially in the bathhouses. "I think," he wrote, "that it is politically important that sexuality be able to function as it functions in the bathhouses. You meet men there who are to you as you are to them: nothing but a body with which combinations and productions of pleasure are possible. You cease to be imprisoned in your own face, in your own past, in your own identity."

"Limit-experiences" like S/M particularly interested him. On that subject he said, "I don't think that this movement of sexual practices has anything to do with the disclosure or the uncovering of S/M tendencies deep within our unconscious. I think S/M is much more than that; it's the real creation of new possibilities of pleasure, which people had no idea about previously." He returned again and again over the next few years, making his last visit in 1983, after the AIDS epidemic had begun to devastate the bathhouses and after he himself was already (though perhaps unknowingly) infected.

Ten years after his death, Michel Foucault's ideas about the evolution of Western civilization during the last three hundred years exercise tremendous influence. Perhaps no one in the last decade has so profoundly shaped academic thought. His influence on gay consciousness has been enormous, especially through the first volume of *The History of Sexuality.* There he articulates what is known as the theory of social construction: the notion that sexuality, far from being "natural" and unmediated, is instead a cultural construction whose organization varies greatly over time and place. The modern homosexual and heterosexual, he argued, are comparatively recent inventions. Before the eighteenth century, there were no homosexuals (or heterosexuals, for that matter), only homosexual (or sodomitical) and heterosexual acts. Only in the eighteenth and nineteenth centuries did these acts begin to coagulate into an identity. "As defined by the ancient civil or canonical codes," he writes in a famous passage, "sodomy was a category of forbidden acts; their perpetrator was nothing more than the juridical subject of them. The nineteenth-century homosexual became a personage, a past, a case history, and a childhood, in addition to being a type of life, a life-form, and a morphology, with an indiscreet anatomy and possibly a mysterious physiology.... Sodomy had been a temporary aberration; the homosexual was now a species." In other words, the sexuality that we like to think constitutes our very identity, the core of our being, the essential truth of our nature—one of our most cherished and fundamental ideas—is only a historical construct, which, because we are so thoroughly inside it, we cannot see clearly. By analyzing the power that organizes our sexuality— through medicine, psychiatry, religion, the law—and the resistances to that power, Foucault provided the discursive tools for everyone from the burgeoning queer theorists of the academy to AIDS activists in the streets. His revolutionary thought, in his final years, lay in the direction of what he called "a hyper- and pessimistic activism." His influence will almost certainly continue to grow.

Michel Foucault died of complications resulting from AIDS on June 25, 1984, at the Hôpital de la Salpêtreiere in Paris. It is not clear whether, in those early days of the epidemic, he ever knew that he had AIDS. His final weeks are recorded, in barely disguised form, in his young friend Hervé Guibert's harrowing 1990 novel *To the Friend Who Did Not Save My Life*.

I have grouped Foucault here on this list along with ANDY WARHOL [33] and JOHN CAGE [34]. Put simply, all three men revolutionized their respective disciplines. That Foucault is ranked first among these three very significant figures indicates my sense that his work is more immediately relevant—indeed, absolutely central—to contemporary issues of gay/lesbian identity.

33

Andy Warhol

1928–1987

Andrew Warhola was born on August 6, 1928, in Forest City, Pennsylvania. His parents were immigrants from Czechoslovakia, and his father worked as a coal miner. Little is known of his early life. In 1949 he graduated with a degree in pictorial design from the Carnegie Institute of Technology in Pittsburgh. Moving to New York City, he changed his name to Warhol and began working as a fashion illustrator for stores such as Tiffany & Co. and Bonwit Teller, and magazines such as *Vogue* and *Glamour.* By the mid-1950s his success in commercial work had enabled him to buy a town house in midtown Manhattan. He was not content, however, and wanted to try his hand at painting. In 1960 he produced a series of pictures based on comic strips such as *Superman* and *Dick Tracy,* but these met with little success. It was not until 1962, with an exhibition in Los Angeles of his paintings of Campbell's-soup cans, that he became an overnight sensation. Pop art had been born. Warhol was at the forefront of the movement, which included such other artists as Roy Lichtenstein, Robert Rauschenberg and Jasper Johns (the latter two were lovers for six years).

The 1962 soup cans still reveal brushstrokes. By 1963, Warhol had settled into the medium that was to characterize his work for much of his career: silk-screen prints. Utterly depersonalized, and capable of being mass-produced, silk-screening was ideal for his purposes. As art critic Robert Hughes wrote: "Painting a soup can is not in itself a radical act. But what was radical in Warhol was that he adapted the means of production of soup cans to the way he produced paintings, turning them out *en masse*—consumer art mimicking the process as well as the look of consumer culture."

To underline this aspect of mass production, Warhol took to calling his studio "the Factory." During the midsixties, the Factory became a hangout for all sorts of talents and personalities such as Edie Sedgewick, Holly Woodlawn, Viva, and Ultraviolet. Artwork would be produced collectively under Warhol's direction by a team of associates.

During this period, Warhol began making films—or perhaps they should be called antifilms—plotless paeans to boredom and erotic invention that sometimes lasted as long as twenty-five hours. These included *Eat, Blowjob, My Hustler, The Chelsea Girls,* and *Blue Movie.*

On June 5, 1968, a disaffected follower of Warhol's named Valerie Solanas shot and seriously wounded the artist. He spent a year recuperating and never entirely recovered from his wounds ("Since I was shot, everything is such a dream to me. I don't know what anything is about. Like I don't know whether I'm alive or whether I died"). Abandoning his wilder followers, in the 1970s Warhol began to gravitate toward the fashionable world of celebrities. He entered his most sustained period of creativity during this decade, turning out garish, iconic silk screens of figures such as Marilyn Monroe, Liza Minnelli, Jimmy Carter, and Chairman Mao. He also collaborated with filmmaker Paul Morrissey on such films as *Trash* and *Lonesome Cowboys.* Starring the beautiful and sexually provocative Joe Dallesandro, these films were more ambitious than the ones Warhol had made solo in the 1960s.

In the 1980s Warhol began to take on more in the way of commissioned and commercial works. He also befriended and mentored emerging young artists like Keith Haring and Jean-Michel Basquiat.

Warhol the man was something of an enigma. A quiet, shy individual, he was always open about his sexuality, though he claimed to prefer to watch or read about sex rather than actually participate in it: "Fantasy love is much better than reality love," he declared. "Never doing it is very exciting." He liked to surround himself with flamboyant hangers-on, but gave the impression of being always alone. He hated giving interviews, sometimes asking interviewers to tell him what they wanted him to say and he would say it. His persona was a carefully constructed façade, as studiously impersonal and banal as his art. Often he would send a Warhol look-alike to deliver lectures in his name.

The day after a routine gallbladder operation, on February 22, 1987, Warhol died of a heart attack in his sleep at the New York Hospital–Cornell Medical Center in Manhattan.

Andy Warhol was without doubt the most influential artist of his generation. He was fascinated by contemporary culture in all its banality and blatant consumerism. He was obsessed by the notion of art as business, observing that "being good in business is the most fascinating kind of art." As art critic John Russell wrote in a tribute to Warhol, he "turned everything upside down and inside out and got away with it. He made paintings that bore no trace of the human hand, let alone of traditional skills. He made sculptures that looked just like the boxes that came up with the delivery boy. He made motion pictures in which almost nothing moved....As for the uniqueness of the work of art, he thought nothing of it....As for the celebrity that traditionally accrues to successful high art, he devalued that also, saying he would like everyone in the world to be famous for fifteen minutes."

In many ways Warhol's achievement in the visual arts is analogous to that of JOHN CAGE [34] in music: both men revolutionized our notions of what constitutes art, Warhol by elevating the most trivial images to the status of "art," Cage by broadening the definitions of music to include all types of noise and even silence. Is it possible that their gayness, their permanent status as outsiders, is what allowed them to ask such fundamental and far-reaching questions about the very nature of art?

34

John Cage
1912–1992

John Cage was born on September 5, 1912, in Los Angeles, California. The son of an inventor, he manifested his own inventiveness early on: by the age of twelve he was hosting a radio program on KNX, Los Angeles, featuring himself on piano. In 1928 he enrolled at Pomona College, but left after two years for Paris. There he painted, wrote poetry, and composed music while working for an architect with ties to Marcel Duchamp, the dadaist artist whose work would greatly influence Cage's development. Returning to California in 1931, he worked as a cook and gardener while beginning to study the twelve tone music of Arnold Schoenberg. Schoenberg's radical departure from traditional harmonies and tonal relationships interested Cage, and in 1934, when Schoenberg moved to Los Angeles as a refugee from

Nazi persecution (his music had been denounced there as "decadent"), Cage persuaded the composer to give him free composition lessons. But their styles and philosophic attitudes quickly diverged: Schoenberg was interested in a music of total control, whereas Cage was after something quite different, only he was not yet sure what. Schoenberg must have sensed this when he declared his young student to be "not a composer but an inventor of genius." It was an assessment that Cage always liked.

While living briefly in Seattle in 1937, where he studied and worked as an accompanist for dance classes at the Cornish School of the Arts, Cage met the dancer/choreographer Merce Cunningham, with whom he would collaborate in art and life for the next fifty-five years.

Joining the faculty at Mills College in Oakland, California, in 1938, Cage began in earnest to move into uncharted musical territories of his own devising. In 1939 he wrote a landmark piece for piano, cymbal, and variable-speed turntables. In 1940 he began his work with "prepared" piano—a piano whose strings Cage altered in various ways to produce novel sounds. The 1940s also saw Cage touring extensively with Merce Cunningham in their performance collaboration "Credo in Us."

Settling in New York City, Cage took courses in Zen Buddhism at Columbia University, a study that had important consequences for his evolution as an artist. In 1950 his interest in non-Western modes of thought was further enhanced when he became acquainted with the I Ching, the ancient Chinese "book of changes" in which the toss of coins is an important guide to action. Cage was deeply influenced by this notion of the profound role of chance in affairs both cosmic and human. Among the important works that resulted from this interest in the procedures of chance was "Imaginary Landscape 4" (1951), a piece for twelve radios whose tuning and volume are minutely notated, but whose content is determined by whatever happens to be on the airwaves at the moment. Perhaps the culmination of this period of Cage's experimentation was the famous "4'33" for piano" (1952), in which the four minutes and thirty-three seconds of silence on stage, divided into three movements, seek not to impose some kind of controlling order on the world, but rather to create a space in which sonic events—passing traffic, stray coughs from the audience, the sounds of one's own breathing— are allowed to happen. Audiences, of course, were mixed in their reaction, and Cage's music was often booed—sometimes even by the musicians themselves.

Throughout his long and productive career, Cage's questing and mercurial imagination illuminated whatever new territory he turned to next. In "Williams Mix" (1952) and "Fontana Mix" (1958), he carried out early and pathbreaking experiments with recorded tape. Other important works include "Ellipticalis with Winter Music" (1964); "Hpschd" (1969) for seven harpsichords, fifty-one tapes, slides, films, and colored lights; "Roaratorio" (1979), based on sounds from James Joyce's *Finnegans Wake;* and "Europera 5" (1987–90), a massive multimedia meditation on electronic and operatic sounds.

Cage was married briefly in the 1940s. From 1970 until his death on August 12, 1992, he and Merce Cunningham lived together in New York City.

Writing about Cage in the *New York Times* in 1967, the critic Richard Kostelanitz observed, "Perhaps no living artist has such a great influence over such a diverse lot of important people. Nowadays even those critics who disagree with him respect his willingness to pursue his ideas to their 'mad' conclusions, and he was impoverished for too many years for anyone seriously to doubt his integrity."

A writer and philosopher as well as composer, Cage's books included *Silence* (1961), *A Year From Monday* (1967), *Empty Words* (1979), *Theme and Variations* (1982), and *X* (1983).

Cage is ranked high not only because of his immeasurable influence on other composers, but also because of the impact of his ideas on painting, dance, performance art, and poetry. By redefining the very nature of music—all sound, in his cosmology, was music—he left our sonic landscape irrevocably changed. After Cage, we would never hear our universe in quite the same way.

35

Ruth Benedict

1887–1948

Ruth Fulton Benedict was born on June 5, 1887, on a farm in the Shenango Valley in upstate New York. Her father, a brilliant and promising young surgeon, died when she was an infant, and she was raised by her mother and grandparents. Following in her mother's footsteps, she enrolled at Vassar College in Poughkeepsie, New York, in the fall of 1905. After receiving her BA in English in 1909, she traveled for a year in Europe, then taught for three years at girls' schools in California. In 1913 she met Stanley Benedict, a medical student, and they were married in 1914. Benedict settled into the life of a housewife in the Long Island suburb of Douglas Manor, but found suburban life stultifying and soul-destroying. To occupy herself—to salvage herself—she wrote poems (a number of which she published under the pseudonym Anne Singleton) and a biography of MARY

WOLLSTONECRAFT [11], the first in a series of projected biographies of what she called "restless and highly enslaved women of past generations." The work was rejected by Houghton Mifflin in 1917 and remained unpublished in Benedict's lifetime.

In 1919 she took the important step of enrolling in some courses at the New School for Social Research in New York City. Encouraged by her teachers, she went on to study with the great anthropologist Franz Boas at Columbia University, where she received her PhD in 1923 with a dissertation titled "The Concept of the Guardian Spirit in North America." As Boas's assistant and chosen successor, she remained at Columbia and was eventually made professor of anthropology there.

In 1922, while working as Boas's teaching assistant at Barnard College, Benedict met a senior named Margaret Mead. The two became intimate friends and by 1925 were lovers (even though Mead had married in 1923). It was both a physical and emotional relationship and an intellectual collaboration so profound that the two eventually claimed that they were unable to distinguish who was responsible for what particular idea. Their relationship also affected the nature of their work. Biographer Margaret Caffrey writes: "Benedict found the study of misfits congenial to her personally, having felt herself a misfit in American society since early childhood. Now she and Mead were faced with questions the new psychology raised about their love—were they sick, were they neurotic, were they abnormal, did they deserve to be social outcasts? Within this general context, and within the specific context of their feelings toward each other, during 1926, when Mead and Benedict worked together at Barnard and Mead wrote *Coming of Age in Samoa,* they began to explore the idea of deviance and ultimately subtly attempted to change the idea of the deviant from a totally negative one to one possessing positive value." To facilitate this, they came up with the notion of positive and negative deviancy: women who loved women were positive when they accepted their love as a healthy alternative to society's conventions; they were negative only when they internalized the homophobia of their society and hated themselves as a consequence. The deviant, Benedict argued, is "not some type to be specified and described on the basis of a universally valid abnormal psychology." Instead, the deviant is simply "the type not capitalized in the society to which he was born."

Although Benedict's and Mead's physical relationship cooled with time, their intellectual rapport remained constant for the rest of Benedict's life. Mead moved on to other lovers, both male and female, and to two more husbands. Benedict fell in love, in 1931, with Natalie Raymond, and the two stayed together for the next eight years. Caffrey explains: "For Ruth Benedict her relationship to Margaret Mead acted as a revelation. It apparently affected her so deeply that from that time forward she became a woman-loving woman." She and her husband formally separated in 1931.

One of Benedict's goals as a woman-loving woman was to change the social attitude concerning homosexuality. In particular, she took on the psychology and psychiatry establishment that defined homosexuality as a disease. To that end she published, in 1934, an article called "Anthropology and the Abnormal" in the *Journal of General Psychology*. She began by questioning the idea of "normal" and "abnormal" as absolute categories and demonstrated that "whenever homosexuality has been given an honorable place in any society, those to whom it is congenial have filled adequately the honorable roles society assigns to them." In particular she pointed to the culture of ancient Greece, and to those Native American societies with a tradition of the berdache. Furthermore, she argued, just as certain values that are considered abnormal in our society are normal in other societies, so other societies value as ideal certain behaviors that are considered reprehensible in our own. As examples she offered the Dobu people of New Guinea, for whom individuals "of sunny, kindly disposition who liked work and liked to be helpful" were considered "silly and simple and definitely crazy"; and the Kwakiutl of British Columbia, for whom what we would diagnose as megalomaniac paranoia is "an essential attribute of ideal man." The result, she argued, is to "force upon us the fact that normality is culturally defined."

Benedict expanded her concept of cultural relativity in *Patterns of Culture* (1934), a landmark book that was translated into fourteen languages and sold over 1.5 million copies. Caffrey writes: "*Patterns of Culture* had a multiple impact on American thought. It acted as a signal of and a catalyst for the final acceptance of a profound paradigm change in the social sciences and in American society and set in place the new twentieth-century paradigm or world view which had been taking shape up to that time.... At the beginning of the decade biology was firmly entrenched as the primary motivator of humanity. Biological determinism allowed no leeway for change.... Benedict's demonstration of the overwhelming role of culture in creating three different lifestyles, those of the Zuñi, the Dobu, and the Kwakiutl, provided the final important evidence for replacing biology with culture as the major causal factor in human life."

Benedict's fieldwork among the Zuñi peoples in New Mexico led to the two-volume *Zuñi Mythology* in 1935. Other works include *Race, Science and Politics* (1940) and *The Chrysanthemum and the Sword* (1946), an analysis of the intertwined cultural patterns of aestheticism and militarism in the Japanese national character. During the 1930s she worked against censorship and for individual rights and organized a gathering of signatures for a published condemnation of Nazi science. After her relationship with Natalie Raymond ended in 1939, Benedict fell in love with Ruth Valentine, and the two lived together in New York City until Benedict's death on September 17, 1948.

Ruth Benedict was a major figure in the evolution of the social sciences. Her work provided much of the basis for modern cultural anthropology. Moreover, her notions of cultural relativity, and the importance of culture as opposed to biology in determining identity and values, anticipate in important ways the work of MICHEL FOUCAULT [32] and the arguments about social constructionism versus essentialism that have animated recent gay discourse. By providing a model of culture's role in determining values, Benedict also made possible the hope that our society's firmly entrenched homophobic attitudes are not necessarily immutable givens, but might in fact be susceptible to change.

36

James Baldwin

1924–1987

James Baldwin was born on August 2, 1924, in Harlem, New York. The eldest of nine children, he suffered much under the rule of his minister stepfather, who used to claim that Baldwin was the ugliest child he had ever seen. At age 14, however, he followed in his stepfather's footsteps by becoming a Holy Roller minister at the Fireside Pentecostal Church in Harlem, where for the next two years he was an "out of school" preacher. School was the predominantly white DeWitt Clinton High School in the Bronx, where Baldwin was beginning to feel what he called "the stigma of being a Negro."

After graduating from high school, he moved to Greenwich Village, worked low-paying odd jobs to try to support his siblings, and began to publish reviews and essays in such respected magazines as *The Nation, The New Leader,* and *Commentary.*

Baldwin felt stifled, though, by his double predicament as a black man in racist America and a gay man in the homophobic African-American community. In 1948, with little more than pocket money and a passport, he went to Paris. He spent the next eight years there—but not, he always stressed, as an expatriate: "Only white Americans can consider themselves to be expatriates. Once I found myself on the other side of the ocean, I could see where I came from very clearly, and I could see that I carried myself, which is my home, with me. You can never escape that. I am the grandson of a slave, and I am a writer. I must deal with both." Even after he returned to America in 1957, Baldwin would continue to divide his time between New York City and the south of France.

In France his fiction writing flourished, due to the encouragement of his friend and lover Lucien Happersberger, and in 1953 he published his first novel, *Go Tell It on the Mountain,* an autobiographical work that drew on his early experiences in Harlem. This was followed by *Giovanni's Room* (1956), the story of a white man torn between his love for a man and a woman, and *Another Country* (1962), in which gay and interracial relationships play an important part. These novels brought Baldwin critical acclaim as a powerful new voice in American fiction—but also savage criticism, especially from the black community, for his treatment of homosexuality. The very mention of homosexuality in the black community was taboo to many blacks. Baldwin's subject matter, declared Black Panther member Eldridge Cleaver in a famous diatribe, betrayed an "agonizing, total hatred of blacks" on Baldwin's part. Throughout his career, and even today, Baldwin's enormous contributions as a gay man as well as a black man tend to be downplayed.

Baldwin's greatest influence on the life of his times stemmed from his essay collections: *Notes of a Native Son* (1955), *Nobody Knows My Name* (1960), and especially *The Fire Next Time* (1963), which catapulted him to national prominence as a major player in the civil rights movement. Originally conceived as an article for *The New Yorker* on the Black Muslim separatist movement, *The Fire Next Time* is a stunning and eloquent revelation of black pain, anger, and alienation in white America. White people, Baldwin accused, victimize blacks by investing them with the hatreds and longings of their own guilty imaginations. "At the root of the American Negro problem," he wrote, "is the necessity of the American white man to find a way of living with the Negro in order to be able to live with himself."

Throughout the 1960s Baldwin was a leading spokesman for the burgeoning civil rights movement—though he always disavowed the terms *leader* and *spokesman*. His mission, he said, was simply "to bear witness to the truth." As such he was a maverick, and his opinions owe their richness and sting to his refusal to settle for easy ideological answers. In addition to his work for civil rights, he protested the war in Vietnam and, as an openly gay man, became increasingly outspoken in his condemnation of discrimination against gays and lesbians.

In his later years, Baldwin's failing health and heavy drinking caused a decline in the quality of his output, and such novels as *If Beale Street Could Talk* (1974) and *Just Above My Head* (1979) are generally regarded as disappointing. Nevertheless, his stature as public figure continued unabated during the 1970s and 1980s. In 1986, in recognition of his achievements, he was made a Commander of the Legion of Honor by the French government. He died of cancer on December 1, 1987, in St.-Paul de Vence in the south of France.

"The great difficulty," Baldwin once wrote, "is to say Yes to life." His concern lay always with the difficult quest to be oneself, to be *true*, to say Yes with courage—to accept one's sexuality, one's race, one's bittersweet contradictions. As he said in a 1986 *Advocate* interview: "The inability to love is the central problem, because that inability masks a certain terror, and that terror is terror of being touched. And if you can't be touched, you can't be changed. And if you can't be changed, you can't be alive." The awesome challenge implicit in that statement is the key to Baldwin's life and work, and to his continuing influence on the struggle not merely to be gay, or black, but to be human.

37

Hāfiz
1326?–1389?

Muhammed Shams ud-din Hāfiz was born around the year
1326 in the Persian city of Shiraz, capital of the province of Fars
in what is now Iran. Of humble origins, he spent his early years in
poverty; some stories say he supported his mother by working in
a bakery at night while pursuing his studies by day. All in all, little
is known for certain about his life, though legends abound. He
lived during difficult and dangerous times: during his lifetime,
the Arab ascendancy over Persia gave way, often in episodes of
great violence, to domination by the Mongols.

By the age of thirty Hāfiz seems to have established himself
as a court poet, earning an uncertain living by cultivating the
patronage of the powerful. In particular he won favor with Jalal
ud-din Shah Shuja, who appointed him a professor of Qur'anic
and other theological subjects in a mosque school in Shiraz. As a
Persian, Hāfiz belonged to the Shi'a sect of Islam (as opposed to
the hated Arabs, who were Sunnis). He was greatly influenced,

however, by Sufism, an Islamic mystical movement. Though it is
not clear whether he ever became a full-fledged Sufi, he may well
have studied with Shaikh Mahmud Attar. The name Hāfiz, under
which he wrote his poems, denotes one who has memorized the
Qur'an.

Hāfiz's particular verse form, which he brought to perfection, was the erotic ghazal, a lyric poem of six to fifteen rhymed
couplets unified not by logic but by symbols and images: often the
ghazal is compared to a thread of pearls. Love and wine were
traditional themes of the ghazal because they symbolized ecstasy
and liberation from restraint. Hāfiz took these subjects and made
them his own while infusing them with his own brand of Sufi
mysticism and its yearning for a total, obliterating union of the
earthly with the divine. About the Sufi concept of the divine
Hāfiz's translators Peter Avery and John Heath-Stubbs have
written: "It is not improbable that it was from Neo-Platonist
tradition that the Sufis adopted the conception of the Divine as
Absolute Beauty, of which all images of beauty to be discerned in
the natural world are partial and fleeting representations. This
led to the formulation of a conception of romantic love, the germ
of which is to be found in Diotoma's speech to SOCRATES [1] in
Plato's *Symposium*....For the Persians...as for the Greeks, the
earthly expression of that Divine Beauty which the lover con-
templates is embodied primarily in the form of a beautiful
youth."

Although Hāfiz's poems may be read as allegories of Divine
Beauty, they are also resolutely and raffishly earthly. A famous
and often quoted line by Hāfiz admonishes: "The Garden of
Paradise may be pleasant, but forget not the shade of the willow
tree, and the green margin of the fruitful field." It was said he
spurned the mosque in favor of the tavern. His reputation for
leading a dissolute life and his attacks on various orthodoxies led
his patron Shah Shuja to banish him at the insistence of the
religious authorities, though he eventually regained his position
in court.

By middle age, Hāfiz's fame had spread to India and the
Arabic-speaking lands, and though he received offers from
Sultan Ahmed to visit Baghdad and from Mahmud Shah
Bahmani, ruler of the Deccan, to join his court, Hāfiz declined,
preferring to remain in his beloved Shiraz, whose gardens and
haunts and ardent young men he celebrated in his poems.

Perhaps his most famous couplet during his lifetime was the following:

> If that Tartar, that fair-skinned Turk of Shiraz,
>   gets hold of my heart
> I'll give Bokhara and Samarkand for the
>   Indian-black mole on his cheek.

It is said that when the ruthless Mongol leader Tamburlaine entered Shiraz, he ordered that Hāfiz be brought before him. Referring to the famous couplet, Tamburlaine asked, "How is it that when I have depopulated a vast number of cities and provinces in order to increase the glory and wealth of Bokhara and Samarkand, the ordinary places of my residence and the seat of my empire, you, Hāfiz, an insignificant individual, have pretended to give them away in exchange for a mole on the cheek of your boyfriend?"

To which Hāfiz replied, "Sir, it is because of such prodigality that I am as poor as you see."

Tamburlaine was apparently much pleased with the poet's response. That the anecdote is almost certainly apocryphal only goes to show the extraordinary popular esteem in which Hāfiz was held in his day and afterward. Indeed, it is scarcely an exaggeration to say that Hāfiz has been even more popular among the Persian-speaking world than SHAKESPEARE [20] has been among the English-speaking world. Even today Persian speakers unconsciously quote Hāfiz in their everyday speech— phrases like "patience and victory have long been friends"—in much the same way we quote Shakespeare.

In 1389 or 1390 Hāfiz died in his beloved Shiraz, where his tomb remains a pilgrimage site to this day. It is said that he had compiled a collection of his poems—known as a *Divan*—but that it was lost and subsequently recompiled by his friend Muhammed Gulandam. Because of Hāfiz's extraordinary and continued popularity, today there are thousands of poems attributed to him, and thousands of variants of those poems. The more reliable manuscripts contain about five hundred poems, but scholars despair of ever being able to pin down the actual number and the "correct" versions of these poems.

I have not, in general, included in this ranking gays or lesbians who influenced cultures other than our own, as that is a task for a different sort of project. Hāfiz is included here because, despite his relative obscurity in the West today, he has in the past proved influential. If the West can be said to have rediscovered the Greeks and their attitudes toward homosexuality in the eighteenth century with figures such as JOHANN JOACHIM WINCKELMANN [23], so the first translations of Persian poets, appearing around the same time, introduced Europe and England to yet another culture in which the passionate love of men for men was celebrated. Homophobic Western translators were quick to impugn the sexuality of these poems: as an early translator of Hāfiz explained, "To avoid being suspected of disingenuousness, we must here also point out a blemish of our Author, too glaring for disguise, and which, if not explained away, must subject him to the same moral disgrace, which unfortunately attaches itself to some of the first poets, and even to some of the philosophers, of antiquity." Discerning gay readers saw all they needed to. What repelled straight critics about Muslim culture was precisely what compelled gay or bisexual men like BYRON [38], William Beckford, Sir Richard Burton, OSCAR WILDE [3], ANDRÉ GIDE [35], T. E. Lawrence, and E. M. FORSTER [58].

Since Hāfiz's work is little known these days in the West, I close with this exquisite ghazal for your pleasure.

With locks disheveled, flushed in a sweat of drunkenness,
His shirt torn open, a song on his lips and wine cup in his hand—

With eyes looking for trouble, lips softly complaining—
So at midnight last night he came and sat at my pillow.

He bent his head down to my ear, and in a voice full of sadness
He said: "Oh, my old lover, are you asleep?"

What lover, given such wine at midnight,
Would prove love's heretic, not worshiping wine?

Don't scold us, you puritan, for drinking down to the dregs:
This fate was dealt us in God's prime Covenant.

Whatever He poured into our tankard we'll swallow:
If it's liquor of Paradise, or the wine that poisons.

A laughing wine cup, a tangle of knotted hair—
And let good resolutions, like those of Hāfiz, be shattered!

38 Byron

1788–1824

George Gordon Byron was born in London on January 22, 1788. His father, Capt. John "Mad Jack" Byron, was descended from a long line of nobility. His mother was Scottish. Their marriage was tumultuous, and while Byron was still a small boy, his mother spirited him off to Aberdeen in Scotland while, back in London, his father squandered the family fortune and died in 1791.

On the death of his great-uncle in 1798, Byron became the sixth Baron Byron and went to live on the ancestral estate of Newstead Abbey near Nottingham. In 1801 he entered Harrow, the famous public school, where taunts from the older boys about his clubfoot kept him miserable. This did not, however, prevent him from falling in love with his younger classmates. As he recorded of Harrow: "My school friendships were with *me—passions.* That with Lord Clare began one of the earliest and lasted longest.... I never hear the word *Clare* without a beating of the heart even *now,* and I write it with the feelings of 1803–4–5 *ad infinitum.*" Byron spent his school holidays at Southwell, near Nottingham, and there began a hopeless adolescent courtship of his older cousin Mary Chaworth, who was already engaged. This bitter episode apparently colored all his future romantic longings.

In 1805 Byron entered Trinity College, Cambridge, and there conceived what in his words was "a violent, though *pure,* love and passion" for John Edleston, a choirboy whom he first heard sing in Trinity Chapel. "His *voice,*" Byron wrote, "first attracted my attention, his *countenance* fixed it, and his *manners* attach me to him forever.... I certainly love him more than any human being, and neither time or distance have had the least effect on my (in general) changeable disposition." Some of Byron's earliest poems are to Edleston, including "To E_____," "Stanzas to Jessy," and "The Cornelian," which records Edleston's gift to Byron of a cornelian, which Byron kept with him the rest of his life. These appeared in *Hours of Idleness* (1807), Byron's first collection of poems.

The year 1808 seems to have been spent in debauchery in London: "an abyss of sensuality," as Byron characterized it, that threatened to ruin his health. In 1809, accompanied by John Cam Hobhouse, a close friend from Trinity, Byron undertook an extended, life-changing journey to Portugal, Spain, Albania, Greece, and Constantinople. He fell in love with the Mediterranean landscape and with its peoples and their way of life, which seemed to him, after England, earthy, profound, and liberating. Greek boys especially charmed him, and he had liaisons with several, including Eustathius Georgiou and Nicolo Giraud, whom he named his heir upon his return to London. Byron's letters to Hobhouse record the details, often in Latin code derived from Petronius [41].

In 1811 the sad news reached Byron of John Edleston's premature death. Byron wrote: "I have heard of a death the other day that shocked me more than any, of one whom I loved more than any, of one whom I loved more than I ever loved a living thing, and one who, I believe, loved me to the last." In Edleston's memory Byron composed "Thyrza," a series of elegies, though for publication he changed the pronouns to make the sentiments appear more acceptable.

The appearance in 1812 of the first two cantos of *Childe Harold's Pilgrimage,* which he had composed on his Mediterranean journey, made Byron famous. He began to frequent Whig salons (he was now a member of the House of Lords by virtue of his baroncy), carried on a scandalous intrigue with Lady Caroline Lamb, and sampled the "autumnal charms" of Lady Oxford, who encouraged his radical political tendencies. In 1813 he became involved in a dangerous liaison with his half sister, Augusta Leigh. To escape this entanglement he married Annabella Milbanke in 1815, but she left him, amid much gossip and rumor about Byron's homosexual proclivities, after only a year. The ensuing scandal forced Byron to flee England in April 1816, never to return (the penalty for homosexuality in England at that time was death). In Switzerland, on the shores of Lake Geneva, Byron met the poet Percy Bysshe Shelley and his wife, Mary Wollstonecraft Shelley (daughter of MARY WOLLSTONECRAFT [11]), and carried on an affair with Mary's half sister, Claire Clairmont. He also managed to complete a third canto of *Childe Harold's Pilgrimage* and to begin *Manfred.*

The autumn of 1816 found Byron, accompanied by Hob- house, in Venice, where, amid affairs with women married and unmarried, he began *Don Juan,* his mock epic detailing the exploits of the famous and insatiable lover. In 1819 he intervened in the marriage of the twenty-year-old Countess Teresa Guiccioli to a man three times her age: after the breakup, she and Byron settled into a domestic arrangement first in Ravenna, then in Pisa, where he fell again into company with Shelley (OSCAR WILDE [3] maintained that the friendship ended when Byron attempted to make love to Shelley). In any event, Byron grew restless in Pisa, and in 1823 accepted an appointment by the London Greek Committee to act as their agent in Greece, where a war of independence was raging against the Turks. In July 1823, he made his way to the Ionian island of Cephalonia, where he fell in love with a boy named Loukas Chalandritsanos. By January 1824, he and Loukas, whom he had taken along as his page, were in Missolonghi with the forces of Prince Mavrocordatos. Before the Greek offensive against the Turks could begin, however,

Byron was stricken with fever and died on April 19, 1824. His final three poems— "On This Day I Complete My Thirty-Sixth Year," "Last Words on Greece," and "Love and Death"—were searing declarations of his hopeless love for Loukas, who was apparently unwilling to return his affections:

> To thee—to thee—e'en in the grasp of death
>   My spirit turned, O, oftener than it ought,
> Thus much and more; and yet thou lov'st me not,
>   And never wilt! Love dwells not in our will.
> Nor can I blame thee, though it be my lot
>   To strongly, wrongly, vainly love thee still.

Byron was a legend in his own time and continues so into ours. He was a Romantic, but with a darker, more cynical view than his fellow Romantics of the unbridgeable gulf that separates our ideals from our realities. The Byronic hero—convention-defying, doomed, and passionate—has challenged imaginations both gay and straight. From early on, Byron's legend sparked the gay imagination: as early as 1833 a long poem titled *Don Leon* surfaced, filled with homosexual exploits and purporting to be Byron's true and secret biography. Long ignored, the poem's authorship remains a mystery, though it is startlingly accurate on some crucial points of Byron's homosexual love life.

The silence surrounding *Don Leon* for so many years was hardly unique: almost all nineteenth- and much of twentieth-century criticism has resolutely ignored the copious evidence of Byron's bisexuality, and his case represents a reprehensible scholarly cover-up of the kind that is all too common. With regard to any other subject, such a willful exclusion of evidence would be considered a shocking breach of academic integrity—but when the subject is homosexuality, otherwise reputable scholars have, with great regularity, exposed themselves as shameless deceivers. In part, Byron is on this list in order to shame all those so-called scholars who have attempted to "cleanse" their subjects of their homosexual lives and loves.

39

The Ladies of Llangollen
Lady
Eleanor Butler   *Sarah Ponsonby*
1739–1829   1755–1831

Lady Eleanor Butler came from a noble Irish Catholic family and was educated at a convent in France. Returning to Ireland, she showed no interest in marriage and instead immersed herself in study. In 1768 she met thirteen-year-old Sarah Ponsonby, the daughter of a well-to-do Dublin family, and over the next ten years, through letters and visits, the two grew closer. Then in

1778 they did the unheard-of: disguised in men's clothes, they eloped together. After their families pursued them and brought them back, they eloped again, this time successfully. They settled in Wales and bought a small cottage, which they dubbed Plas Newydd, near the town of Llangollen. There they embarked on a rigorous system of "self-improvement," reading to one another every day, and studying foreign languages, literature, and geography. In particular they were passionate about the work of the French romantic Jean-Jacques Rousseau, and in their daily communings with nature and their work in their garden, they sought to emulate his vision of human beings as good and equal in the state of nature, uncorrupted by the evils of the city. Indeed, the world came to see them as Rousseau-esque figures of innocent rural devotion, and they became enormously well-known. They carried on a vast correspondence with the larger world and were visited by many notables of the day, including the Duke of Wellington, Sir Walter Scott, Edmund Burke, Lady Caroline Lamb, Josiah Wedgwood, and Robert Southey. The king of England even granted Sarah Ponsonby a pension in 1787 to augment the small stipends the two ladies received once their respective families had resigned themselves to their living arrangements.

After a visit to Plas Newydd, William Wordsworth composed an enthusiastic poem in their honor, addressing them as "Sisters in love, a love allowed to climb / E'vn on this earth, above the reach of time." He was not the only poet to commemorate their relationship: Southey was inspired by his visit to write a poem as well, as did Anna Seward, who characterized the relationship between the two women as a "Davidean friendship," in reference to the biblical love of DAVID and JONATHAN [40]. In fact, years after their deaths the famous "Ladies of Llangollen," as they came to be known, continued to be the subject of sentimental verse.

A 1790 article in the *General Evening Post* titled "Extraordinary Female Affection" painted this picture of the pair: "Miss Butler is tall and masculine, she wears always a riding habit, hangs her hat with the air of a sportsman in the hall, and appears in all respects as a young man, if we except the petticoats which she still retains. Miss Ponsonby, on the contrary, is polite and effeminate, fair and beautiful." It sounds like a classic butch-femme relationship. The ladies, however, were not particularly

amused by this portrait of themselves. It is interesting to specu-
late why. None of their acquaintances believed they were "sapphists"—perhaps because they genuinely weren't, or perhaps
because their rural habitat safely removed them from the taint of
urban vices with which this newspaper portrait, fond as it might
be, threatened to associate them. When the ladies asked their
friend Edmund Burke whether they could sue the newspaper, he
advised them against it.

We can never know, of course, the true nature of their
relationship, except that Butler and Ponsonby bucked convention
in a remarkable way by choosing to forsake heterosexual marriage and live together. In most other regards, however, they were
far from radical. Historian Lillian Faderman writes, "Their
relationship was considered not only socially permissible but even
desirable. One reason it was so revered was that it was thought to
be nongenital—or rather the sexual possibilities of a life in a
shared bed were not thought of at all.... Their society was happy
to see them as the embodiment of the highest ideals of spiritual
love and the purest dreams of romantic friendship."

Faderman goes on to observe that it was the novelty of
Butler's and Ponsonby's relationship that endeared them: had
their way of life been an option for many women, they would
probably have been regarded as threats to the social order,
"models for a dangerous new lifestyle." Their relationship was
not totally anomalous, however, and Faderman names several
other contemporary "romantic friendships" of great emotional
intensity: between Elizabeth Carter, the esteemed translator of
Epictetus, and another writer, named Catherine Talbot; between
the poet Anna Seward (who lauded the ladies of Llangollen in
verse) and Honora Sneyd; between MARY WOLLSTONECRAFT [11]
and Fanny Blood.

Whatever the true nature of their relationship, Eleanor
Butler and Sarah Ponsonby fired the imagination of the late
eighteenth and early nineteenth centuries in a remarkable way.
As celebrated women intimately involved, aiding and comforting
and supporting one another, inseparable for over fifty years, they
were instrumental in helping create a space in which fulfilling
possibilities at sustained human companionship apart from heterosexual marriage could be imagined.

40

David and Jonathan

c. 1000 B.C.

The biblical story of David and Jonathan is told in the First Book of Samuel in the Old Testament. David first appears in chapter 16, when Saul, the king of Israel, is being tormented by evil spirits. His servants suggest that a little harp music will soothe him, and one of the servants recommends David, "a son of Jesse the Bethlehemite, who is skillful in playing, a man of valor, a man of war, prudent in speech, and a man of good presence." So Saul sends a message to Jesse: "Send me David your son, who is with the sheep."As verse 21 says: "And David came to Saul, and entered his service. And Saul loved him greatly, and he became his armor-bearer....And whenever the evil spirit from God was upon Saul, David took the lyre and played it with his hand."

Samuel chapter 17 seems unaware of the existence of the preceding chapter. Here David is introduced as the youngest of eight sons of Jesse of Bethlehem. His three eldest brothers are

serving in Saul's army, which has been drawn up for battle with
the army of the Philistines at Socoh in Judah. Jesse sends David to
the army encampment to deliver bread and cheese, and to bring
back word of his brothers. When David gets to the encampment,
he finds that the soldiers of the Israelite army are being challenged on a daily basis to a one-on-one with Goliath, the champion warrior of the Philistine army. This has been going on for
forty days, but no one wants to accept Goliath's challenge. So
David volunteers. Saul, who in this chapter seems not to have
heard of David before, offers him armor, but the boy refuses,
instead taking his stand with a slingshot and five smooth stones.
Once he's killed Goliath, David beheads the Philistine with his
own sword and returns in triumph to the Israelite camp. Saul
keeps asking, "Who is this young man?"

Chapter 18 begins, rather abruptly, by asserting, "When he
had finished speaking to Saul, the soul of Jonathan [Saul's son]
was knit to the soul of David, and Jonathan loved him as his own
soul. And Saul took him that day, and would not let him return to
his father's house. Then Jonathan made a covenant with David,
because he loved him as his own soul. And Jonathan stripped
himself of the robe that was upon him, and gave it to David, and
his armor, and even his sword and his bow and his girdle."

Saul soon becomes jealous of David's military successes, and
afraid of David. He tries to give away his daughter Merab in
marriage to David, but David refuses. However, his next offer—
of his daughter Michal—succeeds. Another military victory by
David causes Saul to announce to Jonathan that he plans to kill
David. Jonathan of course warns David and serves as go-between
to patch things up between his father and his friend. After Saul
tries—more than once—to pin David to the wall with his spear
while David is playing the lyre, David prudently decides to flee.
Saul blames Jonathan for aiding and abetting David, accusing
him, "You son of a perverse, rebellious woman, do I not know that
you have chosen the son of Jesse to your own shame, and to the
shame of your mother's nakedness?"

Storming out of the palace, Jonathan goes to find David,
who has hidden himself behind a heap of stones in a field. Seeing
Jonathan, David "fell on his face to the ground, and bowed three
times; and they kissed one another, and wept with one another,
until David recovered himself [or, according to some translations
of the problematic Hebrew word here, *exceeded* himself, which

certain scholars construe as 'ejaculated']." After swearing that "the Lord shall be between me and you, and between my descendants and your descendants, forever," the two part.

Eventually Saul and David are reconciled, and in yet another interminable battle with the Philistines, Saul and Jonathan are killed, beheaded, and their bodies hung from the wall of Bethsan.

In the Second Book of Samuel (1:25–26) the bereft David movingly eulogizes the dead Jonathan: "How are the mighty fallen in the midst of the battle! Jonathan lies slain upon thy high places. I am distressed for you, my brother Jonathan; very pleasant have you been to me; your love to me was wonderful, passing the love of women." David goes on to become the greatest king of Israel, and the ancestor of Jesus.

The story of David and Jonathan is the one biblical narrative that affirms a passionate friendship between men (though in the Middle Ages there was a tradition of a similar relationship between Christ and the apostle John, "the disciple whom Jesus loved"). Over the centuries, the story of David and Jonathan has often been interpreted as homosexual, and the phrase "passing the love of women" long ago entered the vocabulary as a euphemism for love between men. When a medieval biographer of England's notoriously homosexual king EDWARD II [25], for example, described the king's love for Piers Gaveston as being "beyond the love of women," his readers would have known exactly what he meant.

In the Renaissance, the figure of David was appropriated by such gay artists as MICHELANGELO [17] and Donatello to represent youthful beauty, much in the way that Roman artists had used Antinous, the beloved of HADRIAN [15].

Although David and Jonathan are not the only pair of passionately devoted male friends to come down to us from ancient times—two other famous instances are Achilles and Patroclus from Homer's *Iliad* and Gilgamesh and Enkidu from the Babylonian epic *Gilgamesh*—their influence on the centuries upon centuries in which the Judeo-Christian tradition has been with us merit their ranking at number forty on this list. It is an influence that lies not so much in the details of their story *per se,* as in the ways their relationship has served to emblemize the possibility of a powerful emotional intimacy between men "passing the love of women."

41

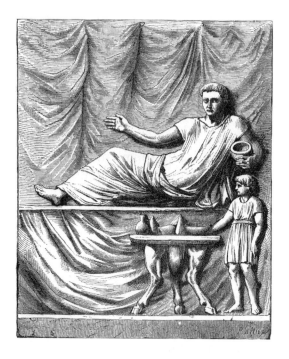

Petronius

died c. a. d. 66

What little we know of Petronius comes entirely from a short passage in the annals of Tacitus so richly atmospheric that it deserves to be quoted in full:

> He spent his days sleeping, his nights in work and the enjoyment of life. That success which most men achieve by dint of hard work, he won by laziness. Yet unlike those prodigals who waste themselves and their substance alike, he was not regarded as either a spendthrift or a debauchee, but rather as a refined voluptuary. Indeed, his words and actions displayed such apparent casualness and unconventional freshness that people found them all the more charming. Nonetheless, as

governor of Bithynia and soon afterwards as consul, he proved himself a capable and energetic administrator. Upon later reverting to a life of vice (or of apparent vice), he was admitted as effective arbiter of taste into the select circle of Nero's intimates. No imperial pastime or entertainment which lacked Petronius' approval could be regarded as either elegant or luxurious. And so Tigellinus, jealous of a rival whose expertise in the science of pleasure far surpassed his own, appealed to the emperor's cruelty (Nero's dominant passion) and accused Petronius of friendship with the conspirator Scaevinus. A slave was bribed to incriminate Petronius; no defense was permitted and most of the prisoner's household was placed under arrest.

At that time the emperor was in Campania. Petronius had gone as far as Cumae when he was apprehended. The prospect of temporizing, with its attendant hopes and fears, seemed intolerable; equally he had no desire to dispatch himself hastily. So he severed his veins and then bound them up as the fancy took him, meanwhile conversing with his friends, not seriously or sadly or with ostentatious courage. And he listened while they talked and recited, not maxims on the immortality of the soul and philosophical reflection, but light and frivolous poetry. He then rewarded some of his slaves and assigned beatings to others. He dined and then dozed so that his death, even though compulsory, might still look natural. Nor did he adopt the conventional deathbed routine of flattering Nero, Tigellinus, and the other worthies. Instead, he wrote out a list of the emperor's debaucheries, citing by name each of his sexual partners, male and female, with a catalogue of his sexual experiments, and sent it off to Nero under seal. He then destroyed his signet ring so that it could not be used later for the purpose of incriminating others.

It's a pity Petronius's catalog does not survive. What does survive, though, are fragments of his *Satyricon,* an immense prose and verse romance detailing the adventures of a bracingly disreputable threesome: sometime lovers Encolpius, Ascyltus, and their catamite Giton. A work that defies classification, the *Satyricon* has been described by its translator, William Arrowsmith, as "a burlesque, a mock-epic, an *Odyssey buffa* or satyr's *Aeneid*." Certainly it is resplendent with gay incident and intrigue. It may also be considered the world's first novel, gay or otherwise, and as such its influence may be said to have been vast.

In the eighteenth century, the name Petronius was a virtual byword for homosexuality. When Hester Thrale wished to fulminate against the excesses of the French court, she wrote, "One hears of Things now, fit for the Pens of Petronius only....The Queen of France [Marie Antoinette] is at the Head of a Set of Monsters call'd by each other *Sapphists*, who boast her example." The poet BYRON [38], writing in 1808 to a friend about his amorous adventures, mysteriously says that nowhere else on earth "can emulate in the capabilities or incitements to the 'Plen. and optabil.—Coit.' the port of Falmouth & parts adjacent.—We are surrounded by Hyacinths & other flowers of the most fragrant [na]ture, & I have some intention of culling a handsome Bouquet to compare with the exotics I hope to meet in Asia. One specimen I shall surely carry off, but of this hereafter." Louis Crompton has pointed out how Byron's code refers to the phrase *plenum et optabilem coitum* in the *Satyricon*, where Eumolpus tricks the boy he is sleeping with into "full and to-be-wished-for intercourse." Once we remember that Hyacinth was the beautiful boy Apollo fell in love with, Byron's interest in botany becomes quite clear.

More than any of the other ancient Roman writers who wrote of homosexual love, including such worthies as Virgil, Horace, and Catullus, Petronius captures the teeming, bawdy, aggressive yet melancholy spirit of the age. And how's this for a first-century lovers' spat?

> When I asked the boy whether he had made our supper, he suddenly burst into tears, collapsed on the bed and lay there wiping his eyes with his thumb. Frantic at seeing him in such a state, I begged him to tell me what had happened. Only much later, after my pleas had turned into threats, did he speak, and even then with great reluctance. "It's that man," he sobbed, "the one you call your brother, your friend Ascyltus. He ran up to my garret a little while ago and tried to take me by force. When I screamed for help, he pulled out his

sword. 'If you want to play Lucretia, boy,' he cried, 'you've met your Tarquin.'"

Furious at such treachery, I rushed across to Ascyltus and shook my fist in his face. "What do you say to that?" I yelled. "You male whore, you! You bugger! Even your breath stinks of buggery!"

At first he pretended to be insulted. Then he started throwing his fists around and yelling at the top of his voice. "Shut up!" he bellowed. "You stinking gladiator! Even in the arena you were a washout! Shut up! Thief! You cheap burglar! When were you ever man enough to take on a real woman? No, first it was me in the garden. Now it's this boy in the inn."

My, my. How things change.

42

The Amazons

Prehistory

In ancient Greek mythology, the Amazons were a tribe of women warriors said to live on the Black Sea coast in northeastern Asia Minor. Their capital was Themiskyra on the banks of the Thermidon River, between present-day Trabzon and Sinop in Turkey. Two legends are told of them. In the first, the hero Herakles must, as his ninth labor, lead an expedition to capture the girdle of Hippolyta, the queen of the Amazons. In a later story, Theseus voyages to Themiskyra, where he rapes an Amazon and carries her back to Athens. The Amazons pursue, invade Attica, and besiege Athens itself. A peace is achieved through the mediations of the captured Amazon, who bears Theseus a son. He deserts her, however, for Phaedra, and when she disrupts the wedding feast, she is slain by Herakles.

In the *Iliad*, Amazons fight with Troy against the Greeks until Achilles demoralizes them by killing Penthesilea, their queen.

The historian Herodotus in the fifth century B.C. thought the Amazons eventually settled in Scythia and intermarried with the Scythians, and that their descendants were the Sauromatae. Most of our information about the Amazons comes from postclassical sources: Didorus Siculus in the first century B.C., who placed the Amazons not in Asia Minor but in Libya, and Strabo of Alexandria in the early first century A.D. Strabo gave voice to the Greeks' anxiety about the Amazons when he wrote: "Who could believe that an army or city or nation of women could be organized without men? Or, that not only could it be organized but even could attack a foreign country, subdue its neighbors as far as present day Ionia, and launch an expedition across the sea as far as Attica? It is tantamount to saying that the men of that day were women, and the women were men."

The Amazon commonwealth was an *ethnos gynaikokratou-menon*, "a nation where women have power." There women fought and refused to be the mothers of sons. It was said that, for breeding purposes, they lived for two months each year with a neighboring tribe. Male offspring were killed, and the girls brought up to be warriors. Amazon society thus offered a matriarchal mirror image of Athenian mores. According to William Blake Tyrrell in *Amazons: A Study in Mythmaking,* the myth of the Amazons may have expressed Athenian insecurity about the weak point in their patriarchy: while they were dependent on women to bear their sons, the Amazons bore their daughters themselves, and their dependence on the opposite sex was thus drastically reduced. It is not uncommon for cultures to tell stories of a distant land where life is organized in ways exactly opposite from their own (see the last part of *Gulliver's Travels* for a more recent example of this).

In 1861, Johann Jacob Bachofen proposed, in his now much discredited *The Mother Right,* that civilization had evolved from matriarchy to patriarchy, and that the Amazon myths repre-sented a collective memory of this transition. Other scholars have suggested that early Germanic tribes and other peoples from the East may have employed women alongside men in combat, thus giving rise to the Amazon legend.

Whatever its origins, the *amazonomachia,* or combat with the

Amazons, was a favorite subject of Greek art and was often featured in conjunction with combat with centaurs. The Amazons are often shown with one breast bared—though never, in classical art, with one breast removed, as is suggested by the false etymology that derives Amazon from *a-mazos*, "without breast," based on the notion that the Amazons cut off their right breast to allow them to use a bow and arrow. Their favored weapon was not the bow and arrow but a double-headed ax called a *labyris*.

The overt association of Amazons with lesbianism is of recent vintage: it would seem, in fact, that NATALIE BARNEY [43] was the first to make this connection in the 1920s when she publicly identified herself as an Amazon and had her portrait painted as such by ROMAINE BROOKS [72]. Since midcentury, lesbians have adopted the image of the Amazon for their own ends in creative and powerful ways. The French writer Monique Wittig's *Les Guérillères*, an experimental novel about a band of women-loving women fighting the patriarchy, is a particularly memorable example of this appropriation.

A miniature Amazonian *labyris* is worn as an emblem by many lesbians today, an indication of the extent to which the Amazon tradition has been reshaped by our century into an influential and empowering origin myth of lesbian identity.

43

Natalie Barney

1876–1972

Natalie Barney was born on October 31, 1876, in Dayton, Ohio. Her father was the heir to a railroad-car fortune, her mother the heir to a whiskey fortune and a talented painter as well. Barney spent her childhood in Cincinnati and later in Washington, D.C., with summers in Bar Harbor, Maine, and numerous trips to Europe. On one of these trips, in Belgium in either 1886 or 1887, she witnessed a scene that made a deep impression on her: a woman pulling a heavy milk cart while her husband walked alongside and smoked his pipe. She dated her feminist consciousness from this moment. When her father returned to the United States, Barney's independent-minded mother elected to remain in Paris and study art with James McNeill Whistler. Barney and her sister were enrolled in the exclusive boarding school Les Ruches.

In 1899, while engaged to one Freddy Manners-Sutton, Barney had her first important lesbian affair—with the famous courtesan Liane de Pougy. With characteristic insouciance, Barney told her fiancé her plan: to marry him in order to free up her $3.5-million trust fund, and to use the money to support Liane. Oddly enough, he seems to have agreed, though the whole thing fell through—affair, marriage, and all. The liaison with Pougy nevertheless yielded Barney's first book of poems, *Some Portraits and Sonnets of Women*. The explicitly lesbian eroticism of the poetry shocked readers, including Barney's father, who bought up all the copies of the book he could find and destroyed the plates. Barney's mother, on the other hand, had provided the work's illustrations—of Barney's female lovers. It wasn't her daughter's lesbianism she disapproved of so much as her indiscretion. Despite some stormy episodes, Barney's mother remained a steadfast ally.

After her breakup with Pougy (and a three-week engagement to, of all people, Lord Alfred Douglas, the former lover of OSCAR WILDE [3]), Barney began an affair with the self-destructive English-born French-language poet and novelist Renée Vivien (1877–1909). Vivien commemorated her first impression of Barney in *A Woman Appeared to Me*, her 1904 novel about their affair: "I evoke that distant hour when I saw her for the first time, and the shiver which ran down my spine when my eyes met her eyes of mortal steel, her eyes which were as sharp and blue as a blade....The charm of peril emanated from her and drew me inexorably." For her part, Barney wrote of Vivien: "She had a thin body and a charming head with straight, mousy hair, brown eyes which often sparkled with gaiety, but when her beautiful, swarthy eyelids were lowered, they revealed more than her eyes—the soul and the poetic melancholy that I sought in her." Needless to say, the ensuing affair, epic in its proportions, was torrid and passionate and doomed. Barney believed in a sapphic ideal of multiple commitments without jealousy, while Vivien yearned for monogamy. Frustrated by Barney's affairs, Vivien eventually allowed herself to be stolen away by Hélene, the Baroness de Zuylen de Nyevelt. The period of Barney and Vivien's relationship, however, was a fruitful one for both their literary careers.

In 1902, Barney and Vivien took the Orient Express to Constantinople and traveled thence to the island of Lesbos to pay homage to the spirit of SAPPHO [2]. There they had the idea of establishing a school of poetry based on sapphic models. Though the project failed to come to fruition, it would later be reincarnated in Barney's Academy of Women.

In 1909, Barney moved her Paris quarters to 20 rue Jacob, where she launched her celebrated literary salon. Open every Friday, this "Lesbos in Paris" was attended by most of the major literary figures in Paris at the time, both male and female, though the emphasis, sometimes to the consternation of male guests, was thoroughly lesbian. Janet Flanner described the scene thus: "introductions, conversations, tea, excellent cucumber sandwiches, divine little cakes Berthe baked, and then the result: a new rendezvous among ladies who had taken a fancy to each other or wished to see each other again." Lesbians in attendance included RADCLYFFE HALL [28] (who portrayed Barney in *The Well of Loneliness* as Valérie Seymour), GERTRUDE STEIN [7], Marguerite Yourcenar, Sylvia Beach, Edna St. Vincent Millay, VITA SACKVILLE-WEST [64], Violet Trefusis, Edith Sitwell, and Wanda Landowska. The salon established Barney as *"l'impératrice des lesbiennes"* of Paris. (Barney's friendly competition during this time was Gertrude Stein's salon, though it tended to attract visual artists rather than writers.)

During World War I, Barney was active in antiwar meetings. In the words of biographer Karla Jay, she was "among the first to connect rape and war, war and machismo." "War," Barney wrote, "—this child men give birth to—they father death as women mother life, with courage and without choice." In 1915, Barney met and fell in love with the painter ROMAINE BROOKS [72]. Together they collaborated on a novel, *The One Who Is Legion, or A.D.'s After-Life,* which was privately printed in London in 1930. This was Barney's only major work in English. The rest, like her landmark 1920 assertion of lesbian identity, *Thoughts of an Amazon,* were written in French.

In 1927, Barney established the Academy of Women as a female answer to the all-male Académie Française. One of the first attempts to organize women writers, the Academy offered salons devoted specifically to women writers—among them, GERTRUDE STEIN [7], Colette, and Djuna Barnes. The Academy also offered publishing subsidies.

During the 1930s Barney and Brooks began to drift toward fascism, and they spent the years of World War II in Italy, at the invitation of Mussolini. Conveniently ignoring the fact that she

was herself one-eighth Jewish, Barney blamed the war on
Churchill and the Jews and went so far as to write that "the Jews
first commercialized the world, then had a hand in running it."
While living in Florence, Barney encouraged fellow expatriate
Ezra Pound to deliver his notorious profascist radio broadcasts
and even presented him with a radio as a token of her appreciation. After the war, Barney and Brooks returned to Paris,
successfully evading the punishment that was meted out to the
hapless Pound.

After 1940, Barney published mostly memoirs, including
Traits and Portraits, Adventures of the Mind, and *Indiscreet Memories.*
Her relationship with Brooks lasted for fifty years, though it was
punctuated by affairs on Barney's part, among them a liaison
with Dolly Wilde, the niece of Oscar. In 1968, when both women
were in their eighties, Brooks bitterly broke with Barney over her
latest affair, and the two women never again spoke. Natalie
Barney died on February 2, 1972, in Paris. The epitaph she
composed for herself read: "She was the friend of man and the
lover of woman, which, for people full of ardor and drive is better
than the other way around."

Barney's influence stems not so much from her writings as
from the figure she cut. A self-proclaimed AMAZON [42], Barney
was a highly visible and successful lesbian whose example served
to help countless others. Through the fifty years of her salon, and
the Academy of Women, she made a great contribution to
women's growing sense of their own collective power and independence as artists and intellectuals.

44

Eleanor Roosevelt

1884–1962

Anna Eleanor Roosevelt was born on October 11, 1884, in New York City. The daughter of Elliott Roosevelt (the younger brother of Theodore Roosevelt) and Anna Hall Roosevelt, she was orphaned at age nine. Raised by her maternal grandmother, she studied at private schools in the United States and abroad. At the age of eighteen, she made her formal society debut in New York City. Three years later, in 1905, she married her fifth cousin, Franklin Delano Roosevelt. They settled at his family estate in Hyde Park, New York, and in the next ten years she bore him six children. While he ran for state office, she was entirely absorbed by the work of raising a family. Shy and retiring by nature, when her husband was crippled by polio in 1921, she was forced to enter the public arena as his liaison with the political world. In 1928, FDR was elected governor of the state of New York, and four years later he won the presidency of the United States.

Eleanor Roosevelt proved to be a controversial first lady, an outspoken activist for women's rights, world peace, and the plight of the planet's underprivileged. In 1933 she gave the first press conference ever by a president's wife. Beginning in 1936, she wrote a syndicated column called "My Day," which focused on social problems, and as a working journalist joined a labor union, the American Newspaper Guild. Her radical recasting of the traditional role of first lady earned her widespread vilification from foes of her husband and his New Deal policies.

In 1941, she was appointed assistant director of defense, and in that capacity she toured U.S. troops in England as well as bases in the Pacific, Australia, and New Zealand during World War II. After FDR died in 1945, Eleanor Roosevelt was appointed by President Harry Truman to be a delegate to the United Nations General Assembly. From 1945 to 1951, she headed the U.N. Commission on Human Rights. She remained in politics throughout the 1950s as one of the leaders of the liberal wing of the Democratic Party, and in 1961, at the request of President John Kennedy, returned to the United Nations as one of the U.S. representatives at the fifteenth Session of the General Assembly.

Eleanor Roosevelt died in New York City on November 7, 1962.

As wife of the president of the United States, Eleanor Roosevelt was clearly restricted in the kinds of public selves she was able to adopt. About the texture and meaning of her private life, we will never be able to know for sure. But what has become clear in recent years is that she led, in many ways and with FDR's full knowledge, a life apart from her husband. As biographer Blanche Wiesen Cook writes: "Over the years, in Greenwich Village and at Val-Kill, Eleanor Roosevelt created homes of her own, with members of her chosen family, distinct, separate from her husband and children." During World War II, she developed particularly close friendships with two lesbian couples: Esther Lape (from whom she rented her Greenwich Village hideaway) and Elizabeth Read, and Nancy Cook and Marion Dickerman.

In later years she was passionately attached both to her male bodyguard Earl Miller and to a lesbian journalist named Lorena Hickock. Roosevelt's ardent letters to "Hick" have survived, though the correspondence was initially suppressed by those who felt it would be "misunderstood." Many other letters to her various intimates, however, have been destroyed.

Cook muses, "How, then, do we assess ER's intimate life? We might begin by acknowledging that the disappearance of so many documents was not an accident, but rather a calculated denial of ER's passionate friendships.... And yet it is now clear that ER lived a life dedicated to passion and experience. After 1920 many of her closest friends were lesbian women. She honored their relationships, and their privacy. She protected their secrets and kept her own. Women who love women...have understood for generations that it was necessary to hide their love, lest they be the target of slander and cruelty. For over a century, scandal and love have seemed so entwined that it has been merely polite to love in private. The romance of the closet, and the perspective of the fortress, became necessary barricades against bigotry and pain."

Known as the "the first lady of the world" because of her engagement in international affairs and her sympathy for the downtrodden of all nations and races, Eleanor Roosevelt was perhaps the most influential woman of her time. As a champion of women's rights and a highly visible symbol of the modern empowered woman, she left a legacy of hope and activism to countless women around the globe. But she stands for more: she stands for a passionate and unconventional private life lived triumphantly in the very shadows of a public role that would seem to forbid such a life.

45

Jean Genet

1910–1986

Jean Genet was born on December 19, 1910, in Paris, France. An illegitimate child, he was abandoned by his mother and raised by a peasant family. At the age of ten he was caught stealing from his foster mother's purse, and he spent most of his adolescence in Mettray, a notorious reform school. Escaping Mettray, he joined the French Foreign Legion, only to desert a few days later. Between 1930 and 1939 he tramped around Europe as a beggar, a male prostitute, and a pickpocket and spent time in French and Spanish prisons. As he said, "abandoned by my family, I found it natural to aggravate this fact by the love of males, and that love by stealing, and stealing by crime, or complicity with crime. Thus I repudiated a world that had repudiated me."

Genet spent most of the Nazi occupation of France in jail. Using a pencil and a brown paper bag, he began to write in 1942 while serving time for burglary at Fresne. When prison guards confiscated his manuscript, he started over. The result was the extraordinary novel *Our Lady of the Flowers* (1944), a blend of mystic lyricism and lush obscenity that was to become Genet's trademark in his fictions that followed: *The Miracle of the Rose* (1946), *Querelle* (1947), and *Funeral Rites* (1947).

In 1948 Genet was convicted of burglary for the tenth time and given an automatic life sentence as an "incorrigible." His case came to the attention of the surrealist Jean Cocteau and the exsistentialist philosopher Jean-Paul Sartre, who launched a successful appeal to the French president to have Genet reprieved.

In 1952, Sartre published a monumental study of Genet's work entitled *Saint Genet, Actor and Martyr*. Summarizing Genet's anomalous career, he wrote:

> I have shown that his work is the imaginary aspect of his life and that his genius is one with his unswerving will to live his condition to the very end. It was one and the same for him to will failure and be a poet. He has never gone back on his pledges, he has never given in, has never abdicated, and if he has won, it is because he has steadily played loser wins.
>
> For he has won. He comes and goes. He is free. It is almost eight years since he was last in prison. He has money, "honorable friends." This common-law criminal lives part of the time in Paris and part in Cannes, leading the life of a well-to-do bourgeois. He is "received." He is taken up by followers of fashion, is admired by others, but as he has not stopped associating with burglars and queers, he goes from drawing rooms to Montmartre bars, plays The Mysteries of Paris all by himself and, because he comes from nowhere, he feels at home everywhere. The finest proof of his victory: two letters he has received, one from a cop and the other from a turnkey, both requesting that he use his influence on their behalf.

Influenced by Sartre, Genet turned his attention to the theater with such plays as *The Maids* (1947), *The Balcony* (1956), *The*

Blacks (1958), and *The Screens (1961)*. In these controversial and shocking plays, Genet reached the height of his powers. According to EDMUND WHITE [92], they "remain, along with the plays of Bertolt Brecht and Joe Orton, the most substantial theatrical legacy of the postwar epoch."

After *The Screens*, Genet wrote little. His lover Abdallah Bentaga, a high-wire artist, died in 1964, and Genet attempted suicide in 1967. In the seventies, he turned out the occasional essay: in one notorious piece from 1977 he defended the terrorist Bader-Meinhoff gang. He refused any involvement in the gay movement, insisting that sexuality was a personal rather than political matter. He was, in Warren Johansson's words, "a rebel, not a revolutionary." That his politics were always frankly and subjectively personal is evidenced by his final work, published posthumously as *Prisoner of Love*, a chronicle of his involvement with the Black Panthers in the United States and the Palestine Liberation Organization in Jordan and Lebanon.

As a cause célèbre of French intellectuals such as Sartre, Genet achieved iconic status, allowing his work to have great influence over a whole generation of writers and thinkers. As a playwright, he has influenced dramatists as diverse as Eugène Ionesco, Amiri Baraka, and Peter Weiss. His investigations of role-playing, drag, and the scripted asymmetries of power involved in sexual relations continue to disconcert readers and audiences. His depictions of gay life are unstinting while at the same time lyrical, even intensely and perversely religious.

Jean Genet died on April 15, 1986, in Paris. In an irony he would have relished, the thief who had spent so much of his life in prison was officially eulogized by no less than the French minister of culture, Jack Lang, who concluded, "Jean Genet was liberty itself."

46

Sergey Diaghilev
1872–1929

Vaslav Nijinsky
1890–1950

The relationship—both professional and personal—between the impresario Sergey Diaghilev and the dancer Vaslav Nijinsky was a brief, volatile miracle.

Sergey Diaghilev was born on March 31, 1872, in Novgorod province, Russia. His father was a major general in the czar's army. His mother, a noblewoman, died giving birth to him. As a child he studied piano and composition with the encouragement of his stepmother. In 1890 he entered the University of St. Petersburg to study law. Soon he and a group of friends, including Alexander Benois and Léon Bakst, were meeting as a small informal salon to discuss the arts. After graduating in 1896 with a law degree, Diaghilev decided to devote himself to music— though he was dissuaded shortly thereafter from a career as a composer by the disastrous public reception of his first publicly performed work. Losing confidence in his abilities as a creative artist, he shifted his goals: he would become, he decided, one of the great and influential partrons of the arts. The only problem was that this required significant capital, which he did not happen to possess. Undeterred, he relied on his wit and charm, both of which he possessed in enormous degree. In 1899 he founded the avant-garde journal *Mir Iskusstva (Art World)*. A major exhibition of Russian art that he organized in 1905 further consolidated his reputation as an important arbiter of taste and champion of the avant-garde.

In 1906 Diaghilev left Russia for Paris. Acting as a cultural liaison between the two countries, he organized exhibitions of Russian art and concerts of Russian music. In 1909 the Grand Duke Vladimir commissioned him to establish the Ballets Russes in Paris. The Ballets Russes was, from the beginning, a hothouse of artistic experimentation. Choreographers Michel Fokine and Léonide Massine, composers such as Claude Debussy, Maurice Ravel, and Igor Stravinsky, and designers, including Diaghilev's old friends from his Russian school days Bakst and Benois, all influenced and were influenced by one another in a grand creative synthesis. The legendary dancers of the Ballets Russes, drawn from the ranks of the Mariinsky and Bolshoi theaters in Russia, included Anna Pavlova, Fokine, and an extraordinary nineteen-year-old named Vaslav Nijinsky.

Born in Kiev on March 12, 1890, Nijinsky was the son of Thomas Laurentiyevich and Eleonora Bereda, both celebrated dancers who had their own dance company. Thus, Nijinsky grew up in the midst of dance, spending much of his time touring with his parents. At the age of nine he was enrolled in the Imperial School of Dancing in St. Petersburg, where he quickly awed his teachers as well as the audiences who saw the boy perform with the Mariinsky Theater. Reviewers called him "the eighth wonder of the world."

After graduating from the Imperial School in 1907, Nijinsky joined the Mariinsky Theater as a soloist, to spectacular reviews throughout Russia, and in 1909 was asked by Diaghilev to join the Ballets Russes, where he danced roles in ballets that have since become the stuff of legend: *Petrushka, Le Spectre de la rose, Les Sylphides, Daphnis et Chloë*.

Nijinsky was probably the greatest male dancer who ever

lived. The French surrealist Jean Cocteau rhapsodized, "In him is reincarnated the mysterious child Septentrion, who died dancing on the shore at Antibes. Young, erect, supple, he walks only on the ball of the foot, taking rapid, firm little steps, compact as a clenched fist, his neck long and massive as a Donatello, his slender torso contrasting with his overdeveloped thighs, he is like some young Florentine, vigorous beyond anything human, and feline to a disquieting degree. He upsets all the laws of equilibrium, and seems constantly to be a figure painted on the ceiling; he reclines nonchalantly in midair, defies heaven in a thousand different ways, and his dancing is like some lovely poem written all in capitals."

Beginning in 1912, Nijinsky choreographed as well as danced, creating controversial and landmark ballets such as the explosive *Le Sacre du Printemps,* whose first performance literally caused a riot in the theater, and *L'Après-midi d'un faune,* in which Nijinsky—clothed in skin-tight leotards with a swaying bunch of grapes attached over his genitals—shocked even sophisticated audiences with his graphic representation of a faun masturbating over a nymph's scarf.

That the young superstar and his impresario were engaged in a relationship more than purely professional was an open secret. As Stravinsky noted wryly about Nijinsky's faun: "Of course Nijinsky made love only to the nymph's scarf. What more would Diaghilev have allowed?" But things did not last: the relationship went sour. Diaghilev was insanely jealous, treating the passive young dancer as his private property, and in 1913, in an act of panic in Buenos Aires, Nijinsky married Romola, Countess Pulszky-Lubocy-Cselfalva. He spent part of World War I interned in Hungary as a Russian subject. In 1919, after a nervous breakdown, he was diagnosed with schizophrenia and lived in various sanitoriums in Switzerland, France, and England until his death in London in 1950.

Diaghilev, in the meantime, continued to shepherd his Ballets Russes from brilliance to brilliance, touring Europe, the United States, and South America. His vast energy and daring spirit took their toll on his health, however, and in 1929, at the height of his success, he collapsed while on holiday in Venice, went into a coma, and died on August 19, 1929. His tomb, next to that of Stravinsky on the cemetery island of San Michele, is still visited by pilgrims, who leave red roses and worn ballet slippers in honor of this man whose vision played such a great role in creating modern dance.

Between them, Diaghilev and Nijinsky practically invented the modern male dancer. Before the Ballets Russes, male dancers played mostly a supporting role to the women—they were lifters rather than dancers. Diaghilev changed that, and the vehicle for that change was Nijinsky. A late-twentieth-century ballet icon like RUDOLF NUREYEV [89] would not have been possible were it not for Diaghilev's and Nijinsky's brilliant innovations during the brief time they were lovers.

Adrienne Rich

1929–

Adrienne Cecile Rich was born on May 16, 1929, in Baltimore, Maryland. Her father was a professor of medicine, her mother a composer and pianist. Rich has characterized her childhood thus: "I was born at the brink of the Great Depression; I reached sixteen the year of Nagasaki and Hiroshima. The daughter of a Jewish father and a Protestant mother, I learned abut the holocaust first from newsreels of the liberation of the death camps. I was a young white woman who had never known hunger or homelessness, growing up in the suburbs of a deeply segregated city."

In 1951, Rich graduated from Radcliffe College, and in that same year her first collection of poems, *A Change of World*, was chosen by the gay poet W. H. Auden for the Yale Younger Poets Award.

Rich married Alfred Conrad, a Harvard economist, in 1953.

Living as a model faculty wife in Cambridge, Massachusetts, she produced three sons between 1955 and 1959. Her 1976 book, *Of Woman Born*, documents her struggle to balance traditional female roles with her chosen life as a poet. Rich's second volume of poems, *The Diamond Cutters*, was published in 1955. Both her early books were distinguished by a quiet elegance, but in the late 1950s Rich's style began to change, and her work of the 1960s—especially *Necessities of Life* (1966) and *Leaflets* (1969)—were marked by a growing political commitment.

In 1966 she began teaching at City College in New York City in the SEEK and Open Admissions programs, an important career move that brought her into contact with the African-American poets Alice Walker and AUDRE LORDE [52], who were also on the faculty. When her 1973 collection, *Diving Into the Wreck*, was awarded a National Book Award, Rich rejected the award as an individual. Instead, in a joint statement with Walker and Lorde, both of whom had been nominated for the prize, Rich wrote that she would accept the award "in the name of all women whose voices have gone and still go unheard in a patriarchal world."

After her husband committed suicide in 1970, Rich became more outspoken as a radical feminist and lesbian separatist. She published her poems not in mainstream magazines but in such feminist journals as *Amazon Quarterly*, *Heresies*, and *13th Moon*. From 1981 to 1983 she coedited, with Michelle Cliff, a lesbian journal called *Sinister Wisdom*.

One of America's most important living poets, Rich has published many volumes of poetry in addition to those already mentioned, including *A Wild Patience Has Taken Me This Far* (1981), *The Fact of a Doorframe* (1984), *Your Native Land, Your Life* (1986), and *An Atlas of the Difficult World* (1991) . Some of her most beautiful lesbian love poems are to be found in "Twenty One Love Poems" from *The Dream of a Common Language* (1978).

Rich is also the author of three highly influential collections of essays that have done much to shape recent feminist and lesbian thought: *Disloyal to Civilization: Feminism, Racism, Gynephobia* (1978), *On Lies, Secrets and Silence* (1979), and *Blood, Bread and Poetry* (1986).

Probably Rich's most influential essay is "Compulsory Heterosexuality and Lesbian Existence," a work that has served as a point of departure for many important lesbian and feminist inquiries. In this essay, Rich argues that "heterosexuality, like motherhood, needs to be recognized and studied as a *political institution*." Heterosexuality is compulsory for most women, according to Rich, because society allows them no other choice. After enumerating the many ways in which male power over women is maintained—by denying women their own sexuality, by forcing male sexuality upon them, by exploiting their labor through the institutions of marriage and motherhood, by terrorizing them and restricting their movement through the threat of rape and other kinds of violence, by stifling their creativity and withholding from them large areas of society's knowledge—Rich is led to conclude that "we are confronting not a simple maintenance of inequality and property possession, but a pervasive cluster of forces, ranging from physical brutality to control of consciousness, which suggests that an enormous potential counterforce is having to be restrained."

Throughout history, however, women have found ways to resist this coercive male power. This resistance—this counterforce—has often taken place within what Rich defines as the "lesbian continuum." The lesbian continuum is "a range, through each woman's life and through history—of woman-identified experience; not simply the fact that a woman has had or consciously desired genital sexual experience with another woman. If we expand it to embrace many more forms of primary intensity between and among women, including the sharing of a rich inner life, the bonding against male tyranny, the giving and receiving of practical and political support; if we can also hear in it such associations as *marriage resistance*...we begin to grasp breadths of female history and psychology that have lain out of reach as a consequence of limited, mostly clinical, definitions of 'lesbianism.'" Because it allows a radical rethinking of women's relationships—and the politics of women's relationships—throughout history, perhaps no single concept has been so useful for lesbian thinkers in recent years as Rich's notion of the lesbian continuum. In powerful and important ways, Rich has succeeded in changing the very rules of discourse about lesbian existence.

Currently professor of English and feminist studies at Stanford University, Adrienne Rich stands at the forefront of contemporary lesbian identity. Her ranking here indicates my sense that, as a major poet and essayist, she is the most influential lesbian alive today.

48

Larry Kramer

1935–

Larry Kramer was born on June 25, 1935, in Bridgeport, Connecticut. His father was an attorney, his mother a social worker. After receiving his BA from Yale and then serving a one-year stint in the army, he trained as an agent with the William Morris Agency in New York City. The next year he began working for Columbia Pictures, first as an assistant story editor in New York, then for four years as a production executive in London. In 1965 he was hired as assistant to the president of United Artists. He was the associate producer in 1967 of the film *Here We Go Round the Mulberry Bush* and in 1969 wrote the screenplay for and produced Ken Russell's film of the D. H. Lawrence novel *Women in Love,* famous for its homoerotic elements. For this project Kramer was nominated for an Academy Award.

Kramer's controversial first novel, *Faggots,* was published in 1978. This satiric chronicle of a gay man's search for love among the bathhouses and bars was roundly denounced by many in the gay community for seeming to offer ammunition to those very forces that were massed against the community. Kramer stood firm by his intentions, however, arguing that he had meant the novel to be a serious critique of the excesses of a certain kind of gay life. In an interview with the *Chicago Tribune* he said, with the kind of brutal insight that has characterized his work and life, "I purposely made the chief characters in my book intelligent, educated, and affluent men who should be role models for the rest of us. Instead, they're cowardly and self-pitying persons who retreat into their own ghetto because they feel the world doesn't want them....It just seems that we should be angry at our own cowardice instead of the world's cruelty."

The advent of the AIDS crisis gave dark relevance to Kramer's musings. One of the first to understand the implications of the epidemic, Kramer raised the alarm in essays in the *New York Native.* In the now famous "1,112 and Counting" he wrote, "If this article doesn't scare the shit out of you, we're in real trouble. If this article doesn't rouse you to anger, fury, rage, and action, gay men may have no future on this earth. Our continued existence depends on just how angry you can get."

In 1982, along with Nathan Fain, Dr. Lawrence Mass, Paul Popham, Paul Rapoport, and EDMUND WHITE [92], Kramer founded Gay Men's Health Crisis (GMHC) to help combat the epidemic. Internal divisions over strategy as well as personality differences forced him to resign little over a year later. In the aftermath he wrote *The Normal Heart,* the 1985 drama that was one of the first and best literary responses to the AIDS epidemic. Imbued with all of Kramer's controversial forthrightness, the play attacked, through the autobiographical character of Ned Weeks, both gay and straight hypocrisy in dealing with the crisis. Although it had been turned down by fourteen agents and numerous directors, producers, and theater companies before being picked up by Joseph Papp's Public Theater, *The Normal Heart* won the 1986 Dramatists Guild Marton Award, the City Lights Award, and the Sarah Siddons Award for best play of the year. Kramer recalls about *The Normal Heart:* "I wrote it to make people cry: AIDS is the saddest thing I'll ever have to know. I also wrote it to be a love story, in honor of a man I loved who died. I wanted people to see on a stage two men who loved each other. I wanted people to see them kiss. I wanted people to see that gay men in love and gay men suffering and gay men dying are just like everyone else."

Kramer continued to agitate publicly for a response commensurate with the enormity of AIDS: "The worst years of the AIDS pandemic," he wrote in 1987, "lie ahead of us. We are woefully unprepared. There are millions of us yet to die. Please etch this thought on your consciousness: THERE ARE MILLIONS OF US YET TO DIE. Three out of four AIDS cases are still occurring in gay men. Many millions of people carry the virus. Three out of four AIDS cases are gay men. THERE ARE MILLIONS OF US YET TO DIE."

In 1987, Kramer was instrumental in founding the AIDS Coalition to Unleash Power (ACT UP). Originally an ad hoc community protest group pledged to concentrate on fighting for the release of experimental drugs, the group's first action was a mass demonstration on March 24, 1987, on Wall Street in New York City. Two hundred and fifty men and women tied up traffic for several hours, and the demonstration and subsequent arrests were, unlike most gay- or AIDS-related stories, covered widely in the media. In the months that followed, ACT UP blossomed into dozens of chapters across the country. Characteristically, when Kramer realized that his impatient leadership style was going to lead to a repeat of the troubles he had experienced with GMHC, he withdrew from active participation in the group. He has chronicled his years of AIDS activism in the 1989 volume *Reports from the Holocaust: The Making of an AIDS Activist.*

In 1988, Larry Kramer learned—as he had suspected for some time—that he was HIV-positive. His response was his critically acclaimed 1992 play, *The Destiny of Me.* A companion piece to *The Normal Heart, The Destiny of Me* traces the development of Ned Weeks from the child to the man. Kramer has written that he wanted to write "a personal history: a journey to acceptance of one's homosexuality. My generation has had special, if not unique, problems. We were the generation psychoanalysts tried to change. This journey, from discovery through guilt to momentary joy and toward AIDS, has been my longest, most important journey, as important—no, more important—

than my life with my parents, than my life as a writer, than my life as an activist. Indeed, my homosexuality, as unsatisfying as much of it was for so long, has been the single most important defining characteristic of my life."

As of this writing, Larry Kramer remains America's most compelling voice of rage—against a system that has doomed so many to untimely death, and against a community that has all too often seemed to allow itself to be victimized. He has been the Jeremiah of our generation: those whom his rage and grief have discomfited are not discomfited by Larry Kramer, but by the truth itself. Rude, opinionated, inconvenient, invaluable, and irreplaceable, he is the most influential gay man in America today. The organizations he helped to found, GMHC and ACT UP, have gone on to become some of the most important institutions in contemporary gay America's struggle to survive. If the community does in fact survive, it will owe that survival in no little degree to Larry Kramer.

49

Tennessee Williams

1911–1983

Tennessee Williams was born Thomas Lanier Williams on March 26, 1911, in Columbus, Mississippi. The son of a traveling shoe salesman, Williams was chiefly raised by his domineering, puritanical mother. As a child he was withdrawn and introspective. Writing, he recalled, "became my place of retreat, my cave, my refuge. From what? From being called a sissy by the neighborhood kids, and Miss Nancy by my father, because I would rather read books in my grandfather's large and classical library than play marbles and baseball...a result of a severe childhood illness and of excessive attachment to the female members of my family, who had coaxed me back into life."

In 1929 he enrolled at the University of Missouri at Columbia to study journalism, but soon dropped out and took a job in a shoe company where for two years he worked by day and, in the evenings, wrote furiously. A nervous breakdown led him to Memphis for treatment, and while there he became involved in a local theater company. Returning to Missouri, he studied at

Washington University in St. Louis, and in 1937, he entered the University of Iowa. The next year, nine years after beginning his college education, he graduated.

Adopting the name Tennessee—over the years he ventured a number of explanations as to why—he moved to New Orleans and its gay milieu. After several failed plays, some encouraging grants, and a brief stint in California as a screenwriter, Williams had his first major success in 1945 with *The Glass Menagerie*. Based in part on his beloved sister Rose—who had been diagnosed with schizophrenia several years earlier and subjected to a frontal lobotomy—the play won the New York Drama Critics' Circle Award for the 1944–45 season. It also irrevocably changed the landscape of American theater. Masterpiece followed masterpiece in quick succession: the Pulitzer Prize–winning *A Streetcar Named Desire* (1947), *The Rose Tattoo* (1951), *Summer and Smoke* (1952), *Cat on a Hot Tin Roof* (1955—Williams's second Pulitzer Prize), *Sweet Bird of Youth* (1959), and *Night of the Iguana* (1961—his fourth Critics' Circle Award). Many of these were made into highly acclaimed movies as well.

Then the luck ran out: in 1963 Williams's lover, Frank Merlo, died of cancer. About their fourteen-year-long relationship, Williams's brother Dakin recalls: "In addition to the sex part, which was mutually good, and the genuine affection they had for each other, they were probably more complementary than most male-female partners. Merlo was, unlike Santo and Rafaello [previous lovers], a steadying influence; he was competent at all the everyday chores of life, at which Tennessee was hopeless. He did the driving, the cooking, the packing, the picking-up, everything, leaving Tennessee free to do nothing but write."

Merlo's death caused serious psychic damage. Williams found it increasingly difficult to write and relied more and more heavily on coffee, drugs, and alcohol to jumpstart his imagination. Through most of the decade he was himself ill, in part as a result of his alcohol and drug abuse.

In 1968 he converted to Roman Catholicism, and in 1969 he was institutionalized briefly after a nervous breakdown. The 1970s saw a renewed vigor and productivity, though new plays such as *Small Craft Warnings* (1972), *Vieux Carré* (1979), and *A House Not Meant to Stand* (1982) failed to meet with much critical or financial success.

In his later years, Williams divided his time between New

York City and Key West and also maintained an apartment in New Orleans's French Quarter, where *A Streetcar Named Desire* had been so memorably set. On February 25, 1983, he was found dead in his suite at New York's Hotel Elysée, having apparently choked to death on a plastic bottle cap from a nasal-spray container.

With the possible exception of Eugene O'Neill, Tennessee Williams was the greatest American dramatist of the twentieth century. In nearly two dozen full-length plays, at least as many one acts, three novels, and two volumes of poetry, Williams created a host of unforgettable characters in predicaments as dark and painful as any the stage has seen. He was the poet of the dispossessed, of those souls too fragile or frightened or tender or broken to live.

Drama critic Frank Rich assesses Williams's contribution to the stage thus: "The daring theatrical innovations and psychological liberation that mark...Williams' breakthrough plays were built on foundations laid by O'Neill and, of course, Freud. In turn Mr. Williams exerted an enormous influence on the generation of writers that followed him. Hardly a month goes by without the production of a new American play that is written in the patented Williams style sometimes referred to, for lack of a better term, as 'poetic realism.' Echoes of his voice can be heard in the works of Edward Albee and Lanford Wilson, to name just his two most prominent successors."

Williams's homosexuality suffused his work, though as a subject more often hinted at than addressed head-on, a darkness lurking at the center of his plays that cannot—or only with great difficulty—be spoken or faced by the characters. And yet audiences *knew*, and from the beginning Williams's dramas helped bring the existence of gay people to the American consciousness in sympathetic and moving ways. By the end of his life, Tennessee Williams was one of our first openly gay celebrities, and his *Memoirs* (1975) addressed gay issues with compelling forthrightness and honesty. If I have ranked Tennessee Williams a step below LARRY KRAMER [48], it is not because Kramer is the better playwright: he is not. Kramer's political presence in the world, however, makes him a more immediate influence on gay and lesbian life—at least in the 1990s—than Williams. To acknowledge that does not in the least diminish Tennessee Williams's immortal contribution both to the American theater and to the gay imagination.

50

Rosa Bonheur

1822–1899

Marie-Rosalie Bonheur was born on March 16, 1822, in Bordeaux, France. Her mother was a musician, her father an artist and art teacher. As a follower of the French social philosopher Saint-Simon, Bonheur's father believed in the emancipation of women and the questioning of conventional sex roles. He also encouraged his children's creativity, and all four of them eventually became artists.

Trained by her father in childhood, Bonheur went on to study with Léon Cogniet in Paris at the Ecole des Beaux Arts. By 1841, at the age of nineteen, she had begun to show paintings regularly at the official Paris Salon. From early on in her career, she specialized in painting wild animals—an academic genre whose conventions she honed to perfection. In 1848, when she

193

was twenty-six, a jury that included such well-known artists of the day as Corot, Delacroix, and Ingres awarded her the First Gold Medal for her painting *Ploughing the Nivernais* (now in the Louvre).

Bonheur's work was a great critical and financial success. Her 1853 painting *The Horse Fair* was bought in 1887 by Cornelius Vanderbilt for £4,200—a record sum at the time. A smaller version of the same painting was hung in the National Gallery in London in 1865, the first time a work by a living artist had been thus honored. Also in 1865, Bonheur became the first woman ever to receive the Grand Cross of the Légion d'Honneur. Queen Victoria of England befriended her and proved such a splendid patron that Bonheur's works became highly prized among English aristocratic circles. Such success was just fine with Bonheur: she understood exactly what it allowed her. In words that presage VIRGINIA WOOLF'S [13] feminist prescription of the next century, she clear-sightedly wrote, "I mean to earn a good deal of filthy lucre for it is only with that that you can do what you like."

Her work often took her to the slaughterhouses and horse fairs, and also to the parts of the Bois de Boulogne that in those days were still wild. Arguing that she needed to wear men's clothing in order to avoid being bothered in her work (such cross-dressing was illegal), she convinced the Paris Prefect's Office in 1857 to grant her such permission. Thereafter men's work clothes were habitual with her. She also smoked cigarettes.

At the age of fourteen, Bonheur had begun a friendship with Nathalie Micas, a sickly but talented child two years younger than herself. When they met again in adulthood, they formed a relationship that was to last until Micas's death in 1889. In the house they set up together (in 1860 Bonheur was able, with her earnings, to purchase a château at By, near Fontainebleau), Micas played the part of the wife, tending to the household duties, while close-cropped, masculine-attired Bonheur painted and smoked cigarettes and, for a while, kept a lioness as a pet. In fact, she established a whole zoo of exotic creatures at the château from which to paint.

After Micas's death Bonheur was desolate, but in that same year she met a young American artist whose mother had brought her to Paris in order to experience European culture. Anna Elizabeth Klumpke (1856–1942) was, like Nathalie Micas before her, talented and in delicate health (she had been lame since childhood). In many ways she took up where Micas had left off, and Bonheur referred to her as "my wife." In her will Bonheur named Klumpke her sole heir, and all three women are buried together in Père Lachaise Cemetery beneath the inscription "Friendship is divine affection."

That Bonheur understood quite well the nature of such divine affection is suggested by the account of herself that she sent to MAGNUS HIRSCHFELD [4] as part of his pioneering survey of "intermediate sexual types." She identified herself as a "contrasexual," a member of the "third sex," a "masculinized woman."

Rosa Bonheur died on May 25, 1899, at Melun, near Fontainebleau.

In *The Sexual Perspective: Homosexuality and Art in the Last 100 Years in the West,* Emmanuel Cooper assesses Rosa Bonheur's work and legacy: "The contrast between Rosa Bonheur's academically respectable paintings of animals in which every hair and blade of grass was included, and her highly unusual way of life with an unconventional sexual orientation, expressed both her determination to succeed as an artist and as a woman, whilst acknowledging Victorian ideas about modesty. If her choice of life partner was another woman, the format of the relationship was that of the conventional and devoted marriage. Of equal importance was her career as an artist. Her artistic and financial success placed her in a strong position to determine the way she organized her life."

As one of the most celebrated artists of her day, Rosa Bonheur inspired many women artists—both through her paintings, her independent "butch" image, and her unapologetically unconventional life. Her inclusion in this ranking acknowledges her importance as an exceedingly visible role model for women who were attempting, in the face of a hostile and repressive patriarchy, to establish their own lives. By questioning the options—personal as well as professional—available to women in the nineteenth century, Rosa Bonheur helped begin to dislodge the firmly entrenched verities of her age.

51

Arthur Rimbaud

1854–1891

Paul Verlaine

1844–1896

Paul Verlaine was born on March 30, 1844, in Metz, France. After receiving his *baccalauréat* in 1862, he worked first as a clerk in an insurance company, then for the Paris City Hall while spending his free time writing poetry and frequenting literary cafes. He became associated with the so-called Parnassian Group of writers that included Stéphane Mallarmé, Villiers de L'Isle-Adam, and Anatole France. His poems began to appear in literary journals, and in 1866 he published his first volume of poetry.

In 1869, at the age of twenty-five, he fell in love with sixteen-year-old Mathilde Mauté, and they were married the following year. Poems written during their engagement indicate that he saw her as an escape from "erring ways."

In August 1871, the very embodiment of erring ways came into his life.

Arthur Rimbaud was born on October 20, 1854, in Charleville, France. From an early age he showed great talent as a writer and excelled as a student at the Collège de Charleville, winning first prize for a Latin poem in 1870 at the Concours Académique. His first published poem also appeared that year. His formal education ended with the onslaught of the Franco-Prussian War in July of 1870. After a series of misadventures he finally got himself to Paris, where he lived in poverty for six months before returning to Charleville radically changed in spirit. Gone was the simple joy in existence that he had expressed in his earlier poems, and in its place seethed a daemonic, blaspheming, alchemizing soul. He began to play the local scourge. According to his friend Ernest Delahaye: "He got his kicks by making money in the most repugnant of ways, and by describing various immoral acts in great detail, so that fire from heaven would have had to engulf the cafe." He apparently lived, at that time, off wealthy men who picked him up. In two 1871 letters to Paul Démeny, now known as the *Lettres du voyant,* he articulated his new aesthetics: that the poet must destroy the restraints that define the conventional self in order to become a seer, a *voyant* in perilous communion with the infinite. He must become like a criminal, must risk everything in what Rimbaud called "a conscious derangement of the senses."

In August 1871, Rimbaud sent some of his recent poems to Verlaine. Dazzled, the older poet immediately sent the boy money to pay his way to Paris. In a burst of enthusiasm before leaving Charleville, Rimbaud produced *Le Bateau ivre* ("The Drunken Boat"), one of the supreme masterpieces of French literature.

In Paris, Rimbaud made the rounds of famous poets, alienating everyone with his behavior except for Verlaine, with whom he became lover. By November, there were rumors in the press about their relationship, and when they showed up together at one literary gathering, the scandalized participants had them thrown out. A tumultuous period of absinthe drinking and

debauchery ensued. There were endless lovers' quarrels, separa-
tions, reconciliations. It all culminated on July 10, 1873, in
Brussels, when Verlaine, drunk on absinthe, shot Rimbaud in the
wrist. Mortified, he then handed the gun over to Rimbaud and
insisted that the boy should kill him. Rimbaud refused, and off
they went to a hospital to have Rimbaud's wound treated. But in
the street Verlaine started another fight, pulled the gun again,
and Rimbaud had to beg a passing policeman for protection.
Rimbaud was taken to the hospital, and Verlaine into custody.
Convicted of attempted murder, the love-besotted poet was
sentenced to two years' imprisonment.

During this turbulent period of their love affair Rimbaud
composed his two most important works, the gorgeous and
terrifying *Une Saison en enfer (A Season in Hell)* and the transcen-
dental prose poems *Illuminations*. Artistically, Verlaine had been
totally outgunned. Hans Mayer assesses the dynamic between the
two poets thus: "It was exactly this that Verlaine had been
incapable of: strong and constant feeling amid the scandalous
experiment. He remained the foolish paramour of hell's consort,
and as 'foolish virgin' never comprehended why everything had
to founder in the end."

They saw one another once more—in 1875, after Verlaine's
release from prison—and quarreled violently. After that, Rimbaud wandered about Europe and the Middle East for some years
before ending up in Ethiopia. There he became the first white
man to venture into the Ogaden region of that country. By 1885
he had set himself up as a gunrunner supplying arms to Menelik
II, King of Shoa. He lived in poverty and obscurity with a local
woman.

In the meantime, during his long absence from France, he
had become famous. Unable to locate his former lover, Verlaine
had taken it upon himself to publish Rimbaud's work (as the work
of "the late Arthur Rimbaud"), to great critical acclaim, and to
write about him in his 1884 book, *Les Poètes maudits (The Accursed
Poets)*. Although Rimbaud apparently heard, circuitously, about
his success in France, he was no longer interested. He had
renounced poetry, had journeyed (in Mayer's words) "from
provocative love of scandal to provocative insignificance."

In 1891, Rimbaud developed a tumor on his right knee that
was diagnosed as bone cancer. When treatment in Aden failed, he
was taken back to France where his leg was amputated. He died

on November 10, 1891, in Marseilles. He was thirty-seven years old.

As for Verlaine, after his break with Rimbaud he reconverted to Roman Catholicism and tried to patch things up with his wife, but in the long run this proved unsuccessful, and he lapsed into drink and bisexual debauchery. His best work lay behind him. He died on January 8, 1896, in Paris.

The passionate, violent, self-destructive love affair between these two poets spawned—especially in Rimbaud—some of the most remarkable and influential poetry in the French language. The haunting saga of Rimbaud's life influenced many imaginations (it has been suggested, for instance, that Joseph Conrad's *Heart of Darkness* was inspired by Rimbaud's final years).

I have included Rimbaud and Verlaine in this ranking because their troubled relationship—at once incandescent and nightmarish—was, with the exception of the affair between OSCAR WILDE [3] and Lord Alfred Douglas, the most publicized gay liaison of the nineteenth century. After these two extraordinary poets, it would be impossible to talk about French poetry without also talking, at some point, about homosexuality.

52

Audre Lorde

1934–1992

Audre Geraldin Lorde was born on February 18, 1924, in Harlem, New York. Her parents were immigrants from Granada who believed, until the Depression, that they would one day return to their Caribbean home. As a result, Lorde's childhood was suffused by a sorrowful nostalgia for her lost "home."

Early on she discovered the wonder of language. As she wrote later, "I used to speak in poetry. I would read poems, and I would memorize them. People would say, well, what do you think, Audre? What happened to you yesterday? And I would recite a poem and somewhere in that poem would be a line or a feeling I would be sharing. In other words, I literally communicated through poetry. And when I couldn't find the poem to express the things I was feeling, that's what started me writing poetry, and that was when I was twelve or thirteen."

Lorde attended Hunter College High School and, after

graduating, moved into her own apartment and supported herself with low-paying, unsatisfying jobs. She had her first lesbian affair with one of her coworkers at a factory in Bridgeport, Connecticut. In 1954 she traveled to Mexico to attend the National University of Mexico for a year—"and for the first time in my life I walked down the streets of a city where most of the people were brown-skinned, everywhere I went. It was like coming into sunlight." Returning to the United States she entered what she called the "gay-girl" scene in Greenwich Village, but was distressed to find herself all too often the only black face in the crowd: "During the 1950s in the Village," she wrote, "I didn't know the three or four other black women who were visibly gay as well. We acknowledged each other's presence by avoiding each other's eyes, and since all too often we were sleeping with the same white women, we recognized ourselves as exotic sister outsiders who might have little to gain from bonding together. It was as if we thought our strength might lie in our fewness, our rarity. That is the way it was downtown, and uptown, meaning the land of black people, seemed very far away, and hostile territory."

Lorde began studying at Hunter College, and working as a librarian, and continued to write poetry. For a time she joined the Harlem Writers Guild, a gathering place for black poets, including Langston Hughes, but the group's homophobia drove her away. In 1959 she received her BA in literature and philosophy from Hunter. Further study at Columbia University's School of Library Service earned her an MLS in 1960, and for the next several years she worked as a librarian, first in the Mount Vernon Library, and later as head librarian at the Town School in New York City. In 1962 she married Edward Rollins, an attorney, and they had two children. Lorde and Rollins were divorced in 1970.

Nineteen sixty-eight was a momentous year for Lorde. She published her first book of poems, *The First Cities*, spent a rewarding six weeks as writer-in-residence at Tougaloo College in Mississippi, and there met Frances Clayton, the woman with whom she would henceforth share her life.

Back in New York City, Lorde taught writing courses in the SEEK program at City College, where her colleagues were Alice Walker and ADRIENNE RICH [47], and courses on racism at Lehman College and John Jay College of Criminal Justice. Her second volume of poetry, *Cables to Rage*, was published in 1970. Neither that volume nor her first had contained any poems about her lesbian experiences. In 1971, however, Lorde publicly read a lesbian love poem for the first time. It was later published in *Ms.* magazine, though her book editor rejected it from inclusion in her third volume of poetry, *From a Land Where Other People Live.* That volume was nominated for a National Book Award in 1974, along with books by her colleagues Alice Walker and ADRIENNE RICH [47]. When Rich was awarded the prize, she issued a joint statement with Walker and Lorde indicating that she was accepting the award not as an individual but "in the name of all women whose voices have gone and still go unheard in a patriarchal world." The nomination won Lorde a great deal of attention, and her next volume of poetry, *Coal,* was picked up by the mainstream publisher W.W. Norton and issued with a preface by Rich. *Coal* and the following volume, *The Black Unicorn* (1978), were widely reviewed and reached a large audience.

In 1980, Lorde published the autobiographical *Cancer Journals,* in which she wrote courageously about her mastectomy and her decision, when her breast cancer recurred, to forgo more surgery in favor of alternative therapies. Other works include the "biomythography" *Zami: A New Spelling of My Name* (1982) and *Sister Outsider* (1984), a collection of essays that has become a feminist classic and staple of women's studies courses. She was editor of the lesbian journal *Chrysalis,* and a founding member of The Kitchen Table-Women of Color Press.

Audre Lorde died on November 17, 1992.

Sadly, people of color have all too often found themselves as shunted to the margins within the gay community as they are within mainstream society: Audre Lorde's life's work was an ongoing protest against this. Not only did she give powerful voice to the sister outsider in all her multiple and expectation-confounding configurations, but she also forced white lesbians and gay men to confront their lingering biases and assumptions. She reveled in her confusion of categories, the supremely human fact that she would not fit easy classification. "I am a black lesbian feminist," she was fond of asserting, while at other times she said, "I cannot be categorized." As she wrote, "I have a duty to speak the truth as I see it and to share not just my triumphs, not just the things that felt good, but the pain, the intense, often unmitigating pain." It is as a great and fierce truth-speaker who influenced a whole generation to see with new eyes that Audre Lorde is commemorated on this list.

53

We'wha

1849–1896

We'wha was born in 1849 in the Anthill at the Middle of the World, the pueblo of Zuñi near the present-day border between New Mexico and Arizona. His parents died when he was a small child, perhaps in 1853, from a smallpox episode that ravaged the pueblo after a party of white American settlers passed through. He and his brother were adopted by their father's sister—which meant, in matrilineal Zuñi society, that We'wha retained membership in his mother's clan, the Badger People, while having lifelong ceremonial ties to his father's clan, the Dogwood People. Since his foster father was a rain priest, his adoptive family was one of the most powerful in the pueblo.

    We'wha's childhood took place in a time of intertribal conflict between the Zuñi and the neighboring Navaho and

Apache peoples. The 1850s and 1860s saw the Zuñi forging alliances with the United States government, providing warriors and provisions for army expeditions in return for much needed weapons and ammunition.

At some point in his childhood, perhaps as early as three or four, We'wha manifested certain traits that the women in his family would have recognized. As Will Roscoe, author of *The Zuñi Man-Woman*, explains: "While the traditional roles of men and women were well defined, the Zuñi viewed gender as an acquired rather than an inborn trait. Biological sex did not dictate the roles individuals assumed. Nor did Zuñi thought limit gender to only two versions. Zuñi berdaches occupied an 'alternative' gender, a status anthropologists have termed berdache and the Zuñis called *lhamana*." The Zuñis were not anomalous in this regard: the existence of the berdache has been documented in over 130 North American tribes.

As a berdache, We'wha was trained by the women in his family to perform women's tasks such as carrying water, tending the vegetable gardens, threshing wheat, and plastering the adobe walls. He was also instructed in pottery-making and weaving and became a particularly talented blanket-weaver.

In 1864, the U.S. army's defeat of the Navahos and the forced removal of tens of thousands of them to distant reservations effectively ended the Zuñi's protracted border skirmishes with their neighbors. The 1870s saw increasing contacts between the Zuñis and white people: in 1876, Mormon missionaries converted over a hundred Zuñis and set up a mission, and two years later the Presbyterians, hoping to counter the Mormon threat, arrived in the pueblo. The Reverend Taylor F. Ealy set up a school, and it was there, in 1879, that the anthropologist Matilda Stevenson found We'wha, a Zuñi "girl" who helped with housework. As she wrote later:

> This person was a man wearing woman's dress, and so carefully was his sex concealed that for years the writer believed him to be a woman. Some declared him to be an hermaphrodite, but the writer gave no credence to the story, and continued to regard We'wha as a woman; and...he was always referred to by the tribe as "she"—it being their custom to speak of men who don woman's dress as if they were women....She was the tallest

person in Zuñi: certainly the strongest, both mentally and physically. Her skin was much like that of the Chinese in color, many of the Zuñis having this complexion....She had a good memory, not only for the lore of her people, but for all that she heard of the outside world....She possessed an indomitable will and an insatiable thirst for knowledge. Her likes and dislikes were intense. She would risk anything to serve those she loved, but toward those who crossed her path she was vindictive. Though severe she was considered just.

An improbable friendship developed between Stevenson and We'wha, and late in 1885, We'wha and several other Zuñis accompanied Stevenson and her husband east to their home in Washington, D.C. There We'wha quickly learned English and soon became the toast of the town—not because he was a berdache (at that point everyone still thought he was a woman), but because Native American women seldom came east. One newspaper raved, "Society has had recently a notable addition in the shape of an Indian princess of the Zuñi tribe....Princess Wawa goes about everywhere at all of the receptions and teas of Washington wearing her native dress....The princess held a regular levee at the house of the handsome Mrs. David Porter Heap the other day. Mrs. Heap, who is one of the most attractive ladies in Washington, suddenly found herself deserted on account of the rival charms of the Indian princess. The ladies crowded about the Princess Wawa and amused themselves endlessly in attempting to converse with her by signs and broken English."

One newspaper did manage to note: "Folks who have formed poetic ideals of Indian maidens, after the pattern of Pocahontas or Minnehaha, might be disappointed in Wa-Wah on first sight. Her features, and especially her mouth, are rather large; her figure and carriage rather masculine." No one at the time, however, guessed the truth. On June 23, 1886, a truly historic occasion, We'wha the Zuñi man-woman met and shook hands at the White House with the president of the United States, Grover Cleveland.

We'wha's visit to the East was a rousing diplomatic success for the Zuñi people. As Roscoe observes: "The image and reputation of the Zuñis—America's industrious, peaceable ally on the New Mexico frontier—was well served by that pueblo's leading berdache. Few tribes could count on the instant recognition that the name 'Zuñi' enjoyed in the 1880's."

The 1890s, however, proved difficult times for the Zuñis. The introduction of whiskey into the pueblo, and the increasing resistance of the Zuñi leaders to U.S. interference in their practices and traditions, led, in 1892, to a confrontation with U.S. troops over the issue of the community's response to a perceived case of witchcraft. We'wha and five other Zuñi leaders were arrested, and We'wha served a month in prison.

In December 1896, after participating in the annual Sha'lako festival, We'wha collapsed and died of heart failure at the age of forty-nine. His death was viewed as a "calamity" by the pueblo—"a death which caused universal regret and distress in Zuñi," as Stevenson wrote. Witchcraft was suspected in such a premature demise, and an old woman was arrested and severely beaten. The incident provided the U.S. government with the excuse it needed to move in and assert its authority once and for all over the Zuñi.

We'wha was the most celebrated and famous berdache, that intermediate gender that has sparked gay imaginations from EDWARD CARPENTER [9] to HARRY HAY [22] to RUTH BENEDICT [35] to JUDY GRAHN [91]. Will Roscoe sums up the importance of the berdache when he writes, "Whether as a role model or as an archetype of wholeness, the multidimensional image of the berdache reminds us that our debates over sex and gender involve ethical choices relative to our own time and place.... In the end, it is hard not to ask who has the greater insight into the psychological and social potentials of human diversity: Western society, which renounced the larger part of the spectrum of gender and sexuality centuries ago, or the people who live in the Anthill at the Middle of the World, who, for just as long, have ensured the representatives of diversity a place in the middle, as valued participants in their social balance?" We'wha is ranked number fifty-three because of the influence the idea of the berdache has exercised in our collective attempts to rethink heretofore hard-and-fast categories. A figure like We'wha—and the culture that produced him—challenge in powerful and liberating ways the "truths" of gender and sexuality that propose to enslave us.

54

Florence Nightingale

1820–1910

Florence Nightingale was born on May 12, 1820, in Florence, Italy, and grew up in Derbyshire, Hampshire, and London. Her family was comfortably off, and she received a classical education at home from her father. From her mother she received constant pressure to conform to society's expectations of a woman's proper role—a role Nightingale resisted from the beginning as impossibly circumscribed.

On February 17, 1837, just as she was about to make her social debut in London, Nightingale heard the voice of God tell her to devote her life to service. Precisely what service He meant wasn't immediately clear, and it would take her nine years to find out. In the meantime, an eighteen-month trip to the Continent served to broaden her horizons beyond the claustrophobic circle of family life. While in Paris she attended the salon of Mary Clarke and was impressed to see women treated as men's equals and friends rather than as wives or lovers. Returning to England and the stifling bosom of her family, Nightingale fell ill. She was nursed back to health by Mai Smith, her father's sister, and the two became passionate friends. Nightingale's biographer, Cecil Woodham-Smith, characterizes their relationship thus: "In spite of the difference in age [Mai] worshipped Florence with the worship of a disciple of a master. She placed Florence above ordinary humanity, above the claims even of her husband and children, and became her protector, interpreter and consoler." According to Nightingale, the two were "like two lovers."

Nightingale's other great love during the 1840s was a cousin named Marianne Nicholson, of whom she later wrote, "I have never loved but one person with passion in my life, and that was her." Marianne, on the other hand, seemed to care only about her brother Henry, who in turn fell in love with Nightingale. Woodham-Smith writes of this period in her life: "[Florence] was deeply, furiously, discontented, with life and with herself. Her infatuation with Marianne was a perpetual torture. She had let Henry fall more in love with her than ever....Her life at home was hateful; impossible that God should have bestowed the gift of time on His female creatures to be used...'faddling twaddling and the endless tweedling of nosegays.'"

After six years of acquaintance, Henry finally proposed, and though Nightingale considered marrying him in order to be close to Marianne, in the end she refused. Furious at what she saw as Nightingale's betrayal of her brother after so many years of courtship, Marianne abruptly ended her friendship with Nightingale. It was a devastating blow, and in its aftermath Nightingale seriously considered giving up the world in order to become a nun.

Desperate to do something useful with her life in a time when careers for women were simply unheard of, in 1846 Nightingale proposed to her family that she be allowed to study nursing at Salisbury Hospital. As she wrote to her friend Hilary Bonham Carter, "I thought something like a Protestant Sisterhood, without vows, for women of educated feelings, might be established. But there have been difficulties about my very first step, which terrified Mama. I do not mean the physically revolting parts of a hosiptial, but things about surgeons and nurses which you may guess." As biographer Dell Richards has observed: "Nursing wasn't a respectable occupation in those days. It was the last resort of drunken women who couldn't keep a job and part-time prostitutes. There was no training, no schools. Women simply sat with the ill or dying, if they weren't actually in bed with them or passed out drunk on the floor." They could scarcely be trusted to carry out the simplest medical duties. Nightingale was adamant, however, and began studying in secret. Within three years, she had become an expert on public health and hospitals. In 1850 she succeeded in entering the Institution of Protestant Deaconesses at Kaiserswerth, Germany, where she took a full course of training as a nurse. In 1853 she was appointed superintendent of the Institution for the Care of Sick Gentlewomen in Distressed Circumstances in London, where her innovations quickly brought her to public attention.

When the Crimean War broke out in 1854, she was appointed by Sydney Herbert, the secretary of war and an acquaintance of hers, to take charge of nursing in the British military hospital at Scutari, on the outskirts of Constantinople. The conditions she found there were appalling—overcrowded, unsanitary, and short of the most basic necessities. With indefatigable energy, she organized a massive overhaul of the hospital. She worked twenty-hour days and insisted on making the rounds of the wounded each night. Grateful soldiers returning home spread the legend of the Lady of the Lamp, as she came to be known. Under her vigorous administration, the death rate in the hospital at Scutari dropped from between 40 and 60 percent to 2.2 percent.

Though she returned to England a national hero, Florence Nightingale shunned publicity and honors. Instead she threw herself into a campaign, against much entrenched opposition, to improve the health, living conditions, and food of the British soldier. A much-sought-after audience in 1856 with Queen Victoria led to the establishment, the next year, of a Royal Commission on the Health of the Army, and the foundation of the Army Medical School.

That same year, Nightingale suffered a major breakdown that left her an invalid for the rest of her long life. Once again, Mai left her husband and family to be by Nightingale's bedside for the next three years. Dell Richards writes: "Most biographers accept [Nightingale's] invalidism at face value, but the fact that she never stopped working places serious doubt on the accepted explanation. Whether she was really ill, whether she had psychosomatic illnesses brought on from overwork, or whether it was a cleverly calculated move, taking to her 'bed' gave her the only control she would ever have over her life. It freed her from her family—and it freed her from the social round her mother and sister were pushing her into.... Taking to her bed even freed her from having to waste time travelling to see people. Suddenly, people were forced to come to her. And she was such an important force by then, they did so gladly."

Using Sydney Herbert, who was by then secretary of state, as her "front" (she preferred working behind the scenes in order to avoid the residual hostility still felt by some for this powerful woman), Nightingale was able to push through any number of reforms, from hospital hygiene to sewage treatment to regularized medical practices. In 1860, she organized the Nightingale School for Nurses in London, the first school of its kind in the world. In her later years she became a major expert on the health and sanitation situation in India, though she had never been there herself. In 1907 she became the first woman ever awarded the Order of Merit by the British government. Florence Nightingale died on August 13, 1910, in London. Characteristically, she refused the offer of a national funeral and burial in Westminster Abbey.

Florence Nightingale's many paradoxes have been summed up by Nancy Boyd: "Rebelling against her parents, she remained in their household for seventeen years. Devoting herself to the saving of military lives, she never questioned the policies that sent them into battle. A woman for whom faith was the overriding concern, she confessed that she didn't believe her own convictions. The weight of her accomplishments and the speed with which she brought them to fruition attest to her energy; yet she remained for forty years a prisoner of her invalid's sofa. Proclaiming the rule of reason, she was destroyed by her emotions. Creating 'a new life for women,' she rejected many contemporary feminist causes."

This brief entry can hardly begin to do justice to Florence Nightingale's many facets. As the founder of nursing as a trained profession for women, she played a vital role in the opening up of legitimate careers for women outside the home and, in this way, helped create the social and economic conditions that made the modern lesbian (and heterosexual working woman) possible. As a woman who shared her emotional life primarily with other women, who adamantly rejected any offer of marriage that came her way, and who, by whatever means available to her—even to the extent of making herself an invalid—worked to carve out a place for herself and her work, Florence Nightingale earns her ranking on this list.

55

Willa Cather

1873–1947

Willa Cather was born on December 7, 1873, in Black Creek Valley near Winchester, Virginia. When she was nine, her father moved the family to a ranch near Red Cloud, Nebraska. After an unsuccessful year of homesteading, they settled in the town itself. A tomboy who was at home in the saddle, Cather grew up with the children of immigrant farmers—Swedes, Bohemians, Russians, Germans. She was educated at home and at schools in Red Cloud and Lincoln. At the University of Nebraska in Lincoln—where she first arrived dressed as William Cather, her opposite-sex twin—she supported herself by writing drama criticism for the *Nebraska State Journal*. While at university, she fell tempestuously in love with Louise Pound, a brilliant fellow student and athlete who would later become the first woman ever elected to the Nebraska Sports Hall of Fame. Some of Cather's passionate letters to Pound survive.

After graduating in 1895, Cather moved back east to Pittsburgh and did editorial work at *The Home Monthly*. In 1901 she quit that job to teach Latin and Greek in a Pittsburgh high school. It was while she was living in Pittsburgh that she met Isabelle McClung, the beautiful sixteen-year-old daughter of a judge who became the love of Cather's life. Though the two became close friends, McClung seems to have been unable to return Cather's passion. Her marriage, in 1916, to a violinist plunged Cather into despair.

Willa Cather published her first book in 1905: *The Troll Garden*, a collection of stories including the celebrated "Paul's Case." The publisher S. S. McClure was so impressed with *The Troll Garden* that he offered Cather an editorial position on *McClure's Magazine*. From 1906 to 1912, as the magazine's managing editor, she succeeded in building up its declining circulation—though she later admitted that its "muckraking" editorial policies were not to her taste.

On a trip to Boston she met the writer Sarah Orne Jewett (herself a lesbian), who advised her to give up journalism for the sake of her writing. It was good advice, which Cather took. She resigned from the financial security of *McClure's* in order to live by her wits and talent. For a while she traveled, both in America, where she returned to Red Cloud for two months to renew her impressions of the place, and in Europe, where she contemplated settling permanently in France. But homesickness drew her back to America, and she settled in New York instead, in an apartment in Greenwich Village that she shared with her companion of the next forty years, Edith Lewis.

Cather's major novels include *O Pioneers!* (1913), *My Ántonia* (1918), the Pulitzer Prize–winning *One of Ours* (1922), *The Professor's House* (1925), and *Death Comes for the Archbishop* (1927). In her last years, she wrote little. She died in New York City on April 24, 1947. In the interests of privacy, she asked that her letters to Isabelle McClung be destroyed.

A reserved and private person, Cather never wrote openly about homosexuality. A number of her works are, nevertheless, classic examples of encoded texts—that is, texts that can be read as heterosexual by the unsuspecting, but that reveal themselves, on inspection by those in the know, to be rich in gay or lesbian subtext. A good illustration of this is "Paul's Case," a story often taught in American high schools as the tale of a sensitive, artistic young man who flees the constrictions of provincial life in order to experience in New York City all his pent-up aesthetic longings for art, beauty, and the artificial world of the theater. But closer inspection reveals Paul to be steeped in the coded signs of the homosexual, from his red carnation to his theatricality to his apparent fling with a wild boy from San Francisco. Similarly, *My Ántonia*'s pallid male narrator, Jim Burden, serves as a disguise to allow Cather the author to freely indulge her fascination with the immigrant girl Ántonia. Cather herself would define as one of the principal qualities of her fiction "the inexplicable presence of the thing not named."

Willa Cather was an important novelist who happened to be a lesbian, and who found herself in circumstances where she felt it was not possible to be open about herself. Her works embody this tension between the need to survive in a homophobic world and the longing to express the inner truths that world forbids. Cather was not alone: other important nineteenth- and early twentieth-century writers such as Herman Melville, Sarah Orne Jewett, and Henry James found themselves in similar predicaments. To what extent this tension limited them and to what extent it drove them to greater creative heights can be endlessly argued. What we *can* say is that writers like Cather were important because their work allowed the presence of a disguised or oblique homosexuality where nothing overt would ever have been tolerated. Their encoded texts are part of that secret history by which gay people have known one another through times of silence and censorship. We may be impatient with such covert tactics today, but we forget at our peril the terrible times in which gay people have often had to live and should remember how important a part their struggle, with all its evasions and subterranean allusions—"the inexplicable presence of the thing not named"—has played in our collective cultural history and survival.

Melville, Jewett, James: all three writers elicit honorable mentions. My choice of Cather over the three of them for inclusion in this ranking reflects my sense that Cather's lesbian sensibility has—to date—been more extensively explored than is the case for these other writers, and that she is thus more widely influential as a gay/lesbian presence within the literary canon.

56

Barney Frank

1940–

Barney Frank was born on March 31, 1940, in Bayonne, New Jersey. After graduating from Bayonne High School in 1957 he attended Harvard University, from which he received his BA in 1962. He stayed on at Harvard to pursue graduate work in political science and was a teaching fellow there from 1962 to 1972. His interest in politics led him to serve, from 1968 to 1971, as the executive assistant to Boston mayor Kevin White, and as administrative assistant to U.S. congressman Michael Harrington during 1971–72. In 1972 he was elected to the Massachusetts House of Representatives, where he served until 1980. Frank received his JD from Harvard in 1977 and was admitted to the Massachusetts bar in 1979. During most of that busy time, he would later recall, he so immersed himself in his work that any possibility of a private life was effectively foreclosed.

In 1980 he successfully ran for the U.S. House of Representatives as a Democrat and began serving in January 1981 as
representative to the 97th Congress from Massachusetts's Fourth
Congressional District. A popular congressman known for his
sharp wit and debating skills, he quickly became one of the
leading voices of liberalism in the House and was reelected easily
in 1982, 1984, and 1986.

In May 1987, a reporter from the *Boston Globe* posed the
question for which Barney Frank had privately been preparing
himself for years. His answer: "If you ask the direct question:
'Are you gay?' the answer is yes. So what? I've said all along that if
I was asked by a reporter and I didn't respond, it would look like
I had something to hide and I don't think I have anything to
hide.... I don't think my sex life is relevant to my job, but on the
other hand I don't want to leave the impression that I'm embarrassed about my life."

The admission made Frank only the second openly gay
member of the House of Representatives in its history, and the
first to come out willingly. Four years before, in 1983, Gerry
Studds (b. 1937), another Democratic congressman from Massachusetts, had admitted his homosexuality after he was accused
of having had an affair with a seventeen-year-old House page ten
years earlier. In order to protect the young man's identity, Studds
waived his right to a public hearing. The House voted to censure
Studds for his conduct. (Another congressman, Republican
Daniel Crane of Illinois, was censured in the same session for his
relationship with a female page.)

According to Barney Frank, his own coming out in 1987 was
motivated by the increasingly public scrutiny brought to bear on
the private lives of politicians: that spring, the presidential
candidacy of Gary Hart had fallen apart due to revelations about
an extramarital affair, and a respected but closeted Republican
colleague in the House, Rep. Stewart McKinney of Connecticut,
had died of AIDS. As Frank observed in a *New York Times*
interview with Linda Greenhouse, "there was such an unseemly
scuffle after [McKinney] died. I'm not criticizing the press; the
problem was the way it was handled. I have no reason to expect
anyone to be reading my obituary anytime soon, but I do fly
home on weekends, and we can all be hit by a truck, and I don't
want the focus to be: Was he or wasn't he, did he or didn't he. I
just wanted to get rid of it."

Reaction to Frank's announcement was overwhelmingly positive, both from his colleagues in the Congress and from his constituents, who reelected him in 1988 with 70 percent of the vote.

Trouble was brewing, however. In August 1989, the right-wing *Washington Times* ran an article charging that Frank had hired a male prostitute named Steven Gobie to run errands for him, and that Gobie had operated a prostitution ring out of Frank's Washington, D.C., apartment. Frank admitted that he had, in fact, responded to an escort-service advertisement in a local paper and paid $85 to have sex with the young man one time in 1985. Thinking he could help rehabilitate Gobie, who had a police record for numerous offenses, Frank hired him out of his own pocket and wrote letters on House stationery to Gobie's probation officer in Virginia indicating that Gobie was employed—one of the conditions for his parole. When he came to suspect that Gobie had not changed his ways, he dismissed him in August 1987. Gobie, it turned out, had for some time been trying to peddle his story for money.

In order to spare his fellow Democrats a tough decision, Frank himself called for a House Ethics Panel investigation of his actions. In July 1990, nearly a year after the story first broke, the Ethics Panel, having dismissed all but two minor charges against Frank, urged a formal reprimand of the representative. The full House voted 390–38 against expulsion (moved by homophobe William Dannemayer of California), 287–141 against censure (moved by Republican whip Newt Gingrich, this would have meant loss of committee chairmanship), and finally 408–18 in favor of reprimanding him.

Many forecasters saw Frank's reprimand as the end of his political career, but voters returned him to office in both 1990 (with 66 percent of the vote) and 1992 (with 68 percent). Today he remains a force in the House, where he continues to campaign for a variety of liberal causes. His legislative accomplishments include getting the House to pass a bill redressing Japanese Americans interned during World War II, expanding immigration limits, fighting against the provision barring HIV-positive people from entering the country, and successfully lobbying for amendments to the fair housing bill for those with AIDS and HIV. He is a perennial sponsor of gay civil rights legislation. Though he alienated some of his gay supporters in 1993 with

what was seen as a premature willingness to compromise on the
issue of gays in the military, his is nevertheless an important voice
for gays and lesbians not only in his own district but throughout
the country.

Honorable mention here should go to Roberta Achtenberg,
the assistant secretary for fair housing and equal opportunity at
the U.S. Department of Housing and Urban Development, who
is the highest-ranking openly gay person ever to serve in a
presidential administration, and to Gerry Studds, whose absence
from this ranking is not meant to slight his considerable accomplishments on the Hill in working for gay and lesbian causes, but
merely reflects my sense that, of these three prominent political
figures, Barney Frank is the more well-known and influential on
a national level.

57

Bayard Rustin

1910–1987

Bayard Rustin was born on March 17, 1910, in Chester, Pennsylvania. He was raised by his grandfather, a caterer, and his grandmother, a Quaker who founded the black day nursery in Chester and was head of the local NAACP chapter. After graduating from high school, he worked a series of odd jobs, traveled, and studied for five years at Cheyney State Teacher's College in Pennsylvania, Wilberforce University in Ohio, and City College in New York City without ever getting a degree. In 1936 he joined the Young Communist League—"they seemed the only people who had civil rights at heart," he recalled later—but resigned in 1941 to work for an antiwar group, The Fellowship for Reconciliation. That same year he began working for the Congress of Racial Equality (CORE) as a field secretary, helping A. Philip Randolph organize a civil rights protest march on Washington, D.C., the prospect of which pressured President Franklin Delano Roosevelt into ending racial discrimination in the war industries. More radical than Randolph, Rustin criticized the union leader openly during the 1940s, but later became one of his most loyal followers.

A Quaker and pacifist, Rustin spent two and a half years in prison as a conscientious objector during World War II. After the war, in 1947, he organized the first freedom rides in North Carolina to protest segregation on buses, for which he was arrested and spent several weeks on a prison chain gang. In all, Bayard Rustin would be arrested or jailed over twenty times during his lifetime for his civil rights and pacifist activities. A different kind of arrest took place in 1953: while in Pasadena, California, organizing demonstrations against discrimination in restaurants and hotels, he was entrapped, arrested on a "sex perversion" charge, and sentenced to sixty days. In an interview with the *Village Voice* shortly before his death, Rustin reflected on the effect his homosexuality had on his work in the civil rights movement: "There is no question in my mind that there was considerable prejudice amongst a number of people I worked with. But of course they would never admit they were prejudiced. They would say they were afraid it would hurt the movement."

From 1953 to 1955, Rustin was the executive director of the War Resisters League, and from 1955 to 1960 he worked as a special aide to Martin Luther King, Jr., helping King to organize the Montgomery bus boycott, drafting the original plan for the Southern Christian Leadership Conference (SCLC), and master-minding civil rights demonstrations in 1960 at both the Republican and Democratic national conventions. Perhaps his greatest accomplishment was planning the 1963 March on Washington for Jobs and Freedom which brought over two hundred thousand people to the nation's capital to demonstrate for civil rights. Once again, his homosexuality became an issue. As he recounted it in the *Village Voice* interview:

> Mr. Randolph had asked me to organize the march. I proceeded to line up people; it was always a matter of boxing in the civil rights leadership, because each had his own turf. In any event, it was Mr. [Roy] Wilkins [executive director of the NAACP], whom I admire greatly, who raised the question this time. He called me

to his office and said, "I don't think you should lead this march—because they will try to stop it, and the most important thing they have to stop it with is that the director of it is gay." I said, "Roy, I just disagree with that, and I think that the time has come when we have to stand up and stop running from things. And I don't believe that if this is raised by the Southern Democrats, that it will do anything but spur people on. We can issue a statement which says they will use anything to try to stop us in our march to freedom, but no matter what they use we will win." He disagreed and called a meeting of all the civil rights leaders. Finally, a compromise was reached. Mr. Randolph would be the director of the march, but he made me his deputy.

Then, Strom Thurmond [a senator from South Carolina] stood in the Senate speaking for three-quarters of a hour on the fact that Bayard Rustin was a homosexual, a draft dodger, and a communist. Newspapers all over the country came out with this front-page story. Mr. Randolph waited for the phone to ring. And it did indeed ring. I went immediately to Mr. Randolph, and we agreed he would make a statement for all the civil rights leaders, which basically said, "We have absolute confidence in Bayard Rustin's integrity and ability." He read this statement to the labor leaders and the Jewish and Catholic and Protestant leaders involved in the march and they all agreed to it.

The march went ahead as planned and became, in the words of author Columbus Salley, "the crossing of the Rubicon in the African-American quest for equality."

From 1964 until his death, Rustin was the head of the A. Philip Randolph Institute, a New York–based educational, civil rights, and labor organization. He advocated coalition-building among black, gay, Jewish, liberal/leftist, and labor-union constituencies and enunciated the following principles: "(1) nonviolent tactics; (2) constitutional means; (3) democratic procedures; (4) respect for human personality; (5) a belief that all people are one."

In his interview with the *Village Voice* he said, "I think that the gay community has a moral obligation...to do whatever is possible to encourage more and more gays to come out of the closet. God knows, people stay in the closet because it's very painful to come out. But we cannot play the political role we could play, because we don't have the numbers."

His companion, assistant at the Randolph Institute, and adopted son for the last decade of his life was Walter Naegle. Bayard Rustin died of a heart attack on August 24, 1987, in New York City.

Bayard Rustin merits his ranking on this list because of his paramount role in the black civil rights movement—a role that has been obscured because of his homosexuality. His situation was analagous in many ways to that of JAMES BALDWIN [36]—both suffered the pain of being reviled for their homosexuality by many in the same African-American community whose cause they worked so tirelessly to advance. It is useful to remember that in the 1960s many gays and lesbians worked in the black civil rights movement because they could not openly work for their own civil rights. In the process of the struggle for one people's rights, they acquired the valuable tools that would later enable them to strive for their own. In this sense Bayard Rustin—and the movement he helped build—served to enable the development, beginning with STONEWALL [5] in 1969, of the gay civil rights movement.

58

E. M. Forster

1879–1970

Edward Morgan Forster was born on January 1, 1879, in London. His father, an architect, died when Forster was an infant, and Forster was raised by his mother and aunts. His years at Tonbridge School, Kent, were unhappy and laid the basis of his later criticisms of the English public-school system. In 1897 he entered King's College, Cambridge, with whose tolerant intellectual climate and homoerotic emotional atmosphere he fell in love. He also fell in love with fellow classmate H. O. Meredith, whom he would later portray as Clive in his novel *Maurice*. In 1901 he was elected to The Apostles, Cambridge's most exclusive intellectual club, where, under the influence of the philosopher G. E. Moore, the Apostles' chief luminary, Forster began to form his notions concerning the value of the individual and the primacy of personal relationships.

After graduating, Forster traveled (with his mother) to Italy, and later to Greece, where he fell in love with the "pagan" culture of the Mediterranean. Returning to England, he lived with his mother and composed his first three novels, *Where Angels Fear to Tread* (1905), *The Longest Journey* (1907), and *A Room with a View* (1908), all of which received excellent press on publication and established Forster as one of England's most promising young novelists. The publication of *Howards End* in 1910 marked Forster's arrival in the foremost ranks of English literature. Success was difficult for him, though, and he found himself artistically paralyzed. In large part this paralysis stemmed from what he called "weariness of the only subject I both can and may treat— the love of men for women & vice versa." Progress on his next novel, *Arctic Dreams*, foundered, and he began, in secret, to write erotic stories, "not to express myself but to excite myself." These stories were posthumously published in the collection *The Life to Come*.

A trip to India in 1912–13 did little to stir him from his artistic slumber. But in 1913–14 he paid a visit to the home of homosexual rights advocate EDWARD CARPENTER [9] and his working-class lover George Merrill. At one point in the visit, Merrill affectionately patted Forster's buttocks, and the result was prodigious. The repressed Forster wrote, "The sensation was unusual, and I still remember it, as I remember the position of a long vanished tooth. It was as much psychological as physical. It seemed to go straight through the small of my back into my ideas, without involving my thoughts. If it really did this, it would have acted in strict accordance with Carpenter's yogified mysticism, and would prove that at that precise moment I had conceived."

What resulted from this moment of conception was the gay novel *Maurice*, which Forster wrote in a bout of creative euphoria. Its ending—the upper-middle-class Maurice disappearing into the greenwood with his working-class lover Alex Scutter—paid tribute to the relationship between Carpenter and Merrill. The realization that he couldn't publish *Maurice*— certainly not as long as his mother was alive, and probably never—served to deepen his creative depression. He dedicated the novel "To a

Happier Time," and it remained unpublished during his lifetime.

When World War I broke out, Forster was determined to *do* something with a life that seemed increasingly dead-ended, and so spent three years serving with the International Red Cross in Alexandria, Egypt. In 1917 he met and fell in love with a handsome tram conductor named Mohammed el Adl. Their affair, which lasted until Mohammed's marriage in 1919, was the first satisfying sexual relationship of Forster's life, and perhaps its emotional high point as well. Forster never really recovered from his grief at Mohammed's death from tuberculosis in 1922.

In 1921, Forster made a second journey to India and served for a year as the private secretary to the maharajah of Dewas. The two became fast friends, and when the maharajah learned of Forster's sexual orientation, he charmingly provided a resident catamite for his guest's pleasure. Forster's Indian experiences culminated in his first novel in a decade—*A Passage to India* (1924)—which was immediately acclaimed as his masterpiece. Privately, he knew he would never write another novel.

His attention turned increasingly to political and social issues, especially to questions of censorship and civil liberties. In 1928 he was a leading voice of protest against the suppression of the controversial lesbian novel *The Well of Loneliness* by RADCLYFFE HALL [28]. During the 1930s, Forster spoke out against the rise of fascism and became the first president of the National Council for Civil Liberties. His 1938 essay "What I Believe" was a stirring account of his belief in the paramount value of human relationships in the face of institutions of all kinds and contains the famous formulation "if I had to choose between betraying my country and betraying my friend, I hope I should have the guts to betray my country."

During World War II Forster gained great respect for his radio speeches on the BBC, in which he steadfastly enunciated the humanist principles that lay behind the struggle against fascism and totalitarianism; at the same time he articulated his fears that, in order to defeat totalitarianism, England would have to become totalitarian itself. His essays on this subject were collected in *Two Cheers for Democracy* (1951).

In 1946, after the death of his mother and the loss of his longtime home in Abinger, Surrey, an honorary fellowship from King's College allowed him to live in rooms at the college. In his later years he continued to produce nonfiction, as well as the libretto for the 1951 opera *Billy Budd* by BENJAMIN BRITTEN [73].

Beginning in the 1930s, Forster's circle of friends widened to include working-class men as well as the Cambridge set he was used to. Particularly nourishing for Forster was his forty-year relationship with Bob Buckingham, a married policeman whose wife grew to accept Forster's presence in the family. Forster died on June 7, 1970, at Buckingham's home in Coventry, Warwickshire. *Maurice* was finally published in 1971.

Forster's influence has been twofold: he was one of the important novelists of the first half of the twentieth century, and *Maurice* (which was made into a film by the production team of Ismail Merchant and James Ivory in 1987) is a landmark of gay literature; second and perhaps even more important, Forster became an eloquent spokesperson for the values of a skeptical and secular humanism. For people like CHRISTOPHER ISHERWOOD [60], the E. M. Forster of the 1930s was a potent symbol of those values, which found themselves everywhere under siege. Attacking the media's adulation of Prime Minister Neville Chamberlain during the Munich crisis of 1938, Isherwood wrote: "Well—*my* England is E. M.; the anti-heroic hero, with his scraggly straw moustache, his light gay blue baby-eyes and his elderly stoop.... While the others tell their followers to be ready to die, he advises us to live as if we were immortal. And he really does this himself, although he is as anxious and afraid as any of us, and never for an instant pretends not to be. He and his books and what they stand for are all that is truly worth saving from Hitler..."

E. M. Forster was one the most humane public figures of the twentieth century. His continuing influence on the gay imagination stems from the tolerant, beneficent, humanistic spirit that suffuses both the words he wrote and the life he lived.

59

Martha Carey Thomas

1857–1935

Martha Carey Thomas was born of wealthy parents on January 2, 1857, in Baltimore, Maryland. Even as a child, she had a clear vision of herself that was at odds with the self society expected from her: "I ain't going to get married and I don't want to teach school. I can't imagine anything worse than living a regular young lady's life," she is reported to have said.

After attending a Quaker boarding school for girls, she went on to college—over her father's objections. It was fine, he argued, for middle-class girls to go to college but improper for wealthy ones. Thomas earned her BA from Cornell in 1877. Her attempt to do graduate work at Johns Hopkins, however, was rebuffed when she was barred access to the classrooms. Undeterred, she and her "devoted companion" Mamie Gwinn went to Europe, and in 1882 Thomas was awarded a PhD from the University of Zurich.

Returning with Gwinn to the United States, Thomas became the dean of English at the newly founded women's college of Bryn Mawr. In the meantime, a wealthy philanthropist named Mary Garrett had fallen in love with Thomas. She promised to give millions to the college if Thomas became its president, and so in 1894, at the age of thirty-seven, Thomas was appointed Bryn Mawr's second president. She remained in that post for the next twenty-eight years.

How Thomas managed to balance the competing attentions of Gwinn and Garrett is evidenced by an account left us by the British philosopher Bertrand Russell, who visited Thomas in 1896: "[Thomas] had immense energy, a belief in culture which she carried out with a businessman's efficiency, and a profound contempt for the male sex....At Bryn Mawr she was Zeus, and everybody trembled before her. She lived with a friend, Miss Gwinn, who was in most respects the opposite of her....At the time we stayed with them, their friendship had become a little ragged. Miss Gwinn used to go home to her family for three days in every fortnight, and at the exact moment of her departure each fortnight, another lady, named Miss Garrett, used to arrive, to depart again at the exact moment of Miss Gwinn's return."

When Mamie Gwinn ran off with a male philosophy professor in 1904, Mary Garrett moved in and lived with Thomas until Garrett's death in 1915.

Thomas's long tenure as president of Bryn Mawr was not without its storms. Autocratic and conservative, she took an active role in shaping the curriculum at the college and faced frequent faculty revolts over the years. But she held firm to her conviction that a women's college must have the same demanding standards as its male counterparts: "girls," she wrote, "can learn, can reason, can compete with men in the grand fields of literature, science and conjecture." In contrasting Thomas with JANE ADDAMS [26], historian Lillian Faderman writes, "Thomas' philosophical thrust was not in demonstrating that women could redeem the world because they were different from and better than men, but rather in showing how they were like men, as good as men, and hence deserving of equal treatment."

Thomas was keenly interested in women's education in all forms. With the help of Garrett's millions, she endowed Johns Hopkins Medical School, stipulating that women be admitted there as well as men. In 1921 she instituted the Summer School for Women in Industry, a pioneering program in the liberal arts aimed at urban working women. A friend of SUSAN B. ANTHONY's [12], she was also extremely influential in the suffragist movement, serving in 1908 as the first president of the National College Women's Equal Suffrage League. Especially after 1920, she advocated the policies of the National Woman's Party. She was also an early and articulate supporter of the need for an equal rights amendment to the U.S. Constitution.

Thomas died on December 2, 1935, in Philadelphia.

M. Carey Thomas was a key figure both in the history of American education and in the creation of modern lesbian identity. By helping to build the institution of the women's college, she enabled tens of thousands of middle-class women to acquire the skills necessary for careers. Careers entailed the ability to lead independent lives, which in turn made possible the personal choices that helped create modern lesbian existence. Furthermore, women's colleges often provided safe havens where lesbians could flourish—much to the consternation of outside commentators, who often decried these environments as hotbeds of deviancy. The experience of an all-female college environment, with its systems of intellectual and emotional support, was often a powerful, life-changing influence on those women lucky enough to attend. If there was a lesbian nation in America in the years before World War II that created the conditions that led to the development of the contemporary lesbian community, it was most likely to be found on the campuses of Bryn Mawr, Mount Holyoke, Smith, and Vassar.

60

Christopher Isherwood
1904–1986

Christopher Isherwood was born on August 26, 1904, at High Lane, Cheshire, England. His father was an army officer who was also a talented musician, amateur actor, and watercolor painter. During Isherwood's early life, his family lived in several locations around Britain due to his father's military transfers.

Isherwood was educated at St. Edmund's School, Hindhead, where he met and became lifelong friends with a fellow student named W. H. Auden. In 1924, Isherwood entered Corpus Christi College, Cambridge, with a history scholarship, but left the next year without a degree. For the next few years he worked as a private tutor, studied medicine for two semesters, and then in 1929 traveled to Berlin to visit Auden, who had been sent there by his parents to learn German. Thrilled by Berlin's thriving underworld of gay bars and boy prostitutes, Isherwood stayed on, teaching English and gathering the material that would eventually comprise *Mr. Norris Changes Trains* (1935) and *Goodbye to Berlin* (1939). These "Berlin stories," featuring the inimitable Sally Bowles, were the basis for John van Druten's successful 1951 play, *I Am a Camera,* the 1955 film of the same name, the 1966 hit Broadway show *Cabaret,* and the 1972 film of *Cabaret* starring Liza Minnelli.

In 1932, Isherwood fell in love with a working-class boy named Heinz. One of the first writers to fully perceive the implications of the rise of fascism, Isherwood prudently left Germany when Hitler came to power in 1933. For the next four years he and Heinz traveled extensively in the Europe that would soon fall prey to the Nazis. Eventually Heinz returned to Germany, where he was arrested and imprisoned for homosexual activities and later served in the German army. In the meantime, Isherwood and Auden—who since 1925 had been nonromantic sex partners—collaborated on three plays, the most famous of which is *The Ascent of F-6* (1936), and in 1938 traveled to China. That journey resulted in another collaboration, *Journey to a War* (1939).

Nineteen thirty-nine was an important year for both the world and Isherwood: Hitler invaded Poland, and Isherwood moved to the United States, became a pacifist, and first encountered Vedanta, a Hindu philosophy that emphasizes self-abnegation and the illusory nature of the "real" world. Although skeptical of religions in general, Isherwood began to see the need for a spiritual dimension to the material world. His ongoing engagement with Vedanta had a profound impact on all his writing, and for a time he even considered becoming a monk of the Ramakrishna order.

During 1941–42 he worked for the American Friends Service Committee at a hostel for Central European war refugees outside of Philadelphia. Then he moved to California and for the rest of the war was a resident student of the Vedanta Society of Southern California. He supported himself by writing film scripts and editing, with Swami Prabhavananda, two Vedanta publications: *Vedanta and the West* and *Vedanta for Modern Man.* He also continued to write novels, including *The World at Evening* (1954) and his quiet masterpiece *A Single Man* (1964), the best account of a day in the life of a gay man ever written.

In 1953, Isherwood met and fell in love with Don Bachardy, an eighteen-year-old painter and portraitist. Although Isherwood's friends were scandalized by the age difference between the two lovers, the relationship proved extremely stable and long-lasting: Isherwood and Bachardy lived together for the next thirty-three years, until Isherwood's death, at the age of eighty-two, on January 4, 1986, in Santa Monica, California. Bachardy became known and respected as an artist in his own right. Some of his loveliest drawings are of Isherwood.

In 1971, Isherwood published *Kathleen and Frank*, a biography of his parents in which he casually revealed his homosexuality. It had always been implied in his work, but never before stated forthrightly. In television appearances to promote the book, he freely discussed the centrality of his homosexuality to his life and work, and after that became increasingly active in the gay liberation movement, appearing at rallies and fund-raisers. In 1976 he wrote *Christopher and His Kind*, an unstinting look at his homosexuality that has become a classic. By the end of his long life he was, as his biographer Claude J. Summers writes, "a deeply revered icon of contemporary Anglo-American gay culture, a courage-teacher who vigorously protested the heterosexual dictatorship and who unashamedly expressed solidarity with his 'kind.'"

I have included Christopher Isherwood rather than W. H. Auden in this ranking because it is my sense that, while Auden may have been somewhat more significant than Isherwood as a literary figure, his influence on the gay community was less. Isherwood was able to make the transition from being a bad-boy gay artist of the 1930s to taking a forthright stance as a spokesperson for the newly emerging gay movement in the 1970s. Auden remained aloof from the changes that were taking place about him—by the end of his life he had become a jaundiced, alcoholic parody of his former bright self, whereas Isherwood continued to evolve both as an artist and as a gay man. Isherwood is ranked below E. M. FORSTER [58] in acknowledgment of his self-professed debt to Forster (though Forster learned a few things from Isherwood's boldness as well), but is ranked above those more problematic gay artist-figures PIER PAOLO PASOLINI [61] and YUKIO MISHIMA [62].

61

Pier Paolo Pasolini

1922–1975

Pier Paolo Pasolini was born in Bologna, Italy, on March 5, 1922. His father was an officer in the Italian army, and Pasolini was educated in a succession of cities in northern Italy to which his father was posted. He attended the University of Bologna, where he studied art history and literature.

During World War II his family took refuge in the poor northeastern Italian province of Friuli, near the town of Casarsa where Pasolini had spent childhood summers. In 1945, his beloved younger brother, Guido, who had joined the resistance, was killed by Yugoslav partisans during infighting among resistance groups. Pasolini took this death very hard, blaming himself for not keeping Guido at home.

Pasolini's first collection of poetry, published in 1942, was composed in the Friulian dialect of the local peasants, whose old way of life he admired. It was the first manifestation of his lifelong nostalgia for worlds far removed in space and time from the horrors of twentieth-century Italy. His experience of the oppression endured by the Friuli peasants led him to join the Communist Party in 1948, and he was named secretary of the Communist section of San Giovanni, a town close to Casarsa. He also became a respected schoolteacher. Warned by anticommunist clerics in the region that he would suffer if he did not stop his political activities, Pasolini was charged on October 22, 1949, with "corrupting the minors and obscene acts in public." A court acquitted him of the corruption charges but not the obscenity charges—though two years later he was acquitted of the obscenity charges as well. By that time his teaching career was destroyed, however, and he had been expelled from the Communist Party. As he wrote a friend at the time, "my future is not even black; it does not exist."

Calling himself "a Rimbaud without genius," he left Friuli in 1950 for Rome. There he lived with his mother in poverty throughout the fifties, getting himself on a list of film extras at Cinecittà, doing some proofreading here and there, and writing. He became close friends with the writers Alberto Moravia and Attilio Bertolucci (father of the young filmmaker-to-be, Bernardo Bertolucci, who looked up to Pasolini as a mentor). Pasolini also, in those years, began the pattern of random sexual encounters that would characterize his search for love. As he wrote: "A normal person might resign himself (terrible word) to chastity, to lost opportunities; but in me, the difficulty of loving has made the need for loving an obsession." Rome suited him in this regard. He wrote ecstatically: "Here I am in a life that is all muscles, turned inside out like a glove, which always unfolds like one of those songs that I used to hate...in human organisms so sensual as to be almost mechanical; here none of the Christian attitudes—forgiveness, humility, etc.—are known, and egotism takes legitimate, virile forms....Rome, ringed by its inferno of *borgate*, is stupendous right now."

It was in these *borgate*, the desolate outlying districts of the Eternal City, that Pasolini cruised for the young men he loved. His two novels from that decade—*The Ragazzi* (1955) and *A Violent Life* (1959)—are peopled with an underworld of thieves, hustlers, and prostitutes drawn from his experience of the streets. These works made him famous, but also created scandal and were charged with obscenity. In addition to novels, his literary output included several highly regarded volumes of poems, including *Gramsci's Ashes* (1957), *The Religion of My Time* (1961), and *Poem in the Form of a Rose* (1964).

Convinced that cinema was the medium of the future, Pasolini began to make movies in the 1960s. Bernardo Bertolucci said of watching him direct his first film, *Accattone* (1961): "I felt as if I were present at the invention of cinema." This film and his next, *Mamma Roma* (1962), inhabit the poor urban world of his novels. *The Gospel According to Saint Matthew* (1964) is an austere, Marxist retelling of the life of Jesus that is one of the indisputable masterpieces of the screen. It was followed by *Hawks and Sparrows* (1966), *Oedipus Rex* (1967), *Medea* (1969), and the highly acclaimed *Teorema* (1968), in which an erotic angel played by Terence Stamp makes his way through a bourgeois family with devastating effect.

Highly publicized prosecutions for obscenity and blasphemy dogged Pasolini's career—in all, a total of thirty-three legal accusations against him in the course of twenty years. Nine of his films faced major censorship problems, and he himself was often accused of personal—and invariably unproven—improprieties. He was acquitted each time.

In the early seventies he traveled to Iran, Yemen, and Nepal to film his ambitious *Trilogy of Life,* consisting of *The Decameron* (1971), *Canterbury Tales* (1972), and *Arabian Nights* (1973). In these gorgeous, bawdy films Pasolini attempted, in his words, to "oppose both this excess of politicalization and utilitarianism on the part of the leftists as well as the unreality of mass culture. To make films where you could find the existential sense of the body, of what is physical, the *élan vital* which is being lost." But after completing the trilogy, Pasolini bitterly repudiated the films, claiming that such sexuality does not exist. There is no escape from the prisons that enclose us except in escapism, and Pasolini's last film, *Salò: The 120 Days of Sodom* (1975), is a nightmarish, unrelenting vision of sadomasochistic sex, fascism, and power.

Pasolini was one of Italy's most prominent public figures in the 1960s and 1970s. In his regular column in a Milan newspaper, he often startled the public by challenging not only right-wing views, but modern liberal thought as well. In the student demon-

strations of May 1968, he sided with the police—sons of the poor
caught on the wrong side—rather than the privileged students.
He deplored Italy's 1974 law that legalized divorce as a victory for
"the hedonistic ideology of consumerism" and also wrote against
abortion. The sexual revolution, he lamented, had transformed
sex into "a convention, an obligation, a social duty, a social
anxiety, and an inevitable part of the consumer's quality of life."

On the morning of November 2, 1975, in a vacant lot in
Ostia, one of the *borgate* on the outskirts of Rome, a carpenter
discovered the body Pier Paolo Pasolini. He had been blud-
geoned to death and then run over by his own Alfa-Romeo. A
seventeen-year-old boy named Giuseppe Pelosi was charged with
murder after the police stopped him for speeding in Pasolini's
car. He claimed self-defense. "He wanted to have sexual relations
with me," Pelosi said, "and I did not want to." He was one of those
boys whose desperate lives Pasolini had chronicled in the novels
he had written and the films he had made twenty years before.

Pasolini's critique of modern bourgeois society—in his novels, his films, his essays—resonated far beyond his native Italy.
His death shocked the world and was a brutal reminder of the
punishing violence that lurks in the heart of that society Pasolini
so often scandalized. He is a difficult figure in many ways, and a
troubling one. His politics, his sensibility, his sexuality—none are
precisely containable in terms most of us would be content with.
Pasolini's refusal to fit the categories, combined with his vigorous, passionate questioning of them, makes both the example
of his life and the legacy of his work an ongoing challenge to the
comfortable certitudes of gay and straight alike. Like JEAN GENET
[45] and YUKIO MISHIMA [62], Pasolini was an outlaw in the most
valiant sense of the word.

62

Yukio Mishima

1925–1970

Hiraoka Kimitake was born on January 14, 1925, in Tokyo, Japan. The son of a high-level civil servant, he was educated at the prestigious Peers School in Tokyo. He began to write early and published his first short story under the pseudonym Yukio Mishima when he was sixteen. When World War II began, he tried to join the army but failed to qualify and instead spent the war working in a factory in Tokyo and writing. After Japan's defeat, he studied law at the University of Tokyo and during 1948–49 was employed in the banking division of the Ministry of Finance. The publication in 1949 of his second novel, *Confessions of a Mask,* brought the young Mishima immediate fame. The story of a boy who comes to recognize his homosexuality and the need to conceal it behind a mask, the novel was taken as a sensitive coming-of-age tale by Japanese audiences, who seemed to have missed its homosexual themes. Other novels followed, including *Forbidden Colors* (1953), *The Temple of the Golden Pavilion* (1959), *The Sailor Who Fell from Grace with the Sea* (1963), and *Sun and Steel* (1968). Mishima also wrote numerous plays, including the famous *Madame de Sade*, as well as works for the Kabuki theater and modern No drama.

In 1966, Mishima directed and starred in the film *Patriotism*, based on his short story of the same name. Both film and story focus—in loving and morbidly riveting detail—on a young Japanese military officer and his devoted wife as they prepare for and commit the ritual suicide known as seppuku. The effect is mesmerizing and deeply unsettling:

> With only his right hand on the sword the lieutenant began to cut sideways across his stomach. But as the blade became entangled with the entrails it was pushed constantly outward by their soft resilience; and the lieutenant realized that it would be necessary, as he cut, to use both hands to keep the point pressed deep into his stomach. He pulled the blade across. It did not cut as easily as he had expected. He directed the strength of his whole body into his right hand and pulled again. There was a cut of three or four inches.
>
> The pain spread slowly outward from the inner depths until the whole stomach reverberated. It was like the wild clanging of a bell. Or like a thousand bells which jangled simultaneously at every breath he breathed and every throb of his pulse, rocking his whole being. But by now the blade had cut its way through to below the navel, and when he noticed this he felt a sense of satisfaction, and a renewal of courage.
>
> The volume of blood had steadily increased, and now it spurted from the wound as if propelled by the beat of the pulse. The mat before the lieutenant was drenched red with splattered blood, and more blood overflowed onto it from pools which gathered in the folds of the lieutenant's khaki trousers. A spot, like a bird, came flying across to Reiko and settled on the lap of her white silk kimono.

Mishima was increasingly drawn to the militaristic samurai past of Japan as an antidote to what he saw as the materialism of the modern world. In *The Sea of Fertility* (1969–71), his greatest work, he used the image of the barren "seas" of the moon to capture the sterility of contemporary Japan. *The Sea of Fertility* consists of a quartet of novels: *Spring Snow, Runaway Horses, The Temple of Dawn,* and *The Decay of the Angel.* He was also attracted to and celebrated the venerable tradition of homosexual love between samurai warriors (sixteenth-century Jesuit missionaries had been particularly shocked by it). Taking up karate and kendo, a traditional Japanese form of swordsmanship, this formerly delicate youth who had failed to qualify for the army built up his own private army, the controversial Shield Society, which was meant to defend the emperor in the event of a leftist uprising or Communist attack that Mishima's paranoia feared was growing more likely in the late 1960s.

Although married, Mishima patronized gay bars in the Ginza district of Tokyo. He despised effeminate men and was what the Japanese call "a bearer of two swords," meaning he kept the company of both men and women, though he preferred men. His marriage preserved the necessary façade of propriety—a façade his widow maintained after his death by censoring all press reports concerning her husband's homosexuality.

On November 25, 1970, Mishima and four young followers from the Shield Society broke into the National Defense Headquarters in Tokyo. Armed with swords, they made their way to the building's roof, where Mishima made a ten-minute speech to some thousand servicemen gathered below. He attacked the Japanese constitution—with its prohibition on national rearmament— for having betrayed the spirit of Japan: "We see Japan reveling in prosperity," he exhorted his audience, "and wallowing in spiritual emptiness....Is it possible that you value life, given a world where the spirit is dead?" His audience was unimpressed. In the samurai tradition of suicide protest, Mishima then committed seppuku. In accordance with tradition, one of his disciples—Morita, who was said to be Mishima's lover—decapitated his master with his sword.

Yukio Mishima was the most important writer of postwar Japan. In his work, including the shocking act of his suicide, he crystallized Japan's national agony, the tensions between longing for traditional ways of life and the persistent demands of encroaching westernization. His presence in this ranking is in part an indication of how widely disseminated his work and symbolic death have been in the West as well as in the East.

Both the gay rightist Mishima and the gay leftist PIER PAOLO PASOLINI [61] fought against what they perceived to be the sterility of the modern bourgeois world. Both sought other ways of living that would be richer, more full of meaning: Mishima in the traditions of samurai Japan, Pasolini in his *Trilogy of Life*, with its nostalgic vision of peasant and third-world "free" sexuality. Both failed in ways that are instructive and sobering.

63

Rock Hudson

1925–1985

Rock Hudson was born Roy Scherer, Jr., on November 17, 1925, in Winnetka, Illinois. His father was an auto mechanic and his mother a telephone operator. During the Depression, his father lost his job and abandoned the family. His mother remarried, and her son adopted his stepfather's last name of Fitzgerald.

In 1944, Roy Fitzgerald joined the Navy and worked as an airplane mechanic in the Philippines. After the war, he drifted through a series of odd jobs—piano mover, vacuum-cleaner salesman, truck driver—but his ambition was to be an actor. In 1948, thanks to his persistent agent Henry Willson (who had

242   T H E   G A Y   1 0 0

supplied the fledgling actor with a stage name and persona), he
landed a small part in the movie *Fighter Squadron*. Hudson's big
break came in 1954, when he played opposite Jane Wyman in
Magnificent Obsession (1954). This was followed in 1955 by another
movie with Wyman, *All That Heaven Allows*.

At six foot four, with dark eyes and a deep voice, Rock
Hudson was the quintessential romantic hero, and it was in that
role that he flourished in the 1950s: melodramas like *Giant* (1956),
which earned him an Academy Award nomination, *Written on the
Wind* (1956), and *Tarnished Angels* (1957).

His career took a surprising turn, however, with the 1959
Pillow Talk, costarring Doris Day. Critics praised Hudson's comic
sense and timing, and other comedies followed: *Lover Come Back*
(1961), *Man's Favorite Sport?* (1963), and *Send Me No Flowers* (1964).
In all, Hudson made sixty-two motion pictures. He also starred in
the television series "McMillan and Wife" in the 1970s and was a
recurring character on the series "Dynasty" in the 1980s.

What was carefully kept from the public during all this time
was Rock Hudson's homosexuality. When rumors began to spread
in the midfifties, Hudson's protective agent married him off to
Phyllis Gates, his secretary. Predictably, the marriage was on the
rocks within three years, and Hudson continued his secretive
affairs with men.

In July of 1985, while in Paris, Hudson collapsed in the lobby
of the Ritz Hotel and was taken to the American Hospital. The
official story was that Hudson was suffering from liver cancer,
but then word got out that he was in Paris to undergo an
experimental treatment for AIDS. The news profoundly shocked
many people: although thousands had already died of AIDS,
Hudson was the first person whose case galvanized the threat of
the epidemic in the collective consciousness. The impact was
twofold: first, no one was immune to AIDS, and second, intertwined with that, if manly heartthrob Rock Hudson could turn
out to be gay, then who else might not be gay as well? It was all
confusing and threatening and sad. Newspapers obsessed over
the contrast between earlier images of the handsome, virile
Hudson and the gaunt, disease-ravaged face in recent
photographs.

It is of course deplorable that these convulsions ever had to
take place: that it took someone of Rock Hudson's popularity to
legitimize concern about a public health crisis of the magnitude

of AIDS. But at the same time, it is undeniable that Hudson's plight was directly responsible for both increased public awareness and increased governmental spending on the epidemic.

In September of 1985, an AIDS fund-raiser in Los Angeles garnered $5 million—a sum directly attributable to Hudson's revelations a month earlier. Too ill to attend, Hudson sent a telegram: "I am not happy that I am sick. I am not happy that I have AIDS. But if that is helping others I can at least know that my misfortune has had some positive worth." He died on October 2, 1985, in Beverly Hills, California.

Rock Hudson's fate is full of ironies. This man spent his life hiding his sexuality from the world, and yet his influence rests precisely in the terrible revelation, through his illness, of that sexuality. The revenge of the closet: he was influential in death in ways he had spent his whole life trying to avoid.

64

Sir Harold Nicolson 1886–1968

Vita Sackville-West 1892–1962

In this entry I pay tribute to that peculiar but sustaining phenomenon, the marriage of a lesbian and a gay man.

Harold George Nicolson was born on November 21, 1886, in Teheran, Persia (Iran), where his father was British chargé d'affaires. Due to his father's diplomatic postings, his childhood was variously spent in central Europe, Turkey, Spain, and Russia. Graduating from Balliol College, Oxford, he followed in his father's footsteps and joined the Foreign Office in 1909. For the next twenty years he served in the diplomatic corps in such cities as Madrid, Teheran, and Berlin. He played an important part in authoring the Balfour Declaration during World War I and was a junior adviser at the Paris Peace Conference, which launched the League of Nations.

During his spare time, he wrote voluminously, publishing over 125 books in his lifetime: biographies, travelogues, mystery novels. His officially commissioned biography of King George V led to his being knighted in 1953.

In 1910 he met Vita Sackville-West, and they married in 1913.

Victoria Sackville-West was born on March 9, 1892, at Knole Park, England. The daughter of the third Baron Sackville, she was educated at home on the family's ancestral estate. By the "technical fault" of her sex, she was barred from inheriting Knole, and the estate passed into other hands.

Sackville-West's first great lesbian love occurred five years after her marriage to Nicolson, when she "rediscovered" a friend from childhood named Violet Keppel Trefusis. In 1919, while Nicolson was involved with peace negotiations at Versailles, the two embarked on a stormy affair that Sackville-West memorialized in her unpublished 1924 novel *Challenge*. In 1922 she met VIRGINIA WOOLF [13], and the two began an affair that lasted through most of the 1920s and a fast friendship that lasted till Woolf's suicide in 1941. Their relationship led Sackville-West to write *Seducers in Ecuador* (1924), which was published by the Woolfs' Hogarth Press. On Woolf's part, she presented Sackville-West with *Orlando*, a fiction in which she restored the lost estate of Knole to her lover. Woolf's and Sackville-West's letters to one another represent one of the great correspondences on record.

Though little read today, Sackville-West's novels were quite successful in their day and include *The Edwardians* (1930), *All Passion Spent* (1931), *The Dark Island* (1934), and *Easter Party* (1953). She also authored several biographies, including a volume on a Renaissance playwright, *Aphra Behn* (1927), and *St. Joan of Arc* (1936).

Stephen O. Murray describes the complex dynamics of Nicolson's and Sackville-West's forty-nine-year marriage thus: "Nicolson's liaisons with younger aristocrats were emotionally cooler than his wife's passions for Virginia Woolf and Violet Trefusis. He was quite devoted to her, while she was less promiscuous than he and more devoted to the women she loved than to her husband."

Nicolson retired from the diplomatic service in 1929 to devote his time to writing and creating formal gardens. Together he and Sackville-West turned the grounds of their home at Sissinghurst Castle into perhaps the most famous gardens of the twentieth century. Harold was the genius "with square-ruled drawing paper, india-rubber, control of temper, stakes and string." Vita was the gardener who made things grow. The Sissinghurst gardens, especially the all-white garden, have been endlessly admired, studied, and imitated by serious gardeners around the world. Long after their many books have been forgotten and their many loves laid to rest, it is as gardeners extraordinaire that their benign influence continues to this day.

Vita Sackville-West died at Sissinghurst Castle, Kent, on June 2, 1962. Bereft, Harold Nicolson survived her by six years. He died at Sissinghurst on May 2, 1968. One of their two sons, Nigel, published a frank and moving account of his parents called *Portrait of a Marriage* (1973).

The intertwining lives of Harold Nicolson and Vita Sackville-West were, by our standards, complex. They managed to accommodate the conventional demands of their time while simultaneously fashioning rich personal lives of their own. Theirs was a relationship that may seem curious to us now, but I think it would not be amiss to suggest that marriages of this type were early examples—within a different cultural context from ours— of the common cause that lesbians and gay men often feel today. It is as elegant exemplars of that common cause that I place Harold Nicolson and Vita Sackville-West in this ranking.

65

Elsie de Wolfe

1865–1950

Elsie de Wolfe was born on December 20, 1865, in New York City. Her father was a prosperous physician, her mother a Canadian of Scottish descent. As de Wolfe wrote later, "he was as extravagant and impractical as my mother was thrifty and practical. He was as gay as she was austere. A constant gambler, he liked to live as dangerously as she did securely, and our family budget was like a weathervane with Mother always blowing against the wind." In 1881, de Wolfe was sent to Scotland to complete her education and in 1885 made her society debut in London, where she was formally presented to Queen Victoria. Returning to the United States, she entered New York's fashionable world and began to receive favorable attention as an amateur actress.

In 1887 she met Elisabeth Marbury, a woman eight years her senior who was to become her companion and lover for the next forty years. Marbury would later remember their rather unpropitious first encounter: "There was a buzz of excitement when a slim and graceful young girl passed through the ballroom....I remember that my remark was far from flattering as I was not in the least impressed by her appearance. Her foreign type and her French distinction elicited no admiration so far as I was concerned." Nevertheless, an intense relationship soon developed. De Wolfe's biographer Jane Smith writes: "Like most marriages that are made to last, the relationship coupled romantic fulfillment with certain practical improvements in both their lives." Theirs seems to have been the classic butch-femme dynamic. De Wolfe, who claimed to be unable to add numbers without using her fingers, loved clothes, jewelry, dancing, and decorating. Dressed in dark tailored suits, Marbury was the head of the house and kept the ledger books.

When de Wolfe's father died in 1890, leaving the family practically bankrupt, de Wolfe decided to begin a professional career in acting—a controversial move for a socialite. Marbury, who was beginning to build what would soon become the most influential theatrical agency in the world, became de Wolfe's manager and transformed her from an amateur actress of modest promise into the most fashionable figure on Broadway. Though de Wolfe's acting won little praise from critics, she became famous for showcasing dazzling new designs from the finest Parisian couturiers onstage: one bemused critic called her "the leading exponent of...the peculiar art of wearing good clothes well."

Marbury's clients eventually included OSCAR WILDE [3], George Bernard Shaw, and J.M. Barrie, the boy-loving author of *Peter Pan.*

When de Wolfe and Marbury took a house together, Irving House, they proceeded to host some of the most glittering evenings in New York. Everybody who was anybody would sooner or later be found in attendance. According to Jane Smith, the parties "were so stylish and witty that they were said to have made lesbian households not only acceptable, but positively chic." Their friends began calling them the Bachelors.

By the turn of the century, de Wolfe and Marbury were dividing their time between New York and a small pavilion in

Versailles, and de Wolfe was becoming increasingly interested in furniture styles, especially those of the eighteenth century. When she renovated Irving House, she created a sensation by removing the clutter and lightening the rooms' heavy Victorian gloom in favor of a clearer, more open aesthetic. This redecoration coincided with the Bachelors' increasing prominence as New York's most fashionable hostesses.

Increasingly discontented with the stage, de Wolfe quit the theater for good in 1904. Using her social connections, she forged a new profession for herself as the world's first interior designer. Smith writes, "Newly accustomed to the idea of needing expert advice for both the acquisition and the arrangements of its possessions, the fashionable world was ripe for the arrival of the interior decorator. It was the moment when taste was being transformed from an attitude into an industry, and it was Elsie's good fortune that she was there to take advantage of the change." De Wolfe's first major project was the Colony Club, the first private clubhouse for women in America. The results were spectacular, and de Wolfe was on her way to fabulous success. Since the prices she charged were as astonishing as the interiors she created, financial success was part of the bargain. For the next half century, de Wolfe influenced not only the rich and famous clients of Park Avenue and Palm Beach, but popular taste as well: newspapers and magazines dispensed her advice, which was collected in her best known and most influential book, *The House in Good Taste*. There she advised Americans to eschew ostentation and clutter in favor of simplicity, to dismantle the draperies in order to let in the light, to replace garish colors with beige and ivory. "I believe in plenty of optimism and white paint," she declared, "comfortable chairs with lights beside them, open fires on the hearth and flowers wherever they 'belong,' mirrors and sunshine in all rooms." The rooms that Americans inhabited in the middle of the twentieth century owed much to de Wolfe's tastes.

In 1907, De Wolfe and Marbury met and befriended the heiress Anne Morgan, who would be an important part of their lives for the next twenty years. Together the three women undertook the renovation of the Villa Trianon in Versailles, which became a major showcase of de Wolfe's work. They became known as the Versailles Triumvirate, and their every move titillated the press. When they bought apartments on Manhattan's

Sutton Place, sparking the rise of that heretofore unfashionable neighborhood, the New York gossip magazines buzzed with the news that an "Amazon enclave" had sprung up on the banks of the East River and intimated that sapphic debauches were under way there.

Under Morgan's influence, de Wolfe grew increasingly active in the woman suffrage movement. Marbury, in the meantime, had become a force in American politics and served several terms as Democratic national committeewoman from New York.

In 1926, at the age of sixty, Elsie de Wolfe stunned everyone by announcing her marriage to Sir Charles Mendl, a press attaché at the British embassy in Paris. She had come, apparently, to that time in life when it seemed fitting to acquire a title: she would thereafter be Lady Mendl. Bessie Marbury in particular felt betrayed, though when she learned that Sir Charles had no romantic interest in de Wolfe, would maintain a separate apartment and in no way interfere with de Wolfe's personal life, she was much mollified, and the two women continued on intimate terms until Marbury's death in 1933.

In addition to her work in interior design, de Wolfe was responsible for some other innovations: she popularized the wearing of short white gloves, was the first to tint her graying hair blue (this was in 1924), and invented that noxious cocktail known as a pink lady (grapefruit juice, gin, Cointreau). She was also an enthusiastic early promoter of Noel Coward and Cole Porter. Her spirit is perhaps best captured in her famous remark upon first seeing the Parthenon: "It's beige—my color!"

Elsie de Wolfe never gave up her passion for life. She died on July 12, 1950, at the age of eighty-five, protesting on her deathbed, "They can't do this to me. I don't want to go."

A key player in what her biographer calls the "professionalization of taste" in the twentieth century, Elsie de Wolfe presided over the growth of design as a major industry. That it has been an industry dominated—and quite visibly so—by gay men and lesbians is perhaps no accident. That it has profoundly influenced the physical spaces we live in on a daily basis is undeniable.

66

Liberace

1919–1987

Wladziu Valentino Liberace was born on May 6, 1919, in West Allis, Wisconsin. His father was a specialty grocer who played French horn; his mother was a pianist. He began music lessons when he was four, and by the time he was fourteen he was calling himself Walter Busterkeys and playing honky-tonk piano in local cocktail lounges. In 1936, at the age of seventeen, he debuted as soloist with the Chicago Symphony Orchestra playing Franz Liszt's First Piano Concerto. Three years later, he discovered the shtick that would make him famous. Playing "Three Little Fishies" as a surprise encore at a performance, he knowingly smirked and winked his way through the piece: the audience was delighted, and Liberace was on the road to stardom.

Television was a medium made for a born showman like Liberace, and as host of his own show in the 1950s he became television's first matinee idol, playing what he called "Reader's Digest versions" of the classics: Chopin's "Minute Waltz" in half a minute, Tchaikovsky's First Piano Concerto in four minutes. He specialized, he explained, in "cutting out the dull parts." Further enlivening his performances were his lavish trademark costumes, awash in rhinestones and sequins, and an elaborate gilt candelabra positioned with ritual panache on top of the piano. He started the rage for gold lamé, later adopted by Elvis Presley and still the staple of Elvis impersonators. But gold lamé was only a start for Liberace: his accoutrements included, over the years, jackets with twenty-four-karat gold braid trim, a silvery plum lamé cape with an eight-foot pink feather train, a $300,000 Norwegian blue fox cape with a sixteen-foot train, and even a sequined drum major's outfit with hot pants. His fingers were adorned with huge rings, including one shaped like a grand piano, and he was fond of saying to people who asked him how he played the piano encumbered with all those rings, "Very well, thank you."

All this translated into mind-boggling financial success: Liberace earned $5 million a year for twenty-five straight (or not so straight) years.

There were rumors in the press, even outright attacks. He had showed an interest in drag back in his high school days and apparently began to have gay sex in the 1940s. In 1956, a catty columnist for London's *Daily Mirror* wrote in a shrill review that Liberace "is the summit of sex—the pinnacle of masculine, feminine and neuter. Everything that he, she and it can ever want." The American tabloid *Confidential* took it from there, running a cover story entitled "Why Liberace's Theme Song Should Be 'Mad About the Boy.'" In a move reminiscent of OSCAR WILDE [3], Liberace sued both publications for libel. The difference is, he won.

He was not so lucky in 1982, when his former chauffeur Scott Thorson initiated a $113-million palimony suit against the entertainer, claiming the two had been lovers. The suit was settled a month before Liberace's death for $95,000.

Liberace's last public performance was in November 1986 at Radio City Music Hall. Further concerts were canceled, and rumors surfaced that the performer was suffering from AIDS, though this was strenuously denied. But on February 4, 1987, Liberace died in Palm Springs, California, of cardiac arrest due to congestive heart failure brought on by AIDS-related subacute encephalopathy.

At the time of his death, Liberace owned five homes, twenty cars, and eighteen pianos—as well as the hearts of countless fans. Liberace personified show business—Mr. Show Business, he in fact called himself. An influence on entertainers as different as Elvis Presley and Elton John, the man couldn't possibly have been a bigger success at what he did if he'd wanted to. He was schmaltzy and campy and utterly artificial and so transparently gay that it seems astonishing that his audience, which consisted largely of older straight women, seemed bent on taking him at his word when, stepping out of his usual self-deprecating spirit of fun, he fiercely denied everything.

Liberace's achievement remains this: that in the heart of the repressive 1950s, he managed to bring *gay* into the living rooms of America without ever committing the indiscretion of mentioning it by name. He merely personified it—albeit extravagantly—for all to see.

67

Allen Ginsberg

1926–

Allen Ginsberg was born on June 23, 1926, in Newark, New Jersey. He grew up in Paterson, where his father was a high school English teacher and poet. His mother, a Russian Jewish émigré, had a precarious hold on reality and spent many years confined in mental hospitals. During high school, Ginsberg was a self-defined "mystical creep." He entered Columbia University in a prelaw program in 1943, but was expelled two years later. The official charge, that Ginsberg had been caught writing obscenities on a dorm window, obscured the real reason: he had been discovered in bed with fellow student Jack Kerouac. Ginsberg and Kerouac moved into an off-campus apartment that they shared with William Burroughs, and their digs soon became a gathering place for the so-called beat movement. One of their frequent visitors was the legendary Neal Cassady—who became Dean Moriarty in Jack Kerouac's classic novel, *On the Road,* and with whom Ginsberg fell madly in love. They became sexual partners, though Cassady couldn't reciprocate the passion Ginsberg brought to the relationship, and their breakup was bitter.

After completing a four-month program at the Merchant Marine Academy in Brooklyn, Ginsberg took to sea for seven months in 1946, and again in 1947 when he sailed to Africa. On his return he was readmitted to Columbia and graduated in 1948. During this time he began to have his famous visions, in which the poet William Blake seemed to be speaking to him. The experience forever changed Ginsberg's notions of reality, and he began to seek, through drugs among other things, heightened states of being.

In 1949, an escapade involving stolen goods being transported in a stolen car landed him an eight-month stay (in lieu of prison) at Rockland State Hospital for psychoanalysis and therapy. In Rockland he met Carl Solomon, the "lunatic saint" to whom *Howl,* Ginsberg's first collection of poems, would be dedicated.

The publication of *Howl* in 1956 was a cultural bombshell. As Ginsberg said in the introduction to the volume: "Hold back the edges of your gowns, Ladies, we are going through Hell." Written—in part—when he was on peyote, and in a style he described as "Hebraic-Melvillean bardic breath," the poem became the manifesto of the beat movement, a literary revolution that celebrated what Kerouac called "spontaneous style"—or as Ginsberg put their credo: "First thought, best thought." Unimpressed by literary revolutions, the San Francisco police declared the poem obscene and arrested its publisher, Lawrence Ferlinghetti. The obscenity trial garnered national attention, with prominent literary figures defending the poems' literary merits. Judge Clayton R. Horn declared that *Howl*—despite its "angel-headed hipsters" "who let themselves get fucked in the ass by saintly motorcyclists, and screamed with joy, / who blew and were blown by those human seraphim, the sailors,"—was not in fact obscene.

Antimaterialist, a self-declared "Space Age anarchist," and increasingly interested in the nonviolent principles of Buddhism, Ginsberg became one of the most visible gurus of the counterculture that was coalescing in 1960's America. He was the creator of "flower power," a strategy by which flowers, music, and chanted mantras were to be used to confront the forces of violence and destruction. In 1966 he composed the "Wichita Vortex Sutra," which was intended to end the Vietnam War through magic incantation. In 1967 he organized the first hippie festival, called "The Gathering of the Tribes for a Human Be-In." In 1969 he devised a mantra for the exorcism of the Pentagon. All this he did with extraordinary zest and tenderness, and sometimes it got him into trouble. He was thrown out of Cuba in 1965 for protesting the condition of gays in that country. The same year, after being crowned "King of May" by one hundred thousand Czechoslovakian students in Prague, he was thrown out of the country for being "sloppy and degenerate." He was arrested at a 1967 antiwar rally in New York City, teargassed at the 1968 Democratic National Convention in Chicago, arrested at a demonstration against Richard Nixon at the 1972 Republican Convention in Miami, and in 1978, along with his longtime companion Peter Orlovsky, for a sit-in at the Rocky Flats Nuclear Weapons Plant in Colorado.

Through it all he continued, prolifically, to write the poems collected in *Kaddish* (1961) about his mother's death, *Reality Sandwiches* (1963), *Planet News* (1968), *The Fall of America* (1972) which won a National Book Award, *Mind Breaths* (1978), and *White Shroud* (1986). He also made numerous recordings of his poems.

Beginning in the early 1970s, Ginsberg studied with the Venerable Chagyam Trungpa, a Tibetan Buddhist abbot who had established a Buddhist University called the Naropa Institute in Boulder, Colorado. Meditation, Ginsberg discovered, could deliver a heightened state of consciousness far more profound than that offered by mere drugs. In 1972, Ginsberg made his Buddhism official by taking the bodhisattva vows. With the poet Anne Waldman he established, as a branch of the Naropa Institute, the Jack Kerouac School of Disembodied Poetics in 1974. As he explained, "Trungpa wants the presence of poets at Naropa to inspire the Buddhists towards being articulate, and he also sees the advantage of having the large-scale Buddhist background to inspire the poets to silence."

Allen Ginsberg is the poet laureate of gay love, one of the elder statesmen both of American poetry and the gay movement. Throughout his long career he has been outspokenly gay, and his compelling presence in the antiwar movement of the sixties guaranteed an influential and public gay voice that was heard by millions in those troubled times. Today he lives modestly in a small apartment on the Lower East Side of Manhattan, donating nearly all of his considerable earnings as a world-famous poet to the Jack Kerouac School of Disembodied Poetics. A proud member of NAMBLA, the North American Man-Boy Love Association, Ginsberg continues to move boldly and provocatively on the forefront of the gay imagination.

68

Marlene Dietrich

1901–1992

Marlene Dietrich was born on December 27, 1901, in Berlin, Germany. Her father was a police lieutenant, and her mother came from a merchant family. As a child, Dietrich called herself Paul and fancied that she resembled her father rather than her mother. At the age of sixteen she made her debut as a violinist— performing in drag at a Red Cross pageant. In 1918 she graduated from the Auguste Victoria School for Girls and the following year entered the Weimar Konservatorium to prepare for a career as a violinist. A wrist injury dashed these hopes, however, and she returned to Berlin, where she began work as an actress and studied at the Max Reinhardt Drama School. Her film debut came in 1923, in *Der kleine Napoleon*. The next year she married

Rudolf Sieber, a casting assistant, and they had one daughter. It was Sieber who first suggested that Dietrich wear men's clothes and a monocle when performing. For the next five years Dietrich played bit parts in various forgettable films, as well as appearing in stage performances. It was during the run of one of these stage shows that she was initiated into lesbian sex by her costar Claire Waldoff, who is also credited with teaching Dietrich the fine art of how to get a song across when one has no real singing voice.

Eventually Dietrich was discovered by the Austrian director Josef von Sternberg, who cast her as Lola-Lola, the tuxedo-sporting cabaret singer in *The Blue Angel* (1930). The critical success of the film established both their reputations instantly. The two moved to the United States, and a series of masterful collaborations ensued: *Morocco* (1930), *Dishonored* (1931), *Blonde Venus* (1932), *Shanghai Express* (1932), and *The Scarlet Empress* (1934). Sternberg carefully cultivated Dietrich's androgynous image. As he put it, "I had seen her wearing the full-dress regalia of a man, high hat and all, at a Berlin shindy, and so outfitted her [in *Morocco*]. The formal male finery fitted her with much charm, and I not only wished to touch lightly on a lesbian accent…but also to demonstrate that her sensual appeal was not entirely due to the formation of her legs."

Marlene Dietrich's legs. About them she would eventually say, "My legs, always my legs! Yet for me they have only one purpose; they make it possible for me to walk." Nevertheless, they were insured for a million dollars.

When Hitler came to power, Dietrich was asked by the Nazis to return to Germany and continue her career in the fatherland. It was even rumored that Hitler wished her for his mistress. She demurred, however, insisting that she would return only if Sternberg, who was a Jew, could direct her in films there.

Dietrich and Sternberg's last film together, *The Devil Is a Woman* (1935), was such a commercial disaster that Dietrich became known as "box office poison." She resurrected her career, however, with *Destry Rides Again* in 1939. During World War II she entertained Allied troops in France, Italy, and the United States, and made anti-Nazi radio broadcasts in German. For her services, she was awarded a U.S. Medal of Freedom.

After the war she starred in such films as *Stage Fright* (1950), *Rancho Notorious* (1952), *Witness for the Prosecution* (1957), *Touch of Evil* (1958), and *Judgment at Nuremberg* (1961). None of these films approached the camp splendor of her collaborations with Sternberg in the 1930s. Her last film was *Just a Gigolo* in 1979. Starting in the 1950s, Dietrich appeared in numerous successful cabaret and one-woman Broadway shows.

Although she never divorced her husband, they lived apart for most of their lives, and Dietrich was famous for her many liaisons with both men and women. The women included Hollywood scriptwriter Mercedes de Acosta (who also had a well-known liaison with Greta Garbo), chanteuse Edith Piaf, and a certain famous Hollywood socialite during the mid-1950s. At the age of seventy-three, Dietrich was being accompanied on her tours by Ginette Vachon, a Canadian woman in her twenties. Her last years were spent in seclusion in Paris, where she died on May 6, 1992.

The critic Kenneth Tynan formulated Dietrich's appeal in an oft-quoted aperçu: "She has sex but no particular gender." Elsewhere he summed up her enchanting convolution of gender roles when he reminisced that she was "the only woman who was allowed to attend the annual ball for male transvestites in pre-Hitler Berlin. She habitually turned up in top hat, white tie and tails. Seeing two exquisite creatures descending the grand staircase, clad in form-hugging sequins and cascading blond wigs, she wondered wide-eyed: 'Are you two in love?' '*Fräulein*,' said one of them frostily, 'we are not lesbians.' This Marlene lives in a sexual no man's land—and no woman's, either. She dedicates herself to looking, rather than to being, sexy. The art is in the seeming. The semblance is the image and the image is the message. She is every man's mistress and mother, every woman's lover and aunt, and nobody's husband except Rudi's—and he *is* her husband, far off on his ranch in California."

Marlene Dietrich was influential because she introduced to American audiences the Continental tradition known as *la garçonne:* the provocative boy/girl ambiguity that so enthralled Paris and Berlin in the 1920s and 1930s. Her trademark white tie, tails, and top hat have been much imitated and remain so today by entertainment figures as different as Liza Minnelli, Julie Andrews, and Annie Lennox. Indeed, her celebrated androgyny has had even wider influence, helping to make the everyday questioning of gender images a more acceptable part of our culture.

69

Quentin Crisp

1908–

"In the year 1908," writes Quentin Crisp, "one of the largest meteorites the world has ever known was hurled at the earth. It missed its mark. It hit Siberia. I was born in Sutton, in Surrey." His original name was Denis—"before I dyed it." He spent his childhood endlessly and creatively seeking attention from his parents, who lived not in poverty but in debt. In his fantasy games with the little girls of the neighborhood, he first entered into what he called "an exotic lifelong swoon"— "to me fantasy and reality were not merely different; they were opposed. In the one I was a woman, exotic, disdainful; in the other I was a boy. The chasm between the two states never narrowed."

After prep school he went "on a very poor scholarship to a public school on the border of Staffordshire and Derbyshire....It looked like a cross between a prison and a church and it was." It was during his four years there that he learned the only thing he

261

was ever able to use in adult life: "I discovered that my great gift was for unpopularity." After graduating, he briefly attended King's College, London, where he studied journalism but left without a degree. Returning to live at home, he took to wandering the streets of London's West End—and discovered he was not alone in the world. He and his kind hung out at a cafe they called the Black Cat where with lady-like sips, they made their cups of tea last for hours while trying on one another's lipstick. When they'd get thrown out of the cafe, they would cruise the neighborhood "in search of love or money or both." Failing any of those, they'd return to the cafe and put on more lipstick.

The only thing that bothered Crisp was the coarseness of the situations he found himself in: "Courtship consisted of walking along the street with a man who had my elbow in a merciless grip until we came to a dark doorway. Then he said, 'This'll do.' These are the only words of tenderness that were ever uttered to me."

It was during this time that Crisp decided to become a missionary. "The message I wished to propagate was that effeminacy existed in people who were in all other respects just like home. I went about the routine of daily living looking undeniably like a homosexual person." The reckless courage, even the madness, of such a gesture was not lost on him. In his attempt to look like a homosexual person, he began wearing makeup, let his fingernails grow, and teased his increasingly long hair into adventuresome disguises. He continued living at home, and when his parents moved to High Wycombe, he went with them. There he attended art school for a while and met with some minor success: an instructor mistook his sketch of a frog for some draperies. In 1931 he moved out of his parents' house and into a shared flat in Baron's Court, where he began to live a life of "Soho" poverty ("It comes from having the airs and graces of a genius but no talent"). Meanwhile, his appearance progressed from the effeminate to the bizarre: "Blind with mascara and dumb with lipstick, I paraded the dim streets of Pimlico with my overcoat wrapped around me as though it were a tailless ermine cape. I had to walk like a mummy leaving its tomb."

People reacted with outrage, slapping his face as he stood in line for the bus, stomping on his toes if he wore sandals, following him like a mob. Then they started beating him up.

He was undeterred. He was a missionary. The great work had begun.

He worked a series of odd jobs and lived in a series of odd apartments. As he reported, "life was a funny thing that happened to me on the way to the grave." Then the war came. "Apart from getting a good supply of cosmetics," he remembered, "I made up my mind to ignore the war as completely as I could." He was called up for service in the army, however, and appeared before the medical board. "You've dyed your hair," the examining physician told him. "This is a sign of sexual perversion. Do you know what those words mean?" Crisp replied that, in fact, he did. The army, he was sternly told, would never want him.

It was during the war that he began to work as an artist's life model. "It required no aptitude, no education, no references, and no previous experience.... The war was on and I was almost the only roughly male person left with two arms and two legs."

War, it turned out, was heaven.

[I]nto the feast of love and death that St. Adolf had set before the palates of the English—parched these long dark twenty-five years—Mr. Roosevelt began, with Olympian hands, to shower the American forces. This brand new army of (no) occupation flowed through the streets of London like cream on strawberries, like melted butter over green peas. Labelled "with love from Uncle Sam" and packaged in uniforms so tight that in them their owners could fight for nothing but their honor, these "bundles for Britain" leaned against the lamp posts of Shaftesbury Avenue or lolled on the steps of thin-lipped statues of dead English statesmen. As they sat in cafés or stood in the pubs, their bodies bulged through every straining khaki fiber toward our feverish hands. Their voices were like warm milk, their skins as flawless as expensive India rubber, and their eyes as beautiful as glass. Above all it was the liberality of their natures that was so marvellous. Never in the history of sex was so much offered to so many by so few.

All goods thing, unfortunately, must come to an end, and the postwar years were dreary. Plus, Quentin Crisp was getting old. He began dying his hair blue. He had become one of the stately homos of England.

The appearance, in 1968, of his wickedly funny autobiography, *The Naked Civil Servant,* finally, after all those years of Soho poverty, made him wildly famous. A TV-film version starring John Hurt won accolades and awards. Crisp became perhaps the most recognized homosexual in the world, an elder statesman of a certain vintage type of homosexuality, gravely wounded but endlessly resilient. Other books followed the success of *The Naked Civil Servant,* including *Love Made Easy* (1977), *Chog: A Gothic Fable* (1980), and *How to Become a Virgin* (1982). He traveled to and fell in love with America, where he toured as a popular one-man show. He was in much demand.

Perhaps the culmination of Crisp's long career came with his 1992 film debut: in Sally Potter's *Orlando,* an otherwise mediocre film based on the novel by VIRGINIA WOOLF [13], the eighty-five-year-old Quentin Crisp steals the show with his performance as the aged Elizabeth I. It is a perfect crowning moment for England's finest queen.

Quentin Crisp earns his place in this ranking as a courageous, outrageous warrior on the front lines of the ongoing struggle of gay and lesbian people simply to *be.* Enduring insults, mockery, physical violence, he has, in his inimitable way, given the ideals of civil disobedience and nonviolent protest an entirely new meaning. Bless you, Quentin.

70

H.D.

1886–1961

Hilda Doolittle was born on September 10, 1886, in Beth-lehem, Pennsylvania. Her father was a professor of astronomy. Her mother came from a long line of Moravians, a religious sect founded in the eighteenth century, whose rituals exercised a profound influence on the young H.D.'s imagination. She was mostly educated in private schools and attended Bryn Mawr College for a year and a half before dropping out in 1906—not, as she liked to claim, because of a "slight breakdown," but because she had failed English. She spent the next five years living at home, reading Greek and Latin literature and writing poetry. She also fell in love with Frances Gregg, a family friend. During this time she saw much of her neighbor Ezra Pound, who was a year older than she. He encouraged her in her writing, and when he went abroad in 1908, she eventually followed, settling in London in 1911. There the two were briefly engaged; in 1913, however, she married the poet Richard Aldington. She and

265

Pound remained close, however, and Pound included three of her poems in his 1914 volume *Des Imagistes:* at his suggestion, she signed her work "H.D. imagiste." Together with Aldington, they formed the imagist movement in poetry. Their aim, as enunciated in their "Imagist Credo," was "to produce poetry that is hard and clear, never blurred nor indefinite...concentration is of the very essence of poetry."

The years of World War I brought H.D. to the brink of the abyss. She suffered a miscarriage, her beloved older brother was killed in combat, her marriage with Aldington collapsed, her father died. "Death!" she wrote at the time. "Death is all around us!" She found herself alone, seriously ill, and pregnant again. It was at that point that Annie Winifred Ellerman entered her life. The daughter of one of the wealthiest men in England, "Bryher" (as she called herself) had read *The Sea Garden* (1916), H.D.'s first published volume of poetry. Not only had she read it, she'd memorized it. Although married—in an unconsummated arrangement with the bisexual American writer Robert McAlmon—Bryher instantly fell in love with H.D.: "So madly," wrote H.D. on first meeting Bryher, "it is terrible. No man has ever cared for me like that." Bryher wanted to rescue the poet (and her newborn daughter, Perdita), and H.D. consented, albeit reluctantly, to be rescued. Together they traveled in Greece (1920) and Egypt (1923) before more or less permanently settling in Switzerland. The publication of *Collected Poems* in 1925 established H.D.'s reputation as one of the major modern poets. Included in this volume were several poems based on fragments from SAPPHO [2]. Over the next decade and a half H.D. published, in addition to poetry, novels, including *Palimpsest* (1926) and *Hedylus* (1928), the verse drama *Hippolytos Temporizes* (1927), and several highly acclaimed translations, including *Euripides' Ion* (1937).

She seems not to have been completely content in her relationship with Bryher, but felt she owed her her life. In 1926 she began an affair with Kenneth MacPherson, which the by-now-divorced and extremely wealthy Bryher nipped in the bud by proposing to MacPherson herself, and what ensued was, in H.D.'s words, "a very static and 'classic' and peaceful relationship with Bryher and MacPherson. I admit, I am at times very lonely, not that they do not understand." The marriage remained unconsummated.

Owing to her continuing mental distress and unhappiness,

in 1933 H.D. traveled to Vienna to be psychoanalyzed by Sigmund Freud. In her *Tribute to Freud* (1956) she wrote, "I did not specifically realize just what I wanted, but I knew that I, like most of the people I knew in England, in America, and the continent of Europe, was drifting.... I would (before the current of inevitable events swept me right into the main stream and so on to the cataract) stand aside, if I could (if it were not already too late), and take stock of my possessions. You might say that I had—yes, I had something that I specifically owned. I *owned* myself. I did not really, of course. My family, my friends, and my circumstances owned me. But I *had* something. Say it was a narrow birch-bark canoe...with the current gathering force, I could at least pull in to the shallows before it was too late, take stock of my very modest possessions of mind and body, and ask the old Hermit who lived on the edge of this vast domain to talk to me, to tell me, if he would, how best to steer my course." The sessions with the old Hermit were successful—H.D. was particularly impressed by his understanding of dreams as a universal language. They were also, apparently, quite frank: Freud declared H.D. to be "that all-but-extinct phenomenon," the perfect bisexual.

During World War II, H.D. lived in London and produced a trilogy of war poems: *The Walls Do Not Fall* (1944), *Tribute to Angels* (1945), and *The Flowering of the Rod* (1946). After the war she returned to Switzerland and Bryher. Her final years saw the expansive poetic sequence *Helen in Egypt* (1961). In 1960 she was the first woman ever to receive an Award of Merit Medal for Poetry from the American Academy of Arts and Letters. She died in Zurich, Switzerland, on September 27, 1961.

H.D.'s career was long and varied, and as a poet she moved far beyond the early imagist poems for which she is best known. Little of the work published in her lifetime was overtly lesbian in content, though three unpublished autobiographical novels from the 1920s are emotionally quite explicit—*Paint It Today* (1921), *Asphodel* (1921–22), and *Her* (1927), published in 1981 as *Hermione*. Despite this, H.D.'s work has attracted the attention of contemporary lesbian readers, who have found her reshaping of classical myths for modern purposes a compelling project. It is because of the current interest in the lesbian implications of H.D.'s work that I have chosen to include her in this ranking rather than such other important twentieth-century lesbian poets as Amy Lowell, Edna St. Vincent Millay, and Elizabeth Bishop.

71

Dr. S. Josephine Baker

1873–1945

Sara Josephine Baker was born on November 15, 1873 in Poughkeepsie, New York. Her father was a lawyer, and her mother had been in the first graduating class of Vassar College. When Baker was sixteen, her father died of typhoid, which he had contracted from Poughkeepsie's drinking water. Discovering that the family finances were ruinous, Baker's mother nevertheless managed to pull together enough money to send her daughter to school, and in 1898 Baker received her MD from the Women's Medical College of the New York Infirmary for Women and Children. After a year's internship at the New England Hospital in Boston, she returned to New York to enter the practice of medicine, augmenting her meager income by working as a medical inspector for the New York City Health Department. Assigned to Hell's Kitchen and the midtown slums, she later wrote: "I climbed stair after stair, knocked on door after door, met drunk after drunk, filthy mother after filthy mother, and dying baby after dying baby."

Alarmed by the high infant-mortality rate in the city, in 1908 she established the Division of Child Hygiene, the first public agency in the world to address issues of children's health and a model for similar programs throughout the United States. At first male doctors refused to work with her, but eventually she won them over. Emphasizing the importance of preventive medicine, Dr. Baker introduced public-school health programs, infant-health clinics, and special schools designed to train midwives. In the first five years of the Child Hygiene Project, the infant mortality rate in New York City dropped from 144 per one thousand births to 105 per thousand births. By 1923, when Dr. Baker retired, it had dropped to 66 per one thousand. A statistician estimated at the time that Baker's work had saved, between 1908 and 1923, over 82,000 infant lives.

In 1916, Baker was invited to give lectures on child hygiene at New York University. She lectured there for fifteen years but was unable to enroll as a student, since the university allowed women teachers but not women students. In recognition of her achievements, New York University awarded her a doctorate in public health in 1917—the first doctorate of its kind ever presented to a woman.

After her retirement in 1923, Dr. Baker served as a representative to the League of Nations on children's health issues. She wrote over 250 articles and five books on child hygiene and in 1939 published her autobiography, *Fighting for Life*.

The writer I. A. R. Wylie, who also published her own autobiography in 1939 (*My Life with George: An Unconventional Biography*), gives us a fascinating glimpse not only into the private life of Dr. Baker, but also into the lives of three "professional women" living together in the 1930s:

> Somewhere in these first years I met Dr. S. Josephine Baker who it seemed had read *Towards Morning* and yearned to meet the author. Unfortunately, I had no idea who she was or that she occupied a unique position in the medical world and New York's civic life. I had never heard of a baby death rate and certainly did not know what she had done to it. So that my opening

gambit, "Are you still practicing, Dr. Baker?" produced a noticeable chill. However, we met again and she forgave my insular ignorance. We drifted into sharing a New York apartment together and years later this pleasant house in Princeton where Dr. Louise Pearce of the Rockefeller Institute and African sleeping sickness fame joined us....

Jo Baker, except for a dozen or so committees, had retired from public life and was not unwilling to prove that she could manage a house just as efficiently as she ran the Bureau of Child Hygiene. She proved it.....

So we are all three quite reasonably happy and I hope not too unreasonably pleased with ourselves.

I don't know what Princeton thinks about us. There is a rumor that we are called "The Girls." If this is so, I now know too much about American terminology to be flattered. There may be other designations mercifully concealed from us. Three professional women, two of them eminent in their respective medical fields, and living amicably and gaily together is an odd phenomenon, especially in a university town given over mainly to male talent.

Dr. Baker is a classic example of a woman operating within the lesbian continuum: we will probably never know—nor do we need to—whether she had genital contact with other women. What is quite clear is that she was a significant and visible example of a woman in the first half of the twentieth century who made her professional life, against great odds, in the public world of men, and her personal life in the nurturing, sustaining, private world of other women.

Dr. S. Josephine Baker died in New York City on February 22, 1945. By that time, over half of the babies born each year in New York City were cared for at the health stations she had established throughout the city. Her pioneering work focused attention on women's and children's health issues in a way that changed the medical profession around the world. A "cultural feminist" in the tradition of JANE ADDAMS [26], Baker's success in bringing hitherto marginalized individuals into a larger continuum of public health initiated a movement that continues to this day. Were it not for her, many of us might not be here today.

72

Romaine Brooks

1874–1970

Romaine Brooks was born Romaine Mary Goddard on May 1, 1874, in Rome, Italy. The child of extremely wealthy parents, she spent what was by all accounts an extremely unpleasant childhood. Her sadistic mother (who had been abandoned by her husband shortly before Brooks was born) treated her like a servant while pampering her brother, who seems, from an early age, to have been certifiably insane. In 1895, Brooks fled to Paris to escape her family and to study music. A year later she went to Rome, where she studied painting for a year, and later rented a studio on the island of Capri, a bohemian haven for artists and eccentrics. For a short time she was married to John Ellington Brooks, a handsome homosexual who had fled England after the trial of OSCAR WILDE [3]. She is also reported to have had a brief affair with Wilde's old lover, Lord Alfred Douglas.

When her mother and brother both died in 1902, the family fortune became hers. In 1905, after leaving her husband with a generous annuity, Brooks chopped her hair, adopted men's clothes, and returned to Paris, where she began painting the portraits for which she became renowned. Her great wealth freed her from the need to please her sitters: she didn't care whether she sold her works or not. Her uncanny ability to depict the truth in people's appearances led her to be called "the thief of souls." A famous anecdote tells that one fashionable lady complained, upon seeing her portrait, "You have not beautified me," to which Brooks replied, "No, but I have ennobled you." She befriended the writer Gabriele D'Annunzio and his mistress, the dancer Ida Rubinstein, becoming the lover of both and using Rubinstein as a model for many of her androgynous, otherworldly female nudes. Art critic Emmanuel Cooper writes: "All Brooks' female nudes have a particular idealisation of the body which is as much an expression of spiritual qualities as of flesh and blood. The pale, wan and bloodless nudes with small immature breasts, no pubic hair and a slim body have the shape more of boys than girls. Their nakedness, which combines eroticism with symbolism, gives them a particular sensuousness, but it is one remove from mortal and physical desire....It is of such paintings that a contemporary reviewer observed that it seemed as though 'the soul is identified with the flesh.'" Brooks's work was heavily influenced by the aesthetic movement.

In 1915, Brooks met and fell in love with the writer and salon patroness NATALIE BARNEY [43], and they began a relationship that would last for fifty years. Together they collaborated on a novel, *The One Who Is Legion, or A.D.'s After-Life*, which was privately printed in London in 1930 with illustrations by Brooks. Over the years Brooks painted many of the famous lesbian habitués of Barney's salon, including Barney as an AMAZON [42] and Lady Una Trowbridge, lover of RADCLYFFE HALL [28]. Many thought the Lady Una portrait cruel, but then Brooks hadn't been particularly flattered by Hall's depiction of her as the artist Venetia Ford in the novel *The Forge*. In 1920, Brooks was awarded the medal of the Legion of Honor from the French government.

Never particularly fond of the salon life, during the mid-1920s Brooks withdrew from the fashionable world of Parisian society. She and Barney built a house together near Beauvallon—actually, two separated houses connected by a common dining room. They called it the Villa Trait d'union, the "hyphenated villa," and this architectural detail tells us much about their relationship: they were often physically apart but emotionally connected, despite Barney's many affairs over the years.

At the onset of World War II, Brooks and Barney moved to Italy, where they spent the war years comfortably ensconced in the Villa Sant'Agnese in Florence. According to George Wickes, "the journal that Romaine kept during the war shows that she...was in sympathy with fascism and had such a phobia about the Russians that she hoped the Germans would defeat them."

After the war, Brooks and Barney lived apart, Barney in Paris, Brooks mostly in Nice, with summers spent in Fiesole, outside Florence. Of the two, Brooks was the more faithful, and in the end—after forty years—Barney's infidelities destroyed the relationship. In 1968, at the age of ninety-four, an increasingly paranoid and eccentric Brooks ended their relationship and refused to have anything to do with Barney for the last two years of her life. She died in December 1970.

After World War II, Brooks's reputation as a painter declined into obscurity, but a retrospective in 1971 led to renewed interest in her work, with art critic Hilton Kramer declaring the exhibition "yet another reminder that the history of American art in this century is still to be written." Feminist attention at the time was just beginning to settle on the question of why there have been no "great" women artists, and Brooks's obscurity became—along with that of her nineteenth-century counterpart ROSA BONHEUR [50]—a celebrated instance of the shadows to which talented women artists have so frequently been relegated by male-oriented histories of art. In the 1970s, the cool, sophisticated sense of lesbian style manifested in Brooks' paintings acted as a potent counterforce to the more butch, down-to-earth aesthetic that prevailed in certain lesbian circles at that time. The lipstick lesbians of the 1980s may, in fact, owe some of their glamour to the Romaine Brooks revival.

73

Benjamin Britten

1913–1976

Benjamin Britten was born on November 22, 1913, at Lowestoft, Suffolk, in England. His father was a dental surgeon, his mother an amateur singer. Britten's musicality manifested itself early. He started composing at the age of five, and by the age of fourteen he had composed ten piano sonatas, six string quartets, three piano suites, and an oratorio. He also studied piano and viola. From 1928 to 1930 he was enrolled at Gresham's School, Holt, and after that at the Royal College of Music, London, where he studied with the composer Frank Bridge.

After leaving the Royal College, Britten worked as a composer of incidental music for film documentaries, completing thirty scores between the years 1935 and 1939. On two of these documentaries, *Coal Face* and *Night Mail*, he collaborated with a schoolmate from Gresham's, the gay poet W. H. Auden. This friendship had a great effect on Britten and served in particular to introduce him to a fuller sense of the artist's political responsibility.

Britten's first popular success came in 1937 with his *Variations on a Theme of Frank Bridge*. But this was not enough to alleviate his growing sense of frustration at his general critical reception in England, and in May of 1939 he left England for the United States. He was accompanied by a young tenor named Peter Pears, whom he had first met in 1937, and with whom he would spend the rest of his life.

Auden had, in the meantime, moved to America as well, and in 1941 Britten collaborated with him on his first opera, *Paul Bunyan*. In 1942, increasingly concerned with the wartime situation in England, Britten and Pears elected to return to their homeland, sailing in a small Swedish cargo ship across the U-boat infested Atlantic. Once there, they both applied for conscientious objector status, Britten declaring, "The whole of my life has been devoted to acts of creation (being by profession a composer) and I cannot take part in acts of destruction." This pacifist bent would be a strong component in his music for the rest of his life.

His next opera, *Peter Grimes* (1945), was a smashing success: critics proclaimed that it ushered in the dawn of a new age for English opera. Britten was quickly anointed the most important British composer since Sir Edward Elgar in the late nineteenth century, perhaps even since Henry Purcell in the seventeenth century. Written for Peter Pears and his inimitable high, clear voice, *Peter Grimes* tells the story of an introverted fisherman who is ostracized by the local community after his three young apprentices die in mysterious succession. The music is by turns dark and luminous, and Britten crafts a moving drama of social conformity and the isolation of the individual. Not left out of the opera were clear hints of an underlying homoerotic impulse in Grimes's relations with his young apprentices.

A series of operas followed the success of *Peter Grimes*, most of them conceived with Pears in leading roles: as the eponymous hero of the comic *Albert Herring* (1947), Captain Vere in *Billy Budd* (1951, with a libretto by E. M. FORSTER [58]), the Earl of Essex in

Gloriana (1953), the sexually ambiguous Peter Quint in *The Turn of the Screw* (1954), the madwoman in *Curlew River* (1964), and Gustav Aschenbach in *Death in Venice* (1973). In that last opera, based on Thomas Mann's novella, Britten finally gave full musical and dramatic expression to the homosexual identity that had heretofore shadowed the margins of many of his stage pieces.

Britten and Pears led a busy professional and devoted personal life together. Their friend Wulf Scherchen left us this reminiscence of their relationship: "[Peter Pears] would restrain Bejamin when Ben was going off the rails, or threatening to go off the rails in some way. He was the wise man in the background....He had this air of stability that Ben didn't have. I mean, Ben was ebullient, outgoing, and Peter was the quiet, steadying influence."

Among their love letters that survive is this one from 1940, written by Pears to Britten during a brief separation: "It was marvellous to get your letter....I was so sad that you were depressed and cold—I wanted to hop into a plane and come over and comfort you at once, I would have kissed you all over & then blown all over you there & then—&—; and then you'd have been as warm as toast!...Ich liebe dich, io t'amo, jeg elske dyg (?), je t'aime, in fact, my little white-thighed beauty, I'm terribly in love with you."

Theirs was one of the extraordinary (and extraordinarily enduring) collaborations in this century. In addition to the operas, works composed for Pears include three church parables, *Les Illuminations* for tenor, horn, and string orchestra (1939), based on poems by RIMBAUD [51], and *Seven Sonnets from Michaelangelo* for tenor and piano (1940).

One of the most important works in the composer's prodigious output was the monumental *War Requiem* (1962), in which the stately certainties of the Latin Mass for the Dead are continually interrupted by searingly intimate settings of antiwar poems by the gay poet Wilfrid Owen (who was killed just days before the armistice that ended World War I).

In 1947, Britten bought a house in Aldeburgh, a small town on the Suffolk coast where *Peter Grimes* had been set, and near his childhood home. The next year he established the annual Aldeburgh Festival of the Arts, which has since become one of the world's major arts festivals. In 1976, Queen Elizabeth II named him a life peer—Lord Britten of Aldeburgh. Britten died in

Aldeburgh on December 4, 1976. Peter Pears survived him by ten years.

Benjamin Britten was the most important English composer of the twentieth century. His operas and the *War Requiem* give urgent voice to the sentiments of liberalism, pacifism, and tolerance while exploring gay themes, at first covertly, but with an increasing honesty over the years that influenced and encouraged many younger artists. The twentieth century has seen quite a constellation of important gay composers who were "out" to a greater or lesser extent during their lifetimes, among them Aaron Copland, Francis Poulenc, Samuel Barber, Leonard Bernstein, Virgil Thompson, Hans Werner Henze, Ned Rorem, David Diamond, and John Corigliano—and, of course, that great genius JOHN CAGE [34], whom I consider in a class by himself. From among the more conventional important composers I have chosen Britten for this ranking due to his celebrated relationship with Peter Pears and his music's use of explicit gay themes. Of all the many gay twentieth-century composers, it was Britten who most successfully integrated his gayness into his art.

74

Rita Mae Brown

1944–

Born on November 28, 1944, in Hanover, Pennsylvania, Rita Mae Brown was adopted in infancy by Ralph and Julia Brown. In 1955 the family moved to Fort Lauderdale, Florida, where Brown attended high school and experimented sexually with both boys and girls. When Brown was sixteen, some love letters she had written to a female schoolmate were discovered by the girl's father, and this led to Brown's being dismissed from the student council and ostracized by her friends. After graduating from high school in 1962, she enrolled at the University of Florida, but in 1964 her scholarship was revoked as a result of her involvement in the civil rights movement and her notorious answer to the taunts of the head of her sorority about being a "nigra lover." "I don't care," Brown is reported to have said, "if I fall in love with a black or a white or a man or a woman or an old or young person." It is that Rita Mae Brown—bold, feisty, and self-assured—that readers will recognize from her novels. Word of her retort reached the dean of the university, who ordered her to attend daily therapy sessions with a campus psychiatrist.

Without her scholarship, Brown was forced to drop out of school. Hitchhiking north to New York City, she lived for a while in an abandoned car with a gay black man and an orphan cat. Baby Jesus, as she named the little creature, remained her constant companion for the next seventeen years.

Brown began attending New York University and in 1967 founded the Student Homophile League there. In 1968 she graduated with a BA in English and classics as well as a cinematography certificate from the New York School of Visual Arts. That same year she joined the New York chapter of the National Organization of Women (NOW) and stirred up much controversy through her insistence that NOW address the issue of lesbian rights—an issue she herself addressed as coauthor of the pioneering Radicalesbian essay "The Woman-Identified Woman" (1970). Frustrated by NOW's homophobia, Brown quit the organization in 1970 to join a more radical feminist group called the Redstockings. In 1971 she was an organizing member of the Furies Collective in Washington, D.C. While in Washington she taught at Federal College and began working on a PhD as a fellow at the Institute for Policy Studies (she was awarded her doctorate in 1976).

In 1973 a small feminist press called Daughters Inc. brought out Brown's first novel. Though the semiautobiographical *Rubyfruit Jungle* had been turned down by mainstream publishers, it sold an astonishing seventy thousand copies—mostly through word of mouth—and Brown emerged as one of the major spokespeople for the lesbian and gay movement. In 1977, Bantam Books bought the rights to *Rubyfruit Jungle* for a quarter of a million dollars and had three hundred thousand copies printed. Brown had proved, spectacularly, what mainstream publishers had been reluctant to admit—that lesbian books could sell, and sell well. She could also now afford to write full-time.

Rubyfruit Jungle was followed by other novels, including *Six of One* (1978), *Southern Discomfort* (1982), *Sudden Death* (1983), *High Hearts* (1986), and *Wish You Were Here* (1990). In addition to these,

Brown has published two books of poetry, a translation of six plays by the medieval nun Hrotsvitha, a collection of essays called *A Plain Brown Rapper* (1976), and *Starting from Scratch: A Different Kind of Writer's Manual* (1988).

In 1978, Rita Mae Brown moved to Charlottesville, Virginia, where for a time she shared a house with Fannie Flagg (author of *Fried Green Tomatoes at the Whistle-Stop Cafe*). In 1979, Brown met the young Czechoslovakian tennis star MARTINA NAVRATILOVA [76], and the two fell in love and bought a mansion outside Charlottesville. The conflicting demands of their two very different careers soon caused fault lines to appear in the relationship, however, and in 1981 Navratilova moved out. Unable to afford the mansion alone, Brown moved to Los Angeles to work as a screenwriter for television and film. Her 1982 ABC series "I Love Liberty" (directed by Norman Lear) won an Emmy nomination for Best Variety Show in 1982. In 1985 she was again nominated for an Emmy for *The Long Hot Summer,* an NBC miniseries. Her film-script credits include *Sweet Surrender* (1986), *Table Dancing* (1987), and the unfortunate Roger Corman-produced film *Slumber Party Massacre* (her script, she insisted, was the true victim).

Eventually she moved back to Charlottesville and, on the basis of her frustrating experiences in trying to get a film of *Rubyfruit Jungle* produced, started American Artists Inc., a company that options novels for film and television. In 1992, after ten years of solitude, she began a much-publicized relationship with Judy Nelson, a former lover of Navratilova's who was suing the tennis star at the time.

As of this writing, Rita Mae Brown is still going strong, a prolific writer whose *Rubyfruit Jungle* remains one of the most popular accounts—and celebrations—of lesbian experience ever written. As one of the first lesbian novels with a happy ending, the book has influenced countless people, for whom it is often a first encounter with lesbian existence. Perhaps more important, its wide commercial availability has ensured that it has found its way into the hands of young lesbians and gays in the desert of the heartland who might otherwise never have come into contact with any gay literature. To them it has offered an invaluable and rousing message of hope.

75

Kate Millett

1934–

Kate Millett was born on September 14, 1934, in St. Paul, Minnesota. Her father was a contractor who absconded when Millett was fourteen. To support the family, her mother sold insurance. Millett attended the University of Minnesota, graduating magna cum laude in 1956. There followed two years of postgraduate work at St. Hilda's College, Oxford, for which she received first-class honors.

In 1961, Millett moved to Tokyo, where she taught English at Waseda University and sculpted. She married Fumio Yoshimura in 1965. On her return to the United States she became active in the civil rights movement and women's causes and in 1966 became one of the first members of the National Organization of Women (NOW). Her first publication, a pamphlet called *Token Learning* (1967), was a feminist attack on the curriculum at women's colleges. In 1968, while beginning work on her doctoral dissertation at Columbia University, she was hired as an instructor at Barnard College, but was fired at the end of her first semester because of her activism in student issues and women's rights. She completed her thesis and was awarded a PhD in English and comparative literature in March 1970. In August, her dissertation was published by Doubleday as *Sexual Politics*. Millett describes the work as "notes towards a theory of patriarchy." She began with the thesis: "Coitus can scarcely be said to take place in a vacuum; although of itself it appears a biological and physical activity, it is set so deeply within the larger context of human affairs that it serves as a charged microcosm of the variety of attitudes and values to which culture subscribes." Sex, in other words, is political. And likewise the oppression of women. By analyzing the various religious, literary, philosophic, and scientific arguments for the dominance of men over women, Millett exposed their biases, ungrounded assumptions, and internal contradictions. As specific examples she investigated what she called the "phallic supremacism" of three famous male "heterosexual" writers, D. H. Lawrence, Henry Miller, and Norman Mailer and contrasted their glorification of patriarchal values with radical subversion of the hierarchies of Western culture to be found in the work of the the gay writer JEAN GENET's [45]. Her work galvanized feminists across the country and sold eighty thousand copies in the first six months—impressive sales figures for a PhD dissertation.

Sexual Politics made Millett a star—and also a target of male outrage and anxiety. She was roundly attacked by male reviewers. Irving Howe fumed, in words that say much about *his* unexamined assumptions, "There are times when one feels the book was written by a female impersonator." But attacks like these were only the beginning.

As recounted by Sidney Abbott and Bernice Love in *Sappho Was a Right-On Woman*, trouble had been brewing within the ranks of NOW for some time over the issue of lesbianism, which RITA MAE BROWN [74] had been instrumental in raising. At the Second Congress to Unite Women in 1970, Brown and about twenty other women disrupted the proceedings. Calling themselves the Lavender Menace, they took over the stage and charged the women's movement with discriminating against lesbians. Then they called on women sympathetic to their cause to join them onstage. The microphone was declared open. Millett—who was well known to the crowd not only as the author of *Sexual Politics* but as chair of the Education Committee of the New York chapter of NOW—took the microphone and declared, "I know what these women are talking about. I was there. In some ways I still am." It was the first time she had spoken publicly about her sexuality.

Soon thereafter, while serving as a panelist at a forum on sexual liberation sponsored by Gay People at Columbia, Millett was challenged by a woman from the group called Third World Gay Revolution, who asked her, "Why don't you say you're a lesbian, here openly. You've said you were a lesbian in the past…"

Millett repeated what she had said earlier on the panel: that she was bisexual. The activist Wendy Wonderful chimed in to say, "I'm bisexual, but it is for my homosexuality that I'm oppressed. Therefore I say I'm a lesbian as a political statement." Millett answered, "Yes, I understand that. I, too, am oppressed for being a lesbian, not for being heterosexual."

What no one knew at the time was that a reporter from *Time* magazine had taped the entire proceeding. The December 8, 1970, issue of the magazine carried a story entitled "Women's Lib: A Second Look," which asked, "Can the feminists think clearly? Do they know anything about biology? What about their maturity, their morality, their sexuality? Ironically, Kate Millett herself contributed to the growing skepticism about the movement by acknowledging at a recent meeting that she is bisexual. The disclosure is bound to discredit her as a spokeswoman for her cause, cast further doubt on her theories, and reinforce the views of those skeptics who routinely dismiss all liberationists as Lesbians."

Although some NOW leaders such as Betty Friedan were vociferous in their denunciation of lesbians in the movement (the lesbian issue was a "lavender herring," "a diversion" from the movement's "true" goals), other NOW activists such as Ti Grace-Atkinson, Gloria Steinem, and Susan Brownmiller rose to defend Millett at a widely covered press conference. When they returned to their individual chapters, however, they were told they had acted inappropriately. A proposal was introduced in the New York chapter stipulating that anyone who spoke on the lesbian issue would no longer be permitted to identify herself as a member of NOW. The proposal was only narrowly defeated. In elections in January 1971, the leadership of the New York chapter was purged for having supported Millett and Brown. Although NOW reversed its stance some eight months later and issued a statement recognizing lesbian concerns as legitimate feminist concerns, the purge left many lesbians bitter about what they saw as betrayal at the hands of their straight comrades. Nevertheless, Millett's—and Brown's—courageous stands as lesbians forced the women's movement to confront the issue of lesbianism, and to recognize that many of their most valued colleagues were in fact lesbian. It was a critical turning point for the women's movement.

Millett went on to write frankly and openly about her sexuality in such autobiographical works as *Flying* (1974), *Sita* (1977), and *The Loony Bin Trip* (1990), this last book an account of attempts to regain control of her life after being diagnosed a manic-depressive. She now lives at the Women's Art Colony Farm, which she founded, outside Poughkeepsie, New York. Her intellectual and emotional honesty over the years has made her one of the most visible figures in the struggle for women's—and lesbian—rights.

76

Martina Navratilova

1956–

Martina Navratilova was born on October 18, 1956, in Prague, Czechoslovakia. Her parents were divorced when she was three, and she was raised by her mother, a ski instructor, who remarried in 1961. Navratilova's stepfather, a tennis instructor, encouraged her in the sport, and by the age of ten she was playing every day. She also played ice hockey and soccer with the local boys.

In the midsixties her stepfather began entering her in summer tournaments around Czechoslovakia, and she started taking lessons with one of the country's most eminent players, George Parma. Her lessons with Parma came to an abrupt end in 1968, when the Soviet Union invaded Czechoslovakia, and Parma, who was in Austria at the time, elected not to return.

In 1969, Navratilova went to West Germany as part of a tennis-club exchange program. The visit was eye-opening: "My first trip out confirmed my suspicion that the West had a style and a freedom that communism couldn't match," she reported in her 1985 autobiography, *Martina*. After a series of attention-getting wins in Germany, she returned home with a reputation

and a large collection of felt-tipped pens, a commodity impossible to find in Czechoslovakia. At the age of fifteen she was
invited to play at Prague's Sparta Club, one of the most famous
sports clubs in Czechoslovakia. A series of tours to other East
Bloc countries in the early seventies—Bulgaria, Hungary, the
Soviet Union (where she was impressed by how much worse
things were than in Czechoslovakia)—made her more well known
abroad than at home.

In 1973 she was granted permission to play the winter circuit
in the United States. Another U.S. tour followed in 1974, during
which she met Fred Barman, a Beverly Hills business manager,
who convinced her to let him represent her—a move that caused
some bitterness back in Czechoslovakia, where people began to
speak of the "Americanization of Martina." On her part,
Navratilova was particularly galled by having to turn over all her
winnings—in American currency—to the Czech Tennis
Federation.

She began to think of defecting, and in August 1975, while at
the U.S. Open in New York, she had Fred Barman contact the
New York office of the Immigration and Naturalization Service.
She stressed that she was not defecting for political reasons, but
rather because "I just want to play the tour, whenever I want and
wherever I want."

In response, the Czech Federation issued a statement: "Martina Navratilova has suffered a defeat in the face of the Czecho-
slovak society. Navratilova had all possibilities in Czechoslovakia
to develop her talent, but she preferred a professional career and
a fat bank account."

One of the developments in Navratilova's new life in America was her realization that she was attracted to women. "When it
finally happened," she reports, "it was with somebody older than
me, a woman I met in the States, and it seemed so natural. I was
pretty much a rookie with women, and I'm shy anyway, so it took
forever for me to get the hints she was throwing at me. Finally,
the way she put it, I was invited over to snuggle, and it went on
from there. She knew what she was doing. I don't remember any
flowers and candlelight, but I do remember feeling relaxed and
happy being there with her, waiting for the next step. When it
finally happened, I said, this is easy and right. And the next
morning—*voilà*—I had an outright, head-over-heels case of infatuation with her."

The affair lasted six months. Other loves followed, including a three-year relationship with Sandra Haynie, with whom she shared a house in Dallas, and who replaced Barman as her manager. Meanwhile, Navratilova had risen to the top of the tennis world. Her 1978 win at Wimbledon made her the number one ranked player in the world, breaking Chris Evert's four-year domination of the sport. That same year, she met novelist RITA MAE BROWN [74], and the two began an intense but short-lived affair. As Brown characterized it afterward: "Some relationships are a marathon and some are a sprint. Ours was more like a sprint." According to Navratilova, Brown made it "clear from the start that she didn't care whether or not I was a great tennis player. Her attitude was almost the opposite: it's only sports. She would say, 'Sports are just to keep your mind off everything else and they don't enhance culture or the mind.'" Such tensions tore the relationship apart. In light of the palimony suit filed against tennis star Billie Jean King by Marilyn Barnett, and the rumor that Avon, a major tennis sponsor, was about to pull out because it didn't want to be associated with homosexuality, Navratilova began to worry how her sexuality might affect both her career and her pending application for U.S. citizenship. She was granted citizenship without incident in 1981, and shortly thereafter the *New York Daily News* ran an interview with her (done earlier but withheld) in which she publicly discussed her relationship with Brown.

Navratilova's private life since then has, unfortunately, been more or less constant fodder for the tabloids: one of the prices of celebrity in a free-press society. She has borne up under these assaults with dignity, and she is ranked here because of her influence as the most highly visible lesbian sports celebrity. Her relationship with RITA MAE BROWN [74] was the most widely talked-about lesbian love affair of recent times (with the possible exception of the pseudoromance between MADONNA [99] and Sandra Bernhardt), and this pairing of two highly successful and attractive women generated positive and widely disseminated images of women loving women. Furthermore, Martina Navratilova's spectacular tennis career—nine singles wins at Wimbledon, four at the U.S. Open, and countless others—has made her a role model for many aspiring women athletes, both lesbian and straight.

77

Barbara Gittings

1932–

Barbara Gittings was born in 1932 in Vienna, Austria, where her father was in the U.S. diplomatic corps. She was educated in Catholic schools in Montreal, Canada. Enrolling at Northwestern University in Evanston to study theater, she became the target in her freshmen year of rumors that she was a lesbian because of her friendship with another female student. The incident led her to realize gradually that she was, indeed, different from others. In a 1974 interview with Jonathan Katz, Gittings recalled: "I went to a psychiatrist in Chicago and told her about myself, and she said, 'Yes, you are a homosexual.' And then she offered to 'cure' me. I didn't have the money for that, so I didn't go back to her. Some people say, 'She shouldn't have given you a label.' I disagree. I think she did me an enormous service, because once I said, 'Yes, that's me, that's what I am,' I was able to work with it. I had been living throughout my high school years and first few months of college with this hazy feeling: 'I don't quite know what's happening to me.' It was a fog of confusion. Now I had something clearcut I could come to grips with. So I stopped going to classes, I started going to the library to find out what it meant to be homosexual." She went through dictionaries, encyclopedias, the chapters in medical textbooks called "abnormal psychology" and "sexual deviations" and "sexual perversions." As she put it: "The overall impression I got was: I must be the kind of person they're talking about, because I am homosexual, and they're describing homosexuals, but I don't recognize much of myself in this."

Having flunked out of college, she returned to her parents' Philadelphia home in disgrace, took a clerical job, and spent her spare time going to the public library and secondhand bookstores. It was in one of the latter that she found and bought a copy of *The Well of Loneliness* by RADCLYFFE HALL [28]. For the first time she was reading something in which she could begin to recognize herself.

When her father found her copy of the book, he wrote her a letter (he couldn't bring himself actually to speak to her about it) telling her to dispose of the book—not by giving it away, since that would contaminate someone else, but by burning it. As she recalled: "Well, I simply hid it better." In search of some kind of community, she found other lesbian novels—by Rosamund Lehmann and Compton MacKenzie and Colette—and she also started going to lesbian bars, though she felt alienated by the butch-femme roles still prevalent in the bar culture of the 1950s. On the advice of Donald Corey, whose *The Homosexual in America* she had read, and who had told her about the existence of the Mattachine Society, she traveled to San Francisco in 1956. There she discovered the Daughters of Bilitis, an organization that had recently been founded by Del Martin and Phyllis Lyon.

The Daughters of Bilitis (DOB) defined itself as "A Woman's Organization for the Purpose of Promoting the Integration of the Homosexual into Society." The word *lesbian* was cautiously avoided. The name of the organization, which was meant to sound like "any other women's lodge," derived from a nineteenth-century collection of poems called *Les chansons de Bilitis* by Pierre Louÿs—supposedly they were translations from the ancient Greek of the work of Bilitis, a sixth-century-B.C. woman from Pamphylia who had journeyed to Lesbos in order to be a disciple of SAPPHO [2]. The DOB had a four-part statement of purpose:

1. Education of the variant...to enable her to understand herself and make her adjustment to society.
2. Education of the public...leading to an eventual breakdown of erroneous taboos and prejudices.
3. Participation in research projects by duly authorized and responsible....experts directed toward further knowledge of the homosexual.
4. Investigation of the penal code as it pertains to the homosexual, proposal of changes...and promotion of these changes through the due process of law in the state legislatures.

When she returned to New York in 1958, Gittings established the New York chapter of the DOB and served as its president for the next three years. In 1962 she was named editor of *The Ladder*, the monthly publication of the DOB. Frustrated by the DOB's general timidity, especially by their habit of inviting homophobic "experts" to speak to them about lesbianism, Gittings took the opportunity to retool *The Ladder* into a much more militant publication. She began to use the word *lesbian* on the magazine's cover, published photos of lesbians taken by her lover, Kay Tobin, whom she had met at a DOB picnic in 1961. In her "Living Propaganda" series, she urged women to come out. Not unexpectedly, she began to antagonize more conservative members of the DOB, especially after the DOB's 1964 convention when she tried to convince the membership that "the only authorities on homosexuality as a way of feeling and living...are homosexuals themselves." She was in particular a great defender of Frank Kameny, the Mattachine renegade who was making waves by urging gays and lesbians to "move away from the comfortingly detached respectability of research into the often less pleasant rough-and-tumble of political and social activism."

In 1966, Gittings was ousted as editor of *The Ladder* by the conservative leadership of the DOB. She and Kay Tobin, left the DOB and went on to work closely with the Homophile Action League while the DOB, which had been for a while a guiding light for lesbians, slowly faded into political irrelevance. After the epochal events at STONEWALL [5] in 1969, Gittings, Tobin, and other activists of their generation were suddenly seen as dinosaurs by the newly formed and militant Gay Liberation Alliance (GLA). While Tobin went on to become one of the founding members of the Gay Activists' Alliance (GAA), Gittings shifted the focus of her activism to the American Library Association, where for fifteen years she worked on the ALA's Gay Task Force. Her ongoing project was, in her words, "to get gay literature into the libraries and into the hands of readers." Along with the redoubtable Frank Kameny, she also lobbied the American Psychiatric Association to drop its listing of homosexuality as a mental illness. When the association did so in 1973, a Philadelphia newspaper story ran the headline, "Twenty Million Homosexuals Gain Instant Cure."

In semi-retirement from movement politics, Barbara Gittings and Kay Tobin (now Kay Lahusen) live together in West

Philadelphia, where Gittings works as a free-lance typist and her companion of thirty years as a real estate agent.

Along with Del Martin and Phyllis Lyon, the founders of the Daughters of Bilitis, Barbara Gittings was one of the formative influences on the early political organization of lesbians in the 1950s and 60s. Her courageous works laid the foundations for later gay organizations—organizations that, all-too-often, have tended to devalue the contributions of those who made them possible in the first place.

78

Martin Duberman

1930–

Martin Bauml Duberman was born on August 6, 1930, in New York City. His father was a Jewish immigrant from the Ukraine, his mother a second-generation Jewish American. As a teenager, Duberman was passionately interested in the theater and even toured with an acting company when he was seventeen, but at his parents' urging he abandoned the idea of a theatrical career. He attended Yale University, from which he graduated Phi Beta Kappa in 1952, and Harvard University, from which he received an MA in 1953 and a PhD in 1957. He returned to Yale as an instructor of history and spent the next five years there. The publication, in 1961, of his revised dissertation, *Charles Francis Adams, 1807–1886,* garnered him a coveted Bancroft Prize (1962) and an assistant professorship at Princeton.

Then he did something rebellious. He began writing plays—
and successful ones at that. His 1963 play, *In White America*,
received rave reviews and the Vernon Rice/Drama Desk Award as
Best Off-Broadway Production.

In 1965 he was promoted to the rank of associate professor
with tenure, and in 1967, after his scholarly biography *James
Russell Lowell* was nominated for a National Book Award, he
became full professor at Princeton.

So much for his academic success story, the public evidence
of his worthiness. In his 1991 autobiography, *Cures: A Gay Man's
Odyssey*, Duberman relates his private, more tortured progress
through life. By the age of twenty-one, his sexual experience had
consisted, as he puts it, of "two blow jobs and two panic attacks."
In graduate school at Harvard, however, he started cruising in
earnest—though not without great guilt. He writes, "I couldn't
shake my mother's ancient injunction *never* to walk through a
park alone for fear of the sick people who lingered within: I had
become the person my mother had warned me about." A series of
mostly short-lived affairs were accompanied by long sessions of
therapy. This therapy, Duberman writes, "would take me to the
brink not of reconstruction but of near-negation. It would so
thoroughly undermine my ability to accept my own nature
that...I would become nearly as homophobic as the culture
itself." Finally, in 1970, in a burst of cathartic energy, he termi-
nated his involvement with therapy: "As I can see in retrospect, a
necessary prelude to becoming an activist myself was taking some
of the anger I vengefully turned inward and putting it where it
belonged—on a repressive culture, and on [my therapist] as its
representative."

The break was decisive and was reflected in both his
personal and professional lives. His plays—in which he had
gradually edged his way toward sexual honesty through the
1960s—began more and more to treat gay themes openly, as in
Payments (1971), an exploration of the world of gay male hustling.
His scholarly work also grew more innovative. The next big
academic project he undertook was a history of Black Mountain
College (1933–56), the experimental community in North Carolina that was in many ways a precursor to the counterculture
that emerged in the 1960s. Duberman writes: "Influenced by the
counterculture myself, I wanted to write what I viewed as a more
honestly subjective kind of history, wanted to let the reader see

the process whereby a particular person grappled with a particular subject and body of evidence. As I was later to write in the introduction to my book, 'My conviction is that when a historian allows more of himself to show—his feelings, fantasies, needs, not merely his skills at information-retrieval, organization and analysis—he is *less* likely to contaminate the data, simply because there is less pretense that he and it are one.'"

Black Mountain: An Exploration of Community was published in 1972. One result of Duberman's approach to his materials was the following admission, during a discussion of gay theater director Bob Wunsch's expulsion from Black Mountain after an arrest for indecent exposure: "It's hard to think well of a place that could cooperate as fully as Black Mountain did in an individual's self-destruction—indeed to have assumed it as foreclosed. But perhaps I exaggerate—a function of my own indignation as a homosexual, a potential victim."

His coming out in print released howls of disapproval: as the *American Historical Review* wrote, "Duberman has thrown the cardinal principles of historical writing to the wind by letting himself get 'personally involved' with his subject." Duberman responded by plunging into the gay activism he had previously withheld himself from: together with fellow scholars Jonathan Katz, Seymour Kleinberg, and Bert Hansen, he established the Gay Academic Union. He sat on the founding board of directors of the National Gay and Lesbian Task Force. He also published widely on gay topics, including an influential article in the *New York Times Book Review* in which he surveyed the history of "scientific" fraudulence and social oppression with regard to gays and lesbians. His groundbreaking scholarly works on gay themes include *About Time: Exploring the Gay Past* (1986), *Hidden from History: Reclaiming the Gay and Lesbian Past* (1989), which he coedited with Martha Vicinus and George Chauncey, Jr., and *Stonewall* (1993). A tireless scholar, he is also author of *Visions of Kerouac* (1977) and the highly acclaimed *Paul Robeson* (1989).

Having resigned from Princeton in 1971 to become Distinguished Professor of History at Lehman College, the City University of New York, Duberman founded CLAGS—the Center for Lesbian and Gay Studies—at the Graduate Center in Manhattan. The first program of its kind in the country, CLAGS sponsors public events and conferences, a regular monthly research colloquium, and research grants to faculty and graduate students.

In the burgeoning field of gay and lesbian studies, Martin Duberman stands as one of the great pioneers. When a historian of his sterling reputation began writing gay history, the act lent great credence to the fledgling field. Historians of every stripe now had to pay attention. More and more, gay and lesbian studies is accepted as an integral and respectable part of the curriculum. Almost singlehandedly, it has at times seemed, Duberman has worked to institutionalize the field within the mainstream academy. If gay and lesbian studies has become a permanent and important part of our collective intellectual life, it is due in no small degree to the unflagging work of Martin Duberman.

79

Gloria Anzaldúa

1942–

Cherrie Moraga

1952–

Gloria Anzaldúa was born on September 26, 1942, on a ranch called Jesus Maria of the Valley in South Texas. Her parents never went to high school; her mother was sixteen when she gave birth to her daughter. Anzaldúa lived on the ranch till she was eleven, when her family moved to Hargill, Texas, a town with "one signal light and thirteen bars and thirteen churches and maybe two minimarts." Her father died when she was fifteen, and the family was forced to go back into the fields to work. They spent a year on the road as migrant laborers, traveling from

South Valley to Arkansas, but then returned to South Texas so the children—especially the boys—could go to school. The boys dropped out, however, and it was Anzaldúa who ended up getting an education—"the only woman, not just the only woman, but the only person from the area who ever went to college." In 1969 she received her BA from Pan American University, followed in 1972 by an MA in English and education from the University of Texas at Austin. She began working as a summer high-school teacher for children of migrant families, traveling with them from Texas to Indiana, where she was hired to teach for a year and a half.

Between 1974 and 1977 she took graduate courses in comparative literature at the University of Texas. When she was rejected as a dissertation candidate because she wanted to write on Chicano or feminist issues, she transferred to the University of California at Santa Cruz to concentrate on feminist theory and cultural studies. In 1979–80 she was a lecturer at San Francisco State. While working for a national feminist writers organization, she met Cherrie Moraga, another Chicana lesbian almost exactly ten years her junior.

Cherrie Moraga was born on September 25, 1952, in Whittier, California. The daughter of a Chicana and an Anglo, she studied at a small, nonsectarian private college in Hollywood and earned her BA in 1974. For the next three years she worked as a high-school teacher in Los Angeles. During this time she enrolled in a writing class at the Women's Building and produced her first lesbian love poems. Her discovery of the poem "A Woman Is Talking to Death" by JUDY GRAHN [91] coalesced in her the need to write not only as a lesbian but as a Chicana, and this politicization was further enhanced by her subsequent meeting with Grahn in person. In 1977, Moraga moved to San Francisco, and in 1980 received an MA from San Francisco State.

In 1981, she and Gloria Anzaldúa coedited the anthology *This Bridge Called My Back: Writings by Radical Women of Color.* The project stemmed from Anzaldúa's attendance at a women's retreat, where she was made to feel "an outsider, the poor relative, the token woman of color." Two months after that experience—in April 1979—she and Moraga sent out a letter soliciting contributions to their proposed anthology. In it they wrote, "We want to express to all women—especially to white middle-class women— the experiences which divide us as feminists; we want to examine incidents of intolerance, prejudice and denial of differences within the feminist movement. We intend to explore the causes and sources of, and solutions to, these divisions. We want to create a definition that expands what 'feminist' means to us."

Unable to find a publisher for the book, Moraga cofounded, along with black lesbian feminist activist Barbara Smith, Kitchen Table/Women of Color Press in New York, the only press in the United States devoted to publishing works by women of color. The anthology was awarded the American Book Award from the Before Columbus Foundation and quickly found a widespread readership, both among women of color and in women's studies classrooms across the country.

According to critic Yvonne Yarbro-Bajarano, "it is difficult to overestimate the timeliness and importance of *This Bridge Called My Back* in the 1980s because it coincided with the coalescing of the organizing activity of women of color, particularly lesbians of color, at the same time that it helped coalesce that activism. The book grew from the need of women of color to express their rage and frustration with the racism and classism of the predominantly white feminist movement. At the same time, it marked the emergence of new connection among Chicanas, Latinas, Afro-American, Native-American and Asian-American women, firmly establishing the term 'woman of color' in the political vocabulary.... *This Bridge Called My Back* was a catalyst in the process of bringing women of color together." The anthology includes, in addition to work by Moraga, Anzaldúa, and Smith, essays and poetry by AUDRE LORDE [52], Pat Parker, Cheryl Clarke, Merle Woo, and Barbara Cameron of the Lakota nation.

Since *This Bridge Called My Back,* Anzaldúa's most important work has been *Borderlands/La Frontera: the New Mestiza* (1987). She writes, "Theory doesn't have to be written in an abstract and convoluted language. Writers like myself are considered low theorists, and writings like *Borderlands* are considered 'low theory'...because it's accessible, people can understand it. It's got narrative, it's got poetry and I do the unforgivable—I mix genres."

Likewise mixing genres is Moraga's 1983 work *Loving in the War Years: Lo que nunca pasó por sus labios.* The first published book of writing by an avowed Chicana lesbian, it explores, in powerful and original language, her multiple identities as Chicana, feminist, and lesbian. Her other work includes the plays *La extranjera*

(1985), *Giving Up the Ghost: Teatro in 2 Acts* (1986), *Shadow of a Man* (1988), and *Heroes and Saints* (1989). She also edited, with Alma Gómez and Mariana Romo-Carmona, *Cuentos: Stories by Latinas,* published in 1983 by Kitchen Table/Women of Color Press.

Gloria Anzaldúa's and Cherrie Moraga's pathbreaking work created an important space in which women of color could, for the first time, articulate their complex identities. As they wrote in their introduction to *This Bridge Called My Back,* "we see this book as a revolutionary tool falling into the hands of people of all colors. Just as we have been radicalized in the process of compiling this book, we hope it will radicalize others into action." It is for this revolutionary tool, this life-changing gift of voice, that Anzaldúa and Moraga are included in this ranking.

80

Mary Renault

1905–1983

Mary Renault (pronounced Ren-OLT) was born Mary Challans on September 4, 1905, in London. The daughter of middle-class parents, she was a tomboy who read voraciously, especially the works of ancient writers. She studied classics with Gilbert Murray at St. Hugh's College, Oxford, and nursing at Radclyffe Infirmary.

After graduating, she worked as a nurse in a series of hospitals, and it was in one of these hospitals, in 1934, that she met a fellow nurse named Julie Mullard. The two women fell in love and lived together until Renault's death forty-nine years later.

In 1939, Renault published her first novel, *Purposes of Love*, a tale of love between two hospital nurses. It was at this time, in order to spare her parents the supposed shame and embarrassment of her subject matter, that she adopted her pseudonym Renault—from the name of a character in one of her favorite plays, the restoration drama *Venice Preserv'd*. Despite, or perhaps because of its theme, *Purposes of Love* was a popular success in England and was followed by other novels written during her off-duty time while serving as a nurse during World War II.

In 1948, Renault's novel *Return to Night* won a $150,000 prize from Metro-Goldwyn-Mayer—the largest financial award in literature at the time. This windfall allowed her and Mullard to leave England and move to South Africa—to take advantage of the better climate. The money was soon lost in a real estate scam, but income from Renault's novels managed to support the two, and she and Mullard moved into a beach house near Cape Town. Despite extensive travel elsewhere—particularly in Greece—Renault never returned to England. In South Africa, she was a member of the Progressive Party and an opponent of apartheid.

In 1953 she wrote the last of her so-called "English" novels, *The Charioteer*, a frank and moving depiction of a young man's homosexual love that went unpublished in America for six years because her publisher, William Morrow, feared that his company might be prosecuted for indecency. It was finally published in the United States in 1959 by Pantheon. By that time, though, many copies had been smuggled into this country by admirers, and the novel had gained a wide underground readership.

After *The Charioteer*, Renault turned her attention to her primary love, the ancient world. Her novels *The King Must Die* (1958) and *The Bull From the Sea* (1962) took as their setting the ancient Minoan civilization and retold the legend of Theseus. Her next two works, *The Last of the Wine* (1956) and *The Mask of Apollo* (1966) concerned themselves with the classical Athens of SOCRATES [1] and Plato. And in her enormously successful trilogy *Fire From Heaven* (1970), *The Persian Boy* (1972), and *Funeral Games* (1981), she told the unexpurgated story of ALEXANDER THE GREAT [14], including his love for his comrade Hephaestion and the eunuch Bagoas. Alexander's character was supposedly modeled in part on a young gay actor Renault was friends with in Cape Town. Mary Renault died on December 13, 1983, in Cape Town, South Africa.

Renault's historical novels are scrupulous in their research and vivid in their imagined textures. Taken together, they represent a remarkable and sustained vision of the classical past. Perhaps most striking is Renault's refusal to "modernize" her characters. She allows them their historical moment, recounting without twentieth-century judgment all their splendors and passions—especially their homosexuality, which she renders with appealing frankness and lyric grace. It is this sympathetic and convincing treatment of homosexual love (male homosexual love, ironically) that earns Mary Renault her ranking in this list.

Although it has been widely known through history that Alexander loved men, conventional biographers had usually been skittish about the subject. It was Mary Renault who, for our century, brilliantly rehabilitated ALEXANDER THE GREAT [14] not so much as the military genius and innovative statesman he undoubtedly was—*that* had already been done—but as a man who loved men.

A figure comparable to Mary Renault, though less well known, especially in the United States, and hence less influential, is Marguerite Yourcenar, also a lesbian, whose moving and eloquent *Memoirs of Hadrian*—more purely literary in intent than Renault's work—does for the Roman Emperor HADRIAN [15] and his beloved Antinous what *The Persian Boy* does for Alexander and Bagoas.

81

Francis Bacon

1909–1992

Francis Bacon—"that man who paints those dreadful pictures," as British Prime Minister Margaret Thatcher once called him— was born on October 28, 1909, in Dublin, Ireland, the son of a horse trainer. Because of his asthma he was mostly educated at home by private tutors. When he was sixteen, his parents discovered that he had had sex with several of the grooms in the stable. When they caught him trying on his mother's underwear, he was banished from home. He fled to London, where he was drawn to the art scene. The Australian painter Roy de Maistre, fifteen years older than Bacon, became his lover and mentor, and Bacon began to paint. In 1930, he and de Maistre mounted an exhibition in the South Kensington garage that Bacon used as a studio.

For the next several years after that, Bacon floated between London and Paris and Berlin, hanging out in transvestite bars with various gangsters and toughs, and painting and selling furniture and rugs of his own design. Little remains from that period since he destroyed most of his early work, preferring to live in more or less complete obscurity. An exhibit in 1945, featuring his triptych "Three Studies for Figures at the Base of a Crucifixion," shocked the art world and put him on the map overnight.

His canvases were—and have remained—controversial. Much of his painting was based on works by old masters. His series of "screaming popes," for example, of which his "Study of Velázquez's Pope Innocent X" (1953) is perhaps the most famous, wrenched the original images of the seventeenth-century Spanish painter Diego Velázquez into anguished, horrifying new forms that are shockingly expressive of our dark century. In one study, a shrieking pontiff is trapped in a glass cage. In another, he is flanked by butchered ox carcasses out of Rembrandt. Although seen as owing much to Picasso, surrealism, and German expressionism, Bacon always maintained that he was simply a realist: "You can't be more horrible than life itself."

Bacon described his technique thus: "You don't know how the hopelessness in one's working will make one just take paint and just do almost anything to get out of the formula of making a kind of illustrative image—I mean, I just wipe it all over with a rag or use a brush or rub it with something or anything or throw turpentine and paint and everything else into the thing."

Although his works eventually sold for millions, Bacon continued to live and paint in a cramped, shabby apartment in South Kensington, London. Painting for him was never so much a vocation as a vacation from his real interests—gambling, boys, and swilling champagne at the Colony room, a run-down Soho drinking club.

In 1964 he fell in love with George Dyer, and the two were together for seven years, until Dyer's death in Paris in 1971 of an overdose of brandy and sleeping pills. Bacon's great "Triptych May–June 1972" takes this death as its subject: in one flanking panel the blurred, distorted figure of Dyer sits on the toilet; in the other, he vomits into a sink. The central panel shows him disappearing in blackness.

The novelist David Plante offers us this glimpse of Bacon and a later lover, an electrician named Bill. The scene is a dark, smoky bar in London:

> Francis kept giving Bill twenty-pound notes to buy
> bottles of champagne. We talked a lot about sex. Bill

said he liked to be fucked, fist-fucked, and he also liked, from time to time, "G.B.H." Nikos asked, "What's that?" "Grievous bodily harm," Bill said, and smiled his smile. "And you've had it?" Francis asked him. "Only a couple of times," Bill said. "Real welts and weals?" Francis asked. "Oh, yes," Bill answered.... "Well," Francis said, "I like a little G.B.H. now and then. I had a friend—he finally killed himself—who had a collection of whips he kept at my place. A while ago, I took someone there who said he was interested in whips, and I showed him the collection." Francis laughed. "Well, I undressed and got on my fish-net stockings—" "Black?" Nikos asked. "Of course black, stupid," Francis said. "And he started to beat me. But he got carried away. He wouldn't stop. I'm a total coward. In nothing but my black fish-net stockings, I ran out into Reece Mews." He laughed loudly.

Bacon was offered a knighthood, but refused.

"I believe in an ordered chaos," he once proclaimed, "the strict rules of chance."

On April 28, 1992, while vacationing in Madrid, Spain, he suffered a heart attack and died.

Bacon has been criticized for recycling a handful of obsessive images, but such criticism misses the point. Unquestionably the greatest British painter of the second half of the twentieth century, he is the author of powerful, unforgettable images. His subject was almost invariably, and unflinchingly, the body—the unbearable stigma of the body, its merciless attractions and visceral repulsions. In a century that has seen the corpses pile up, his was a searing visual conscience that was also unapologetically gay. He moved, with great wit and courage and provocative desperation, outside the norms. "I am an optimist," he declared, "but about nothing." Next to the ferocity and grandeur of Francis Bacon's vision, other openly identified gay artists of stature such as David Hockney, Gilbert and George, Duane Michaels, and even the adventurous Robert Mapplethorpe pale in comparison. They may have had their moment—especially Mapplethorpe—but I hazard to predict that it is Bacon whose influence will loom by far the largest when the history of art in the twentieth century is written.

82

Derek Jarman

1942–1994

Derek Jarman was born on January 31, 1942. His father was an ace Royal Air Force bomber pilot who became, after the war, the director of Engineering Industries Associated. The family lived in Italy and Pakistan before settling in Northwood, Middlesex. Jarman wanted to go to art school, but his father wanted him to get a university education: in the end, a compromise was effected. Jarman attended King's College, London, where he studied art history, history, and English, and after graduating studied art at the Slade School. He did well there, and his paintings showed in several exhibitions, including one at the Tate. He also began doing stage designs, including *Jazz Calendar* for the Royal Ballet in 1968 and *Don Giovanni* for the English National Opera that same year.

Up until the age of twenty-one, Jarman had thought he was, in his words, "the only queer in the world." But in that year he had his first gay affair and after that flung himself into the life. In his 1991 memoir, *Modern Nature*, he wrote, "When I was young, society seemed so totally restrictive I found that the time I did not spend on the piers or bath-houses seemed wasted. The heterosexuality of everyday life enveloped and asphyxiated me."

In 1971, the film director Ken Russell asked Jarman to design the sets for his film *The Devils*. The experience sparked Jarman's interest in the cinema, and he began to make super-8 home movies of his friends. In 1976 his first film, *Sebastiane*, was a controversial success. Complete with Latin dialogue, English subtitles, and steamy homoerotic imagery, the film told the story of the Roman centurion Sebastian who, exiled from Diocletian's orgiastic court to a farflung outpost for refusing to bed down the emperor, experiences visions in the form of a leopard boy and is eventually martyred for his newfound Christianity by his scantily clad colleagues. This was a director who was clearly never going to Hollywood. But Jarman was interested in other things. "My films," he told interviewer Lynn Barber, "are a message of solidarity to people who have been dispossessed. Because when I made *Sebastiane*, there was no way of imaging yourself as gay, you couldn't even see gays on television, so how did you come to terms with yourself?"

Sebastiane was followed by *Jubilee* (1978), *The Tempest* (1979), *The Dream Machine* (1982), *Imagining October* (1984), *The Angelic Conversation* (1985), and *Caravaggio* (1986)—all visually arresting, often hallucinatory adventures in the cinema, and all made on the shoestring budget he became famous for. "All my films were made for peanuts," he told Lynn Barber. "I can promise you that every film I made has been the cheapest film of its year and that is why I have been so lucky as to be able to make so many." Also contributing to his prolific output: "I don't suffer from perfectionism. The thing is you mustn't be precious about things, and then you can get a lot done."

On December 22, 1986, while working on *The Last of England* (1987), Jarman was diagnosed as HIV-positive. A month later he made the diagnosis public, even though friends advised him against it since it would make him uninsurable as a director. But as he recorded in his diary: "I had no choice, I've always hated secrets—the canker that destroys." After finishing his next film,

War Requiem (1989), a treatment of the pacifist masterpiece by
BENJAMIN BRITTEN [73], Jarman announced that he was leaving
film to live a hermit's life at his cottage at Dungeness. In the
shadow of a nuclear power plant he cultivated his herb garden
and contemplated mortality—a task that became the subject of
his next film, *The Garden*. While editing that film, however, his
health broke, and he spent most of 1990 in the hospital fighting
several near-fatal illnesses. He recovered to film *Edward II* (1991),
based on the play by CHRISTOPHER MARLOWE [19], and *Wittgens-
tein*, based on the life of the gay philosopher. He also became an
increasingly visible political leader in the fight against Clause 28,
the infamous 1990 British law that recategorized a number of
consensual gay activities into the same class as rape, thus making
them imprisonable offenses. When the gay actor IAN MCKELLEN
[97] accepted a knighthood in 1991, Jarman bitterly and publicly
attacked him, arguing that gays should not accept honors from a
government committed to oppressing them. Jarman was also
outspoken in his support of OUTrage, the group dedicated to
outing closeted homosexuals, especially members of Parliament.

In 1993, nearly blind from AIDS, he made his final film.
Dedicated to "all true lovers," *Blue* consists of nothing but a
screen of unvarying blue for an hour and a half. "Blue," Jarman
explains, "transcends the solid geometry of human limits." A
voice speaks: "You say to the boy, open your eyes." What follows is
extraordinary: words and music overlap to create the filmmaker's
final confrontation with blindness, with death, with life and love
and the universe. Film critic Paul Julian Smith wrote in *Sight and
Sound:* "At once the most English and the most European of
British filmmakers, Jarman since his first features *Sebastiane*
(1976) and *Jubilee* (1978) has addressed himself alternately to the
decadent state of the UK and to the promise of a mythic
Mediterranean, all light and sensuality. This double focus recurs
in *Blue*, where the horrifying and sometimes grimly humorous
account of Jarman's treatment in London hospitals is juxtaposed
with rapturous fantasies of blue boys on sunlit beaches, of
'ultramarine' strangers bearing exotic gifts."

Derek Jarman died of complications from AIDS on February 19, 1994, at St. Bartholomew's Hospital in London. In his
journal entry for September 13, 1989, he had written, "As I sweat
it out in the early hours, a 'guilty victim' of the scourge, I want to
bear witness how happy I am, and will be until the day I die, that I

was part of the hated sexual revolution; and that I don't regret a single step or encounter I made in that time."

No filmmaker—not PIER PAOLO PASOLINI nor Rainer Werner Fassbinder nor Pedro Almodovar—has been so unstintingly and visibly gay as Derek Jarman. Both his life and his work have played themselves out on the cutting edge of our time. What makes Jarman's legacy so influential is that he has been able to become well-known and respected as a director without compromising his gay sensibility one bit. Though quite different from them in temperament, he opened the door for younger gay filmmakers such as Gus van Sant, Todd Haines, and Greg Araki.

83

Alan Turing

1912–1954

Alan Mathison Turing was conceived in Chatrapur, India, where his father was in the British civil service, and born on June 23, 1912, in London. His parents soon returned to India, farming Alan and his brother out to an English family and visiting them whenever they could. Beginning in 1926, Turing attended the Sherborne School, one of the oldest public schools in England. He found it difficult to adjust to school life, and his headmaster noted, "He is the kind of boy who is bound to be rather a problem in any kind of school or community, being in some respects definitely anti-social." Despite his antisocial tendencies, Turing conceived an intense friendship with a boy one year his senior named Christopher Morrcom, who reciprocated his affections. When Morrcom died suddenly in 1930, at the age of eighteen, Turing was, in the words of one acquaintance, "nearly knocked out from the shock."

At the age of twenty-three, while studying mathematical logic at King's College, Cambridge, Turing wrote an article called "On Computable Numbers, with an Application to the *Entscheidungsproblem*," in which he proved that certain mathematical problems are unsolvable by a fixed process. This article would become a landmark in the development of computer theory, and Turing's concept of a universal machine—today known as the Turing machine—would provide the theoretical underpinnings of the digital computers that began to be developed during the 1940s.

In 1938, the year after that article was published, Turing traveled to the United States to study at Princeton University, from which he received a PhD in mathematics. Returning to England at the onset of World War II, he worked with the British Code and Cypher School and helped to invent the machines that broke Enigma, the key to German war communications. The deciphering of Enigma was a critical intelligence breakthrough that contributed directly to the Allied victory over Germany.

After the war, Turing led the design and construction of a large digital computer called the Automatic Computing Engine (ACE). In 1948 he moved to Manchester to become deputy director of the Manchester Automatic Digital Machine (MADAM), which at the time had the largest memory capacity in the world.

Turing's innovations in computer design and programming were revolutionary. He proposed the possibility of computers that would be capable of thought and suggested that the introduction of certain random elements in the programming could one day enable computer "thinking" to resemble human thought. Turing has been called "the father of artificial intelligence."

In 1952 the first part of Turing's ambitious theoretical study of morphogenesis was published. That same year, he got into some trouble. As he put it in a letter to a friend: "The burglary business was actually worse than an ordinary burglary. I had got a boyfriend, who...put his friends up to my house. One of these has been picked up by the police and has informed against us. When you come to Liverpool perhaps you will stop off to see me in jail." Charged with "Gross Indecency Contrary to Section 11 of the Criminal Law Amendment of 1885," the same one that got OSCAR WILDE [3], Turing guilelessly confessed everything to the police. After being released on bail, he decided to plead not guilty in court but was persuaded, on the basis of his five-page confession, to change his plea to guilty. For that he was given one year probation and ordered to undergo an experimental treatment with female hormones known as organotherapy: basically a kind of chemical castration. As one doctor explained, "in view of the non-mutilating nature of this treatment and the ease with which it can be administered to a consenting patient we believe that it should be adopted whenever possible in male cases of abnormal and uncontrollable sexual urge." Side effects of the treatment included impotence, the development of breasts, and impairment of the central nervous system.

Turing underwent the therapy for the requisite year and tried to continue his work. In the summer of 1953 he undertook a holiday trip abroad and consorted intimately with a number of foreigners he met—a state of affairs that apparently alarmed certain "higher-ups" who were growing to consider Turing something of a permanent security risk because of his "incorrigible" homosexual tendencies. In March 1954, Turing sent a series of enigmatic postcards bearing the inscription "Messages from the Unseen World" to his friend and colleague Robin Grandy. Turing wrote, "The Exclusion principle is laid down purely for the benefit of the electives themselves, who might be corrupted (and become dragons or demons) if allowed to associate too freely." At the time, Grandy didn't know what to make of this; in retrospect, it would seem that Turing may have been trying to tell his friend that he had become too much of a risk to be allowed to travel, to have sex, to communicate with other human beings—even to exist.

On June 7, 1954, ten years after the D-day assault his breaking of the Enigma code had helped make possible, Allen Turing died of potassium cyanide poisoning, possibly self-administered.

His case is a painful one. He wanted to do his work, and he wanted to live his life, and given who he was, that was an impossible contradiction. He embodies not only the contradictions of gay people in straight society but of individuals in the modern security state: he was a victim of the very society his work strove to perpetuate. Turing's biographer Andrew Hodge writes, "Alan Turing's split state prefigured the pattern of growth that he did not choose to live to see: a civilization where the singing and dancing and mating—and the thinking about numbers—would be offered to a wider class, but one built around, and working to provide, methods and machines of inconceivable danger, and in his very silence, he typified the mainstream of collaboration in this policy." Turing's work, "while being as near to pacifism as military work could be, still had the effect of increasing state dependence upon machinery not only beyond the control, but even completely outside the knowledge, of those who paid for it."

In certain ways, Turing's plight resembles that of ROY COHN [84] in that both were loyal servants of a system that had no place for them within it. But where Cohn was an evil genius cunningly manipulating that system for his own gain, Turing was the innocent victim of it.

84

Roy Cohn

1927–1986

Roy Marcus Cohn was born on February 20, 1927, in New York City. His father was a justice in the appellate division of the New York State Supreme Court, and extremely influential within the ranks of the Democratic Party.

Cohn was a precocious child, attending the Fieldstone School and Columbia College. At the age of twenty he graduated from Columbia Law School—too young to take the bar exam. After being admitted to the bar the next year, he used his connections to get on the staff of the United States attorney in Manhattan. There he quickly made a reputation for himself, coming to widespread public attention during the controversial spy trial of Julius and Ethel Rosenberg when his direct and unrelenting examination of Mrs. Rosenberg's brother led him to name his sister as a member of a Soviet spy ring. Chiefly on the basis of the testimony Cohn elicited, the couple were convicted and, despite widespread concern about the fairness of the trial, electrocuted.

In 1952, Cohn moved to Washington as special assistant to the attorney general, where his work soon came to the attention of Joseph McCarthy, the Republican senator from Wisconsin. As chairman of the Senate's permanent investigations committee, McCarthy had undertaken a campaign to "root out Communism in government." Appointed chief counsel to McCarthy's subcommittee, Cohn became the grand inquisitor in McCarthy's ferocious attempts to ferret out "the Communist threat." Together with his close friend David Shine, whom he brought aboard as a consultant, Cohn tirelessly investigated army bases, the State Department, the Voice of America, and Hollywood, destroying the reputations and careers of countless people in government service and the entertainment industry. The McCarthy era was under way, and with it, attempts to eliminate gay men and lesbians—"sexual perverts"— from government jobs as security risks. ("One homosexual can pollute a government office," reported a special Senate committee.)

Oddly enough, in the midst of all the red-baiting and fag-bashing, Cohn, Shine, and McCarthy, all three bachelors, were themselves the subject of homosexual rumor: "Bonnie, Bonnie and Clyde," playwright Lillian Hellman called them.

In 1952, Cohn got himself into serious trouble. When Shine was drafted into the army, Cohn attempted to win his friend an officer's commission. This failed, however, and a furious Cohn threatened "to wreck the army." Word of this got out, and the result was scandal. Both Cohn and Senator McCarthy were formally charged with seeking by improper means to obtain preferential treatment for a serviceman. The televised Army-McCarthy hearings in the Senate were watched by millions. In August 1954, both men were exonerated of wrongdoing. McCarthy's irrational behavior during the hearings, however, had seriously damaged his political reputation. When he was formally censured by the Senate in December 1954, his meteoric career was effectively finished.

Cohn's career was expected to be finished also, but with his characteristic demonic energy he rebounded, joining a New York law firm and using his connections, over the years, to represent an impressive list of high-profile clients: Mafia boss Carmine Galante, Roman Catholic cardinal Francis Spellman, jet-setter Bianca Jagger, artist Andy Warhol, designer Calvin Klein, and real estate executive Donald Trump. Cohn became, over the next thirty years, a power-broker of the first rank.

If LIBERACE [66] was Mr. Show Business, Roy Cohn was Mr. Influence. He prided himself on such powerful friends as Ronald Reagan, FBI chief J. Edgar Hoover, Terence Cardinal Cooke, right-wing columnist William Buckley, and television journalist Barbara Walters. As Cohn said in 1979, "my idea of real power is not people who hold office. They're here today and gone tomorrow. Power means the ability to get things done. It stems from friendship in my case. My business life is my social life." To those who were his friends, he was intensely loyal. To his enemies, he was ruthless. As a trial lawyer, he became known as an attack dog.

His legal dealings over the years led to several indictments against him on charges of extortion, bribery, and mail fraud, but he was never convicted. He claimed there was an ongoing vendetta against him, dating back to his associations with Joseph McCarthy, and that Robert Kennedy was his chief persecutor. As if in confirmation of that, the IRS audited him every year for twenty years, and though he accrued a fortune through his work, he owed the IRS $3 million at the time of his death. He was famous for his high living, his million-dollar expense accounts and fancy cars—all provided by his law firm. During the seventies he was a regular at the notorious and trendy disco Studio 54.

In June 1986, near death from what he said was liver cancer, he was disbarred from practicing law in New York State by the Appellate Division of the State Supreme Court on the grounds that his legal conduct had been "unethical," "unprofessional," and "reprehensible." On August 2, 1986, he died of cardiopulmonary arrest. The death certificate listed secondary causes as "underlying HTLV-3 infections" and AIDS-related "dementia."

Like ALAN TURING [53], Roy Cohn occupies a painful place on this list. He was undoubtedly influential, in ways that were brilliant and monstrous. He was a hypocrite, though not a simple one. His understanding of his situation—like his situation itself—seems to have been complex. That his example continues to resonate darkly in our collective imagination is shown by Tony

Kushner's memorable rendition of Cohn in *Angels in America*—a play that will be remembered long after Cohn himself is forgotten. Cohn's ranking on this list acknowledges the complex position in which many talented gay men of less than sterling principles have found themselves in a society that has no place for their kind. Whether they chose to resolve it with a pact as Faustian as Roy Cohn's is another question altogether.

85

Anna Freud

1895–1982

Anna Freud was born on December 3, 1895, in Vienna, Austria. The youngest daughter of Sigmund Freud, she once said that she was born in the same year as psychoanalysis, since it was in 1895 that Freud began his work on the meaning of dreams—work that would later become the foundation for his theories of the unconscious. She was educated at home and exposed from an early age to the discussions of the Vienna Psychoanalytic Society, which met in her father's study. As a young woman, she taught elementary school for five years, an experience that led her to an interest in the psychology of children. During this time she also entered analysis with her father (these were the fledgling days of psychoanalysis, before there were ethical proscriptions against analyzing relatives and close friends) and accompanied him on his psychiatric rounds at the hospital.

Anna Freud's first paper, "Beating Fantasies and Daydreams," concerning the ways people tried to stop themselves from masturbating, gained her admittance to the Vienna Psychoanalytic Society in 1922. She opened a practice, and among the patients she treated were the son and daughter of a wealthy American named Dorothy Burlingham, who had just separated from her mentally ill husband. Anna Freud soon fell in love with Dorothy Burlingham, and the two began an intense association that would last the remainder of their lives.

In 1927, Freud published *Introduction to the Techniques of Child Analysis*, in which she outlined her pioneering approach to child psychology. Her emphasis on the role of environment in the child's development and on the efficacy of "play therapy" brought her into conflict with many of the leading psychoanalysts of the time and threatened to precipitate a rift between the Viennese and British schools of analysis.

Freud's 1936 work, *The Ego and Mechanisms of Defense*, analyzed repression, which she saw as the principal human defense mechanism, the unconscious process by which the child learns to curb certain behaviors that, if acted on, could prove dangerous. It is considered a landmark in the study of ego psychology and the development of adolescent psychology.

In 1938, just after the Nazi occupation of Austria, Anna Freud was arrested and her father's house ransacked. She was soon released, and three months later she and her father, desperately ill with the cancer he'd been battling for two decades, fled Austria to settle in London. Sigmund Freud died the following year. The loss devastated Anna Freud: her father's constant intellectual companion, she had nursed him through his long and terrible illness. After his death, much of her work was aimed at conserving her father's psychoanalytic principles from inroads by the younger generation of theorists.

In 1941, Anna Freud and Dorothy Burlingham together established the Hampstead War Nurseries, a home for children who had been separated from their parents because of the war. They described their work in *Young Children in Wartime* (1942), *Infants Without Families* (1943), and *War and Children* (1943).

At the beginning of the war, Burlingham had had a brief flirtation with a young man, but then she renounced him, explaining to Freud in a letter: "You know from my letters that I was afraid—afraid of complications, afraid of being forced apart—but it was only now that I was shocked into realizing that I might really lose you—and that the consequences might ruin my life and ours together." Later she would write that her relationship with Freud was "the most precious relationship I ever had."

In 1952, the two women opened the Hampstead Child Therapy Course and Clinic, which became the pioneering institute for the psychoanalytic treatment of children. Freud served as its director for the next thirty years. In 1968 she summed up a lifetime of research and experience in *Normality and Pathology in the Child*. Dorothy Burlingham died in 1979, with Anna Freud by her side. At her death, Burlingham's grandson told Freud, "You were everything to her and she had a most wonderful life with you; how fortunate she was in finding and capturing someone like you."

Anna Freud died on October 9, 1982, in London.

Elizabeth Young-Breuhl, in her psychoanalytic biography of Anna Freud, undertakes to map her subject's psychic makeup when she writes, "[Freud's] masturbation conflict was early on partially sublimated into fantasies that were progressively more liberated—first beating fantasies, then daydreams, then creative work; and partially controlled with somewhat compulsive substitute physical activities like knitting and weaving. She developed a habit of finding acceptable outlets for unacceptable impulses and wishes, ultimately altruistically surrendering her wishes to others....She was able to have a scientific interest in sexuality, but not to be actively sexual in either a heterosexual or a homosexual mode. The crucial fact for her creative life, however, was that her main defense was sublimation—and this also means: not repression." About Freud's primary connections with women throughout her life, Young-Breuhl writes: "The needs expressed to and through these many women were more complex than the needs to love and be like a man that were filled by [her father Sigmund] Freud and Freud only—even if it is taken into account that identifying with her father, being male, might originally have served to deny the intensity of her daughterly love as well as to satisfy phallic wishes."

Whether Anna Freud and Dorothy Burlingham were sexual with one another is something we will probably never know—rumors that they were lesbians persisted throughout their lives, and Burlingham's grandson Michael described them as "the oxymoron, intellectual lesbians." Of course, explicit genital sex-

uality is hardly the most important element of lesbian relationships. According to biographer Dell Richards, Freud and Burlingham saw themselves as "twins, perfect complements in an
'ideal friendship.' The need to prove (or disprove) a sexual
component is a ruse that keeps women out of the historical
lesbian fold. It also misses the most obvious aspect of lesbian
relationships, the 'intellectual' side."

Anna Freud very probably did not consider herself a lesbian
and in fact believed, like most of her contemporaries in the field,
that homosexuality was a disorder that could be "cured." Hers is
a complicated case, and I have included her in this ranking for
several reasons: first, her innovations in the field of child
psychology and her work as conservator of her father's legacy
make her one of the most influential figures in psychoanalysis, a
field that has, for better or worse, greatly affected the way gay
people have been conceptualized (and conceptualized themselves) in the twentieth century. Second, she represents an important configuration available to women who, for whatever reason,
have resisted the conventional arrangements of heterosexuality
and have derived much of their primary emotional support from
other women—namely, the "sublimation" of sexual drives into
creative work. By divorcing herself from a conscious personal
identification with "homosexuality" and by then proceeding to
effect a cure of a condition suspiciously resembling her own, she
illustrates the vexed position in which people of unconventional
sexualities often find themselves. I rank her on this list with
ALAN TURING [83] and ROY COHN [84], two other figures who
reveal the troubled accommodations with the status quo that gay
men and lesbians have been forced, over the years of our difficult
century, to make.

86

Entertainers of Harlem

Gladys Bentley 1907–1960
Ma Rainey 1886–1939
Bessie Smith 1894–1937

In the 1920s, Harlem began to develop as the uptown alternative to Greenwich Village, a place where one could go "slumming" and partake of a bit of bohemia. Particularly popular were Harlem's nightclubs, dispensing hot entertainment to mostly white audiences who went for, among other things, the exotic spectacle of homosexuality. For homosexuals, though, Harlem was not so much a spectacle as part of an awakening realization that gays and lesbians represented an oppressed minority group analogous to American blacks. Three Harlem entertainers were particularly influential in the ways they integrated elements of gay desire into their publicly performed music. By doing so, they helped nurture a gradually evolving gay self-awareness in the first half of this century.

Gladys Bentley

One entertainer willing to oblige her audience's penchant for spectacle was Gladys "Fatso" Bentley, a bisexual three-hundred-pound male impersonator who sometimes performed under the name Bobby Minton. Born on August 12, 1907, in Pennsylvania, she ran away to New York as a teenager and found her way to the clubs of Harlem. There she gained a reputation for improvising risqué songs to popular melodies, adopted her trademark white tuxedo and top hat, and was soon headlining shows at the Clam House. She recorded solo for OKeh Records, and with the Washboard Serenaders for RCA Victor. In the early 1930s she opened The Exclusive Club, where she arranged and directed her own shows, including the famous Ubangi Club Revue. Bentley retained her drag getup offstage as well as on. Dressed in her tuxedo, she married another woman in a New Jersey civil ceremony.

In the early 1940s, she retired to California, where she began a new career as a blues shouter, recording for various independent labels. She died on January 18, 1960, in Los Angeles.

Ma Rainey

"Ma" Rainey was born Gertrude Pridgett on April 26, 1886, in Columbus, Georgia. Her singing career began at the age of twelve when an appearance in a talent show led to an engagement as a cabaret singer. In 1904 she married Will "Pa" Rainey and toured with him in F. S. Wolcott's Rabbit Foot Minstrels and other shows. It was on one of these tours that she met eighteen-year-old Bessie Smith, who became her protégé. In 1916, Rainey and her husband started their own company. Because she was ten years older than most of the other performers, and because of her warm and nurturing personality, she acquired the nickname Ma. She made her first recording in 1923, and over the next five years she made over one hundred records, earning the title Mother of the Blues. A number of Rainey's songs have explicit lesbian content, such as "Prove It on Me Blues."

By the 1920s she and Pa Rainey had separated, and in 1925 she threw a lesbian orgy for her chorus girls at her home. The arrival of the police to investigate noise complaints from the neighbors sent women scrambling for their clothes and fleeing out the back door. In her attempt to escape, Rainey fell down the stairs. Accused of running an indecent party, she was thrown in jail. Bessie Smith bailed her out the next morning.

Rainey left New York in 1935 to retire to Columbus, Georgia, where she was active in the Baptist church. She died on December 22, 1939.

Bessie Smith

Bessie Smith was born on April 15, 1894, in Chattanooga, Tennessee. Her career began in 1912 when she sang in a show with Ma Rainey. Her first recording, "Downhearted Blues," established her as the most successful black vocalist of her time. More than any other performer, she was responsible for introducing the blues into the mainstream of American popular music. She recorded regularly until 1928, touring both the North and the South, and appearing in the 1929 film *St. Louis Blues*. The Great Depression of the 1930s was tough on the recording and entertainment industry, and Smith's career went into a decline. Matters weren't helped by her increasingly frequent episodes of binge drinking. She made her last recording in 1933. After a three-year hiatus in performing, she again began to appear in clubs and shows, but died before another recording session could be arranged. In all she made over two hundred recordings, including some famous duets with Louis Armstrong.

It was commonly asserted that Ma Rainey initiated Bessie Smith into lesbian sex, though there is no hard evidence for this. What is known is that Smith frequently got into trouble with her jealous second husband, Jack Gee, over her affairs with women such as Lillian Simpson, a chorus girl in Smith's touring show, *Harlem Frolics*. Like Rainey, Smith sang songs with explicit lesbian content, such as "It's Dirty But Good" from 1930.

Smith was famous for her excessive appetites—for home-cooked Southern food, for moonshine, and for the tenderloin districts of the cities she performed in. Her cousin Ruby Smith recalled a notorious "buffet flat" that Smith visited whenever she was performing in Detroit: "It was nothing but faggots and bulldykes, a real open house. Everything went on in that house—

tongue baths, you name it. They called them buffet flats because *buffet* means everything, everything that's in the life. Bessie was well known in that place."

Bessie Smith died in an automobile accident on September 26, 1937, in Clarksdale, Mississippi.

Other bisexual black entertainers of the time included Ethel Waters and her lover of many years, Ethel Williams, and Alberta Turner, who married as a cover for her bisexuality but did not live with her husband. Her lover was Lottie Tyler.

Together, these singers formed part of a milieu in which tolerance and acceptance of homosexuality had a historic place. By pushing the envelope of what was acceptable in popular music, they represented one more step in this century's painfully slow movement toward gay/lesbian visibility. When we consider the range of lesbian presence available today in popular music, from the folk-influenced sounds of HOLLY NEAR [88] to the tongue-in-chic antics of MADONNA [99], we should remember that Gladys Bentley, Ma Rainey, and Bessie Smith beat them to the mark by half a century.

87

Dr. Tom Waddell

1937–1987

As a child Tom Waddell studied ballet; as a teenager he took up athletics; at university he dropped athletics in order to pursue his medical studies. A fierce opponent of the Vietnam War, when drafted he managed to avoid going into combat and instead trained, with other military athletes, for the 1968 Olympic Games. What was unusual was that this thirty-year-old trained not for the usual four years, but for a scant three months before heading to Mexico City as a decathlete on the U.S. Olympic team. There he placed sixth—an extraordinary achievement in any event, but especially given these circumstances.

When two U.S. Olympic team members took the opportunity of their gold and bronze medals in the track-and-field competition to give the black-power salute during the playing of the U.S. national anthem, Waddell supported their actions and as a result was threatened with court-martial by an offended military.

In 1980, Waddell, by then a practicing medical doctor, proposed the idea for a gay Olympic games—"a new idea," as he put it, "in the meaning of sport based on inclusion rather than exclusion." Anyone would be allowed to play in the Gay Olympics, regardless of race, sex, age, national origin, sexual orientation, or athletic ability. There would be no minimum qualifying standard, simply the desire to compete and to be one's best. A committed socialist, Waddell believed that the Gay Olympics could help create an "exemplary community" founded on the principles of equality and universal participation. To this end he established, with others, San Francisco Arts and Athletics, Inc., to administer the Gay Olympics.

The United States Olympic Committee (USOC) reacted to news of Waddell's Gay Olympics with outrage and, in 1982, shortly before the first Gay Olympics was set to take place, filed a court action against him, citing the 1978 Amateur Sports Act, passed by the U.S. Congress, which among other items gave the USOC exclusive use of the word *Olympic*. Never mind that the USOC had sanctioned such events as the Rat Olympics and the Dog Olympics—the organizers of the Gay Olympics were forced to change the event's name to the Gay Games.

At the first Gay Games in San Francisco in 1982, thirteen hundred male and female athletes competed in sixteen different sports. Two years later, the USOC filed suit to recover $96,000 in legal fees from their 1982 court case against the Gay Olympics. A lien was placed on Tom Waddell's house.

The 1986 Gay Games also took place in San Francisco, with over three thousand athletes competing in seventeen sports, including basketball, soccer, track and field, marathon, power lifting, swimming, diving, volleyball, softball, and wrestling. As Rita Mae Brown [74] observed at the opening ceremonies to that year's event, the Games showed "the world who we really are. We're intelligent people, we're attractive people, we're caring people, we're *healthy* people, and we're proud of who we are."

Four weeks before the 1986 Gay Games, Waddell was diagnosed with AIDS-related *Pneumocystis carinii* pneumonia. Nevertheless, he participated in the games in track and field and won a gold medal in javelin-throwing. The progress of his disease forced him to give up his post as chief physician specializing in infectious diseases at San Francisco's Central Emergency facility. He spent his last year fighting the USOC's lawsuit against him. A month before his death, the U.S. Supreme Court ruled that the USOC had "the legal authority to bar a homosexual rights group from using the generic word 'olympic' in the name of its games."

Dr. Tom Waddell died at his home in San Francisco on July 11, 1987, from complications from AIDS. He was featured in the 1990 Academy Award–winning documentary *Common Threads: Stories from the Quilt*. In that film, Sara Lewinstein, a lesbian and cochair of the 1982 Gay Games, tells the bittersweet story of her evolving professional and personal relationship with Tom—a relationship that eventually led to their marriage and the birth of their daughter, Jessica.

Three years after Waddell's death, the 1990 Gay Games in Vancouver attracted more than seven thousand athletes from around the world, making it the largest amateur sporting event in history. The 1994 Gay Games, held in New York City, attracted some eleven thousand participants and hundreds of thousands of spectators. Dr. Tom Waddell's legacy lives on in the form of one of the most successful and visible gay institutions in the world.

88

Holly Near

1949–

Holly Near was born on June 6, 1949, in Ukiah, California. She grew up in a musical family and was early on exposed to folk music, country and western, and Broadway tunes. At the age of seven she made her public debut as a singer. By her teens, she had appeared in a number of films and television programs. In the late sixties she traveled east to New York, where she was a lead in the Broadway production of the musical *Hair*. She also became politically active, campaigning against the war in Vietnam and touring that country in the early 1970s with Jane Fonda's contro-versial "Free the Army" show, which demanded U.S. withdrawal from the conflict. Throughout the 1970s, Near performed on the folk music circuit and was considered ripe for a contract with a major record company. Reluctant to give up too much control over her material, which included songs with lesbian themes, she instead established her own label, Redwood Records, and released her first album, *Hang in There*, in 1973. She released three more albums on Redwood and by 1979 had sold 155,000 albums in all—an impressive total for a small, independent label. Throughout the 1970s and 1980s she toured frequently, often in support of political causes such as Women Against Violence Against Women. One of her songs—"Singing for Our Lives," with its refrain "We are gay and lesbian people / And we are singing, singing for our lives"—became the de facto anthem of the gay civil rights movement in the 1980s.

Holly Near earns a ranking on this list as an important representative of the women's music movement that began in the late 1960s in reaction to the male-dominated culture of rock and roll—"cock rock," as some feminists dubbed the genre. Writing in 1973, Joan Nixon described the qualities of women's music as "gentleness, passion, sensitivity and strength—in sharp contrast to the blasting hard rock fed to us by male culture. The themes of our music are self-love, love of other women, love of animals and living things, the damage done to women by the patriarchy and the need to separate from men, the healing powers of sisterhood, ourselves as a spiritual source, the rising tide of feminist power and the creation of a new social order based on feminist principles of nurturance." The idiom generally employed by performers of women's music derives from the folk art tradition.

An important early figure in the movement was Maxine Feldman, whose 1969 song "Angry Athis" told of a woman wanting to hold her female lover's hand in public. Also important for women's music was the establishment, in 1973, of Olivia Records. According to Ginny Berson, one of its founders, Olivia had four principal goals: "(1) to make high-quality women's music (music that speaks honestly and realistically about women's lives) available to the public; (2) to provide talented women-oriented musicians with access to the recording industry and control over their music; (3) to provide music-industry-related jobs for large numbers of women, with reasonable salaries and in unoppressive situations; and (4) to provide industry training for women in all aspects of the recording industry."

Olivia Records was more than a recording company: it was a political organization as well. Uninterested in simply mimicking the structure of male recording companies, Olivia Records was organized nonhierarchically and operated collectively. The basis of the company's collective decision-making was political trust, and the basis of that trust, according to Berson, "comes from the fact that we are all lesbian feminists, who see our present and future intimately connected with the future of all women: we get all our energy from women; we define ourselves in terms of women; we recognize that we are oppressed because we are women and that we will end our oppression with the help of other women, especially women who are willing to make a full-time, lifelong commitment to women's struggles."

Olivia Records became one of the important lesbian institutions of the 1970s. The company's first album was *Meg Christian: I Know You Know,* which included the famous "Ode to a Gym Teacher." That was followed by Cris Williamson's album *The Changer and the Changed.* These two singers, along with the later addition to the company of Holly Near, created the Olivia sound, which flourished through the 1970s and early 1980s. By the mid-1980s, however, Olivia Records was in trouble. Chronically undercapitalized, the company's sales began to flag, and Olivia was forced to abandon some of its original lesbian-feminist principles. By 1989, Ginny Berson could lament: "For the first time in its history at an Olivia Records concert, there were more men than women on stage....I thought I knew that 'Olivia Records Presents' meant something—music about women's lives, music written by women, performed by women. But what we had here were a few songs about women and a lot about horses; lots of songs written by men; and mostly men playing the music."

Ironically—as Arlene Stein has pointed out in her essay "Androgyny Goes Pop: But Is It Lesbian Music?"—by the late 1980s and early 1990s, lesbian artists were more likely to be found on mainstream labels: Tracy Chapman on Elektra, Michelle Shocked on Polygram, Phranc on Island, k. d. lang on Sire. When Michelle Shocked accepted the 1989 New Music Award for Folk Album of the Year—for which Phranc, Tracy Chapman, and the Indigo Girls had also been nominated—she was able to joke on national TV, "This category should have been called 'Best Lesbian Vocalist.'" More pop-oriented singers like MADONNA [99] were also capitalizing on lesbian identity by this point.

Holly Near, meanwhile, has continued to soldier on, playing the college and coffeehouse circuit along with the occasional big rally. Recently she came out—as (gasp) a bisexual, an identity she hid for many years in order not to disappoint her lesbian fans.

If the ruthless laws of the marketplace finally prevailed over the dream of establishing an alternative lesbian-feminist cultural network, Holly Near nonetheless remains as one of a handful of courageous lesbian or bisexual women who resisted the blandishments of commercial success in order to follow her vision of a better world through music. In so doing, she influenced the ongoing quest, in such venues as the annual Michigan Women's Music Festival, to create a nurturing space for women's creativity. For the purposes of this ranking, Holly Near, though less well-known than her latter-day counterparts, is nonetheless more influential than they because her music and political stance—like that of Meg Christian and Cris Williamson—made the next generation's mainstream success possible.

89

Rudolf Nureyev

1938–1993

Rudolf Nureyev was born on March 17, 1938, on a train near Irkutsk, on the borders of Mongolia. His father, descended from Bashkir Muslims, was an itinerant political instructor in the Soviet Army. His mother was a Tartar from Kazan. The family lived in such poverty in the city of Ufa that, as a boy, Nureyev had to wear his sister's dress to school. When he was eight, his mother smuggled herself and all four of her children into a gala performance of the Ufa Ballet: it proved a life-changing experience for the young Nureyev. He started dancing with a folk ensemble at his school and at the age of eleven began his formal training in ballet. His father, who wanted him to be an engineer, tried to discourage his newfound enthusiasm, but Nureyev persisted and by 1955 was a member of the corps de ballet at the Ufa Opera House. That same year he auditioned for the Bolshoi Ballet School in Moscow and the Kirov Ballet School in Leningrad. Though he was accepted into both, he chose the Kirov—despite the fact that one of his auditioners there had told him, "Young man, you'll become either a brilliant dancer or a total failure— and most likely you'll be a failure." At the Kirov School, he studied with the legendary instructor Alexsandr Pushkin, who become a second father to him. When he graduated in 1958, he joined the Kirov Ballet and, bypassing the corps de ballet, was immediately given solo roles. He made his debut in *Laurencia*, dancing with the company's renowned senior ballerina, Natalya Dudinskaya.

Early on, his famous temperament—fiery, arrogant, non-conformist—showed itself in the young dancer's conflicts with the administration, and in his refusal to join the state-sponsored dance collective. In 1961, when the Kirov toured Paris, he won great acclaim for his performances in *Sleeping Beauty, Swan Lake,* and *Giselle*. He also incurred suspicion from the company's management because of his overt fascination with the West. He took to venturing out into Paris unaccompanied, attending concerts and art galleries and developing friendships with French citizens. At the end of the Kirov's Parisian stint, Nureyev was told to return to the Soviet Union to dance at a special performance at the Kremlin. Suspecting that he was being disciplined for his troublesome nonconformity, he feared he might not be permitted to leave the Soviet Union again. On June 17, 1961, as the company was preparing to board their plane at Le Bourget airport, Nureyev bolted toward two French police officers and declared that he was requesting political asylum. His defection brought him international attention, and he did not return to the Soviet Union until 1987, when he received a special visa to visit his dying mother.

During his first year in the West he danced with the De Cuevas Ballet and in a small company formed with Erik Bruhn, a Danish dancer who was one of the major professional and emotional relationships of Nureyev's life. He made his British debut in November 1961, at a charity gala organized by the famous ballerina Margot Fonteyn, who was so impressed that she invited him to dance with her in *Giselle* in February 1962. Their performance together electrified the audience. At the close of the performance, in a now legendary gesture, Nureyev knelt and kissed Fonteyn's hand. Thus began an artistic partnership that made ballet history. Nureyev became a "permanent guest artist" at the Royal Ballet. His association with Fonteyn revitalized the older dancer's career, which many had presumed was nearing its end. "For me," Nureyev declared, "[Fonteyn] represents eternal youth; there is an absolute musical quality in her beautiful body and phrasing. Because we are sincere and gifted, an intense abstract love is born between us every time we dance together." Audiences went wild at the sight of the two dancing together, and their curtain calls became renowned for their fervor and duration. After a performance of *Swan Lake* in Vienna, in fact, the audience called them back so many times that it earned them a place in the *Guinness Book of World Records* for longest curtain call on record.

The partnership of Nureyev and Fonteyn—especially in such classics as *Swan Lake, Giselle, Sleeping Beauty,* and *Le Corsaire*—initiated a flowering of dance in America in the 1960s, with repeated sold-out performances of the Royal Ballet at the Metropolitan Opera House in New York, and extensive national tours. Nureyev became a superstar, attracting the kind of attention and fervent following usually reserved for rock stars. Writing in 1970, Oleg Kerensky commented that "part of Nureyev's sensational success is due to his animal magnetism and sensuality. He appeals to the mothering instinct in middle-aged women, the mating instinct in young ones and the desire of many male homosexuals." And indeed, stories of the dancer's regular attendance at certain notorious gay bars only bolstered his popularity among an important segment of his audience—some of whom were known to chant, "We want Rudi, especially in the nudi."

"There can have been few men in our times," Philip Core writes, "whose physical presence was acknowledged by so many people as a powerful erotic force; I have known men who would have never otherwise considered the idea who were proud to have enjoyed love with Nureyev."

Not content simply to dance the classics, Nureyev performed in contemporary works such as George Balanchine's *Apollo* and Jerome Robbins's *Dances at a Gathering*. During the 1970s he performed with such masters of modern dance as Martha Graham and Paul Taylor. He also restaged traditional works, often emphasizing the role of the male dancers, and sometimes, as in his Freudian *Nutcracker,* offering innovative interpretations of well-worn favorites. A tireless performer, he toured extensively and danced with a wide range of companies, including the National Ballet of Canada, the Australian Ballet, and in 1975, a small touring group called Nureyev and Friends.

The professional longevity of a dancer is notoriously short, and by the late 1970s Nureyev was seen as past his prime. Nonetheless, he continued to dance—often, now, to mixed reviews. He defended his decision to continue by saying, "The main thing is dancing, and before it withers away from my body, I will keep dancing to the last moment, the last drop."

In 1983 he was appointed director of the Paris Opera Ballet. During his tenure he transformed the company, developing world-class dancers, particularly Sylvie Guillem, whom he introduced to London by partnering her for her debut with the Royal Ballet in *Giselle,* twenty-six years after his own debut there. His famous disdain for bureaucratic niceties entangled him in squabbles, though, and he was removed as director in 1989.

A remarkably beautiful man both onstage and off, as a dancer Nureyev was famous for the height and buoyancy of his jumps, his speed, the openness of his chest as if radiating light. In the words of Karen Robertson, "he imported a Romantic sensibility into twentieth-century dance, but allied that with a passionate respect for the classical tradition: the placement of a hand, the accuracy of his return to the fifth position after a jump." Critic Clive Barnes remarked: "People will be writing about Nureyev's stage personality for as long as people remember what a stage was. It was a personality compounded of sensual allure and sexual disdain. Yet he always suggested the loner, which is to say that everything about him, beginning with his androgynous but scarcely asexual looks, seemed to be a harmony of opposites; he was a yin and yang person for all seasons and all manners. No wonder he was compared with NIJINSKY [46]."

Nureyev's last appearance onstage came on October 8, 1992, when, gaunt and unable to walk unassisted, he took a bow following the Paris premiere of his new production of *La Bayadère.* The audience gave him a ten-minute ovation, and he was decorated as a Commander of Arts and Letters by the French minister of culture, Jack Lang. Rudolf Nureyev died of a cardiac complication resulting from AIDS on January 6, 1993, in Paris, France.

Beginning with SERGEY DIAGHILEV and VASLAV NIJINSKY [46], ballet in this century has been a province of gay men: for three decades Nureyev was its reigning fairy prince. His gayness was an open secret, and he brought both ballet and an incomparable gay allure to the attention of the world in ways that earn him his position in this ranking.

90

Freddie Mercury

1946–1991

The son of a government accountant, Freddie Mercury was born Frederick Bulsara on September 5, 1946, in Zanzibar, Africa. By 1971 he was living in London, running an antiques stall in Kensington Market and playing keyboards in a band called Wreckage, when he was invited by guitarist Brian May and drummer Roger Taylor to join their new band, Queen. Along with bassist John Deacon, they began rehearsing their brand of heavy metal. The era of glam rock was just beginning, that cultural/commercial phenomenon that included such bands as the New York Dolls and Kiss, and individual performers as different as David Bowie and Elton John. Flamboyant, outrageous, and flaunting gender stereotypes, glam rock performances usually involved at least a modicum of drag; makeup was de rigueur. Queen became the epitome of glam rock, and Freddie Mercury its reigning highness.

Eschewing the pub and club circuit, Queen performed in showcase venues from the very beginning, and this led to an early record contract. Their first album, *Queen* (1973), got bad reviews, but they received welcome exposure that year by opening for Mott the Hoople on that band's U.S. tour. *Queen II* in 1974 gave them their first hit single, "Seven Seas of Rhye." This album was followed by *Sheer Heart Attack*, with its successful single "Killer Queen." Their breakthrough album came in 1975 with *A Night at the Opera*, said to be the most expensive LP produced in Great Britain since the Beatles' *Sergeant Pepper* in 1967. The seven-minute single, "Bohemian Rhapsody," has been described as "a kitsch epic." Combining hard rock, operatic-style arias, and an ineffable high-camp sensibility, "Bohemian Rhapsody" became the longest-running number one hit in Great Britain in twenty years. In the United States, it reached the number nine slot. The innovative promotional video that accompanied the single was one of the first rock videos and helped inaugurate the practice of releasing videos to accompany singles. Its style influenced numerous videos thereafter. Freddie Mercury's flamboyant, satin-clad stage persona and bravura voice made Queen the gayest of the seventies glam rock bands—at least in image. But then, in glam rock, image is everything. That they were wildly successful with "straight" audiences remains one of the most piquant cultural artifacts of that decade.

Their hits continued with "You're My Best Friend" and "Someone to Love" from *A Day at the Races* (1976). Other albums included *News of the World* (1977), with its hard-rock anthem "We Are the Champions," *Jazz* (1978), and *The Game* (1980), whose disco hit single "Another One Bites the Dust" went to number one in the United States. By the eighties each album generated massive worldwide sales, and the members of Queen were some of the richest musicians ever. They astutely managed their financial affairs as a limited, four-share company: in 1981 they were the highest-paid directors in British industry.

Their music for *Flash Gordon* (1980) broke new ground in that Queen was the first rock band to score a major film. Though the decade of the eighties saw a waning of Queen's popularity, "Under Pressure," Mercury's 1982 duet with David Bowie, rocketed to number one in Great Britain.

In his final years, Mercury lived reclusively and refused to respond to rumors that he was suffering from AIDS. But on November 23, 1991, he released a statement confirming that he had the disease. "I felt it correct to keep this information private to date in order to protect the privacy of those around me," he said. "However, the time has now come for my friends and fans around the world to know the truth, and I hope that everyone will join with me, my doctors and all those worldwide in the fight against this terrible disease." Freddie Mercury died of AIDS-related bronchopneumonia the next day, November 24, 1991, at his home in London.

Soon after Mercury's death, "Bohemian Rhapsody" was rereleased to raise money for AIDS research and soared to the top of the British pop charts once again. A 1992 memorial concert at Wembley Stadium in London featured such glamorous pop luminaries as David Bowie, Liza Minnelli, Elton John, George Michael, Annie Lennox, and Guns N' Roses (a distinctly un-glamorous, homophobic group whose appearance at the benefit was controversial). The extravaganza raised both research money and public awareness of AIDS.

Mercury's death—like that of ROCK HUDSON [63] seven years before—was a highly public death that brought the gravity and immediacy of the AIDS epidemic home to millions of people who might not yet have been touched by the disease. As for "Bohemian Rhapsody," it seems destined for some kind of pop immortality, having been resurrected yet again—with wild commercial success—by the 1992 film *Wayne's World*. What would Freddie Mercury have thought about the delicious spectacle of all those straight boys singing their hearts out to the sound of his overdubbed chorus of "Mama mia, mama mia"?

91

Judy Grahn

1940–

Judy Rae Grahn was born in 1940 in Chicago. Her father was a cook, and her mother a photographer's assistant. She spent much of her childhood in what she describes as "an economically poor and spiritually depressed late 1950s New Mexico desert town near the hellish border of West Texas. There, it seemed to me, virtually everything was prohibited except low-level wage slavery and mandatory, joyless marriage."

At eighteen she "eloped" to be with Yvonne, a student at a small nearby college who first introduced her to the secret gay culture whose history she would later trace. She joined the Air Force, but at the age of twenty-one was given what she calls "a less-than-honorable" discharge for being a lesbian. Her letters and notes were seized and used against her friends in the service, and her parents were notified of her "crime." When she went to a Washington, D.C., library to read about homosexuals and lesbians in an effort to investigate who she might be, the librarians told her such books were locked away, available only to professors, doctors, psychiatrists, and lawyers for the criminally insane. As she would later write, these "constituted some of the serious jolts I experienced in my early twenties concerning the position of Gay people in American society." Such jolts made her "angry and determined enough to use my life to reverse a perilous situation."

In 1963 she was one of fifteen members of the Mattachine Society to picket the White House for gay rights. In 1964 she published, under a pseudonym, an article in *Sexology Magazine* in which she argued that lesbians were normal, ordinary people. Also under a pseudonym, she published some poems in *The Ladder*, the magazine put out by the Daughters of Bilitis. Most of her poetry, she realized, was unpublishable by a mainstream press, so in 1969 she founded, with Wendy Cadden (her lover at the time), the Women's Press Collective. They began by printing on a mimeograph machine in the basement, but in time grew into a complete, productive press.

That same year Judy Grahn was a founding member of the West Coast New Lesbian Feminist Movement. Along with such poets as Susan Griffin, Alta, and Pat Parker, she became an important part of the West Coast women's poetry renaissance of the 1970s. Her volumes of poetry include *Edward the Dyke and Other Poems* (1971), *She Who* (1972), an experiment in feminist scripture, and *A Woman Is Talking to Death* (1974). These three volumes were collected together as *The Words of a Common Woman* and issued in 1978 with a preface by ADRIENNE RICH [47]. Along with Pat Parker, a black lesbian feminist poet, Grahn recorded an album of poetry for Olivia Records, that company's first spoken-word release.

In 1982, influenced by H.D.'s [70] use of myth in *Helen in Egypt*, Grahn published *The Queen of Wands*, the first of a projected quartet of long poems. *The Queen of Swords* appeared in 1987, with *Cups* and *Diamonds* to follow.

In 1984, Grahn published her most influential work, *Another Mother Tongue: Gay Words, Gay Worlds*. In this richly researched and speculative study of gay and lesbian cultural history, she explores the history of words (such as *gay, faggot, dyke, fairy, butch,* and *drag*) associated with gayness. As she puts it, "*Another Mother Tongue* proposes that Gay people have a culture, that it cuts across class, race, gender and even national and tribal categories. It proposes further that Gay people have functions in society that involve, and in fact require, Gay attributes. In short, it says that Gay culture is central to Gay people and that Gay people are central to their societies, even when they occupy a despised or underground position."

According to Grahn, the unique place gay people occupy in any society is in opposition to any stable, one-sided, monochrome perception of the universe: "I believe that Gay culture at its heart is continually, however unconsciously, trying to reveal the other side, sometimes just to reveal the *fact* that there are sides. I believe we do this with regard to the sexes, to work roles, to the world of judgment and value, of aesthetics, of philosophies, of other realms of consciousness. We act out irony, essential humor, and paradox."

Like the work of GLORIA ANZALDÚA and CHERRIE MORAGA [79], *Another Mother Tongue* mixes the genres of poetry, essay, and autobiography to produce a fluent, mutable new form.

In her subsequent work, *The Highest Apple* (1985), Grahn builds on her notion of gay culture to trace a lesbian poetic tradition from SAPPHO [2] through such figures as H.D. [70], Amy Lowell, and GERTRUDE STEIN [7] to contemporaries including ADRIENNE RICH [47], AUDRE LORDE [52], Olga Broumas, and Paula Gunn Allen.

In her latest and most controversial book, *Blood, Bread, and Roses: How Menstruation Created the World* (1993), Grahn undertakes nothing less than a radical reconceptualization of human history and identity. Blood, she thinks, is at the center of culture. As she told *The Advocate*, "it doesn't have to be traumatic blood. It can be natural blood and the rituals that women have always performed that have given us all the things we treasure." Those things include chairs, drinking straws, Greyhound buses, lipstick, and red wedding dresses.

Judy Grahn has been a pioneer in the field of gay cultural history: her explorations not just of the present manifestations of gay life but the origins of its signs and codes have had far-reaching consequences for the gay imagination. Her version of gay culture is very much her own, and perhaps too speculative for stricter tastes. Nevertheless, her life's work—not unlike that of a very different personality, the poet JAMES MERRILL [98]—has been a quest to see the larger picture, to create a gay cosmology, an empowering saga telling us who we are, where we have been, where we might be going. In so doing, she has created invaluable myths—and perhaps even realities—of meaning for gay and lesbian people everywhere.

92

Edmund White

1940–

Edmund White was born on January 19, 1940, in Cincinnati, Ohio. His father was, according to White, "a small entrepreneur who made a lot of money and then lost most of it during the time when small businessmen were being superceded by big corporations." When White was seven, his parents divorced, and he went with his mother and sister to live on the outskirts of Chicago. Summers were spent with his father in Cincinnati. In his 1991 essay titled "Out of the Closet, Onto the Bookshelf," White has written, "As a young teen-ager I looked desperately for things to read that might excuse me or assure me I wasn't the only one, that might confirm an identity I was unhappily piecing together. In the early 1950s, the only books I could find in the Evanston,

Illinois, Public Library were Thomas Mann's *Death in Venice* (which suggested that homosexuality was fetid, platonic and death-dealing) and the biography of NIJINSKY [46] by his wife (in which she obliquely deplored the demonic influence of the impresario DIAGHILEV [46] on her saintly husband, the great dancer—an influence that in this instance had produced not death but madness)."

White attended the exclusive Cranbrook Academy and later majored in Chinese at the University of Michigan. Moving to New York City ("in pursuit of someone I later captured and lived with for five years"), he worked for Time-Life Books from 1962 until 1970. He writes, "I never considered myself a company man. I rushed home from work to my apartment on MacDougal Street, ate something and promptly went to bed. At eleven I would rise, dress as a hippie and head out for the bars." After a year's sojourn in Rome, White returned to the United States, where he served as an editor at *The Saturday Review* and *Horizon*. Beginning in the mid-1970s, he and six other gay New York writers—Andrew Holleran, Robert Ferro, Felice Picano, George Whitmore, Christopher Cox, and Michael Grumley—formed a casual club known as the Violet Quill. Meeting in one another's apartment, they would read and critique one another's work, then move on to high tea. Together they represented a flowering of the kind of gay writing Edmund White as a teenager in Illinois had longed to discover.

White's novels include his allegorical fantasia on Fire Island life, *Forgetting Elena* (1973), *Nocturnes for the King of Naples* (1978), and the first two volumes of a projected autobiographical tetralogy, *A Boy's Own Story* (1982), and *The Beautiful Room Is Empty* (1988).

In 1983 he moved to France; when he returned to America in 1990, it was to a literary landscape devastated by AIDS. Four members of the Violet Quill—Ferro, Grumley, Cox, and Whitmore—had died, as well as numerous other promising young writers such as Tim Dlugos and John Fox. White's two closest friends, the critic David Kalstone and his editor Bill Whitehead, were also dead from the disease. He has written, "For me, these losses were definitive. The witnesses to my life, the people who had shared the same references and sense of humor, were gone. The loss of all the books they might have written remains incalculable."

Although known as a novelist whose work has been widely praised by such writers as Vladimir Nabokov and Susan Sontag, it is as a cultural critic that White has perhaps had his greatest influence. Urbane, knowing, sophisticated, he has chronicled gay life in the seventies through the nineties with wit and insight. He has become a grand arbiter of taste, though he has been criticized for the narrowness of that taste—especially after his 1991 anthology *Gay Short Fiction* contained no writing by men of color. Nevertheless, his 1980 travelogue, *States of Desire: Travels in Gay America*, remains a classic if insouciant (and now poignant) look at gay life at a particular cultural moment just before the onslaught of AIDS. His pioneering 1977 *The Joy of Gay Sex: An Intimate Guide for Gay Men to the Pleasures of a Gay Life*, written with Dr. Charles Silverstein, introduced millions, gay and straight and curious alike, to a brave new world of sexual practices and lifestyle. The cumulative effect of White's presence simultaneously within so many different genres was to begin to define, in the late 1970s and early 1980s, the parameters of "gay culture," whatever that evolving entity might be.

AIDS, of course, has darkened all that, and White, who is HIV-positive, has written of the dilemma facing gay writers today: "Some…think that it's unconscionable to deal with anything [other than AIDS]; others believe that since gay culture is in imminent danger of being reduced to a single issue, one that once again equates homosexuality with a dire medical condition, the true duty of gay writers is to remind readers of the wealth of gay accomplishments. Only in that way, they argue, will a gay heritage be passed down to a post-plague generation."

White's own choice has been clear: his most recent work is a monumental biography of the French novelist and playwright JEAN GENET [45] that celebrates this treasure of our gay heritage and argues for the centrality of Genet's homosexuality to any consideration of his oeuvre. As for Edmund White, he and his work—privileged, literate, sophisticated, hedonistic—remain central to any consideration of gay male upper-middle-class life in late-twentieth-century America.

93

Katherine Philips

1631–1664

Katherine Philips was born on January 1, 1631, in the parish of St. Mary Woolchurch, London. Her father, John Fowler, was a merchant. After his death, her mother married Hector Philips, and Katherine took his surname. At the age of eight, she was sent to the fashionable boarding school at Hackney run by a Mrs. Salmon of royalist persuasion (this was during Oliver Cromwell's Commonwealth). In 1647, Philips married James Philips, her stepfather's son by his first marriage. She was her husband's second wife. Together they divided their time between Cardigan, Wales, which James Philips represented in Parliament, and London.

A studious and disciplined woman, Philips began to write poetry, and in 1651 her first poems appeared prefixed to a volume by Henry Vaughan. Other poems of hers, circulated in manuscript, earned her a considerable reputation among the cognoscenti. She gathered around herself a Platonic Society of Friendship whose members took on playfully exotic names: her husband became "Antenor," Sir Edward Dering was "Silvander," and she herself was known as "Orinda"—or, more popularly, the "matchless Orinda."

The matchless Orinda addressed nearly half of her poems to her friend Anne Owen, whom she called Lucasia. Many of her other poems are to Mary Aubrey, known as Rosania. One of her most famous was titled "Lucasia, Rosania and Orinda Parting at a Fountain, July, 1663," and gives us an intimate look at women's intense friendships in the seventeenth century. Drawing on the passionate language of John Donne's poetry, her verses celebrate with uncommon ardor the joys and sorrows of her love for these women—what she called "friendship's mystery." It is a world centered around the love of women for women, a grave and dignified world from which men are virtually absent. She called Lucasia "my Joy, my Life, my rest." To Rosania she wrote:

> Thus our twin-souls in one shall grow,
> And teach the world new love,
> Redeem the age and sex and show
> A flame fate dares not move.

And this beautiful stanza, from "Orinda to Lucasia," was judged by Philips's contemporaries to rank with the best late-Metaphysical verse:

> Thou my Lucasia art far more to me,
> Than he to all the under-world can be;
>   From thee I've heat and light,
>   Thy absence makes my night.
> But ah! my Friend, it now grows very long,
> The sadness weighty, and the darkness strong:
>   My tears (its dew) dwell on my cheeks,
>   And still my heart thy dawning seeks,
> And to thee mournfully it cries,
>   That if too long I wait,
>   Ev'n thou may'st come too late,
> And not restore my life, but close my eyes.

More than a century after her death, Philips's poems continued to impress no less a poet than John Keats.

In 1662, Philips traveled to Dublin, Ireland, and while there translated Pierre Corneille's *Pompée*, which was produced at the Smock-Alley Theatre during 1662–63 with great success. The play was printed in Dublin in 1663, and two London editions also appeared. In 1664 a London publisher brought out an unauthorized edition of her poems, which so incensed Philips that the publisher took out an advertisement in the January 18, 1664, edition of the London *Intelligencer* apologizing for the edition and withdrawing it from sale.

At the height of Katherine Philips's success and popularity, she was stricken with smallpox and died on June 22, 1664, in London. Her poems were collected and published in 1667, along with a version of Corneille's *Horace* left unfinished at her death.

Katherine Philips was one of those rare women who managed to achieve what VIRGINIA WOOLF [13] called "a room of one's own"—that private space in which a woman, against all the odds of her society, could find the time and economic support and courage to write. As one of the very few women writers—lesbian or otherwise—to achieve widespread recognition in the seventeenth century, Philips is not simply a historical curiosity: her poems have real merit, and their representations of female love and friendship in an earlier age serve as valuable testimony to the existence of same-sex affections that have otherwise gone unrecorded. As a significant precursor to the other lesbian poets in this ranking—ADRIENNE RICH [47], AUDRE LORDE [52], H.D. [70], and JUDY GRAHN [91]—she earns a place in this ranking.

94

Ethel Smyth

1858–1944

Ethel Smyth was born on April 22, 1858, in Marylebone, England. Her father was a general in the British military, and her mother was French. The family was prosperous. In 1877 she enrolled in the Leipzig Conservatory, but soon grew dissatisfied with the instruction there and began taking private lessons from Heinrich von Herzogenberg. Her early chamber works were met with praise, and she was encouraged by such composers as Brahms, Grieg, TCHAIKOVSKY [29] and Clara Schumann, all of whom took her work seriously. Her first major score, the powerful and robust Mass in D Major, made a profound impression on audiences at its premiere in London in January 1893. Women were not, at the time, considered capable of writing music of such depth and range.

Smyth's greatest successes came in the field of opera. Her first, *Fantasio,* for which she also composed the libretto in German, was badly produced in Weimar in 1898 and more competently revived in Karlsruhe in 1901. Smyth came to consider this work an apprentice piece and in 1916 destroyed most of the printed scores. More successful was her ambitious one-act, *Der Wald,* produced in Berlin in 1902, Covent Garden in 1902, and New York in 1903.

Her third opera, perhaps her masterpiece, was *The Wreckers (Les Naufrageurs)* to her own libretto in French, first produced as *Strandrecht* in Leipzig in 1906. It was also staged in Prague in 1906, and London in 1909, where it received great acclaim.

In the first decade of the 20th century Smyth became increasingly involved in the movement for women's suffrage in Britain and composed a "March of the Women," which was frequently sung during street demonstrations. Her next opera, *The Boatswain's Mate* (1916), with its strong female characters, was influenced by her political involvement and became a rousing success, eventually entering the regular repertory of the Old Vic Theatre. An exuberant, even flamboyant figure, Smyth campaigned tirelessly for the equal treatment of women artists. She received an honorary degree from Durham University in 1910 and was created a Dame of the British Empire in 1922.

Her later works include the operas *Fête galante* (1923) and *Entente cordiale* (1925), the Concerto for Violin, Horn and Orchestra (1927), and *The Prison* (1931), a symphony for soprano, bass-baritone, chorus, and orchestra.

Although increasing deafness forced her to stop composing in her later years, she continued to write prose. Her two-volume autobiographical work, *Impressions that Remained,* had been enthusiastically received when it appeared in 1919, and she followed it with eight more books that became famous for their forthright honesty and appealing prose style. Possessing indefatigable energies, resilient self-confidence ("I am the most interesting person I know, and I don't care if anyone else thinks so," she declared in 1935), and a personality that was larger-than-life, Smyth fell in love with numerous women throughout her long life. Reading VIRGINIA WOOLF's [13] *A Room of One's Own* sparked in her a desire to meet the author, which she did in 1930. Seventy-one at the time, Smyth fell in love, recording in her diary, "I don't think I have ever cared for anyone more profoundly. For eighteen months I have thought of little else." She became one of Woolf's most devoted—and demanding—friends and dedicated her volume *As Time Went On* to her in 1936. As for Woolf, we find her writing, in February 1933, after a visit from the by-now-almost-completely-deaf Smyth, "Oh yesterday it was like being a snail & having a thrush tapping till the beak of her incessant voice broke my skull. I always say 'Poor old lady.' For I rather think she came all the way from Woking for the dry brittle hour.... And now she goes to Bath for 5 weeks—yes, to my relief I own. Because I can't bear being a snail shell. And she is so positive, so insistent. Being Ethel is so habitual to her." Nevertheless, Woolf found herself moved by Smyth's "bluff affection."

Ethel Smyth lived at Coign, the house she built near Woking, with her maid and her dog until her death on May 9, 1944.

That rare creature—a woman composer—Ethel Smyth was an important figure in the renaissance of English music that occurred around the turn of the century. Her grand and powerful music was greatly acclaimed by both critics and audiences of the day. For her courageous defiance of convention, for her unceasing struggle to realize both her loves and her musical ambitions against the tide of common practice, she earns her ranking on this list.

95

Halston

1932–1990

Roy Halston Frowick was born on April 23, 1932, in Des Moines, Iowa. After attending Indiana University and the Art Institute of Chicago, he opened a millinery shop at the Ambassador East Hotel in Chicago where, from the very beginning, he was associated with celebrity. His first client was the television star Fran Allison from "Kukla, Fran and Ollie." His shop became an instant success. Soon he was designing hats for the likes of Kim Novak and Shirley Booth, and in 1957, at the age of twenty-five, he moved to New York to work for the famous milliner Lily Daché. From there he went to Bergdorf Goodman in 1959 as their first "name" milliner and designed the famous felt pillbox hat worn by Jacqueline Kennedy at her husband's inauguration as president of the United States.

Unfortunately, the tide in fashion had turned against hats. Bouffant hair was in. Halston expanded his repertoire in 1966 by introducing, for Bergdorf, a line of clothes meant to negotiate the gap between couture and ready-to-wear. In 1968, Halston opened his own couture house on Madison Avenue, where he counted among his clients Elizabeth Taylor, Liza Minnelli, Lauren Bacall, Candice Bergen, and Bianca Jagger.

Halston was at the height of his influence in the early 1970s. In particular, his fall collection in 1971, with its sober, restrained designs and reintroduction of the cashmere sweater sets that had been popular in the 1950s, spelled an end to the antiestablishment look of the previous decade and ushered in an era of chic elegance. He was instrumental in introducing Ultrasuede, an imitation leather made in Japan, to the American market: it proved a staple of the fashion industry for the next several years. His shows became trendy, stylish events, leading his friend ANDY WARHOL [33] to proclaim them "the art form of the seventies." Halston did much to increase the reputation of American designers abroad. In 1971 and again in 1972 he was the recipient of the Coty American Fashion Critics' "Winnie" Award for the most significant influence on fashion, and in 1974 he won the Coty Hall of Fame Award.

In 1973, Halston sold his name and company to the Norton Simon Conglomerate for $16 million. He stayed on as principal designer and diversified his line to include a wide range of items such as furs, cosmetics, perfumes, and luggage. During the successful seventies he became fashion's superstar, an international jet-setter known for his fast-paced lifestyle and trademark black turtlenecks. But things began to fall apart. His stock in the fashion world plummeted in 1982 when he signed a lucrative deal with JCPenney to design ready-to-wear clothes. In response, Bergdorf ended its twenty-five-year association with the designer. The Penney's designs were not a success, and critics speculated that he had taken on too much. His work habits had also changed. By the late seventies and early eighties he was spending time at the trendy but notorious Studio 54 (of which ROY COHN [84] was another habtitué). Instead of working from eight A.M. to midnight, as had been his habit, he partied till four or five in the morning and showed up for work after noon.

In 1984 he tried to buy his business back so that he could once again design under his own name, but his bid was unsuccessful, and the Halston name was acquired by the Beatrice Corporation. Eventually it passed to the Revlon Group. Halston's later work was mostly limited to theatrical design: costumes for Martha Graham's dance company and for Liza Minnelli's Broadway show *The Act*.

Early in 1990, Halston left New York to move to California, in order to be closer to his siblings. He died in San Francisco on March 26, 1990, due to complications from AIDS.

Collectively and individually, gay men have made a greater mark in the fashion industry than perhaps anywhere else. A cliché, perhaps, but it's true: and from the pillbox hat he made for Jackie to his nights in black turtleneck at Studio 54, no one designer was more visible than Halston. No one more influenced the look of the times.

96

Samuel Delaney

1942–

Samuel Ray "Chip" Delaney was born on April 1, 1942, in Harlem, New York, where his family owned a mortuary. As a child he was fascinated by science and math, but also—under his mother's influence—by music, theater, and books.

At the age of ten he discovered that his major sexual preference was homosexual. "Secretly in those years," he would later recall, "I would write down my masturbation fantasies in a black loose-leaf binder I kept beneath my underwear in the tall, stained-oak bureau against the wall in my third-floor room...They were...grandiose, homoerotic, full of kings and warriors, leather armor, slaves, swords and brocade..." His mother's eventual discovery of the loose-leaf binder containing his fantasy-diaries led, predictably enough, to a round of therapy sessions.

Although Delaney thought, in his youth, that his vocation lay in the sciences (he attended the elite Bronx High School of Science), his prodigious creative energies found multiple outlets: in addition to writing novels (his first at the age of thirteen), he composed music, including a violin concerto and a chamber symphony.

In 1961 Delaney married the talented young poet Marilyn Hacker, whom he had made pregnant and to whom he had confessed his homosexuality. Because of miscegenation laws and different age of consent laws for men and women, the nineteen-year-old Delaney and eighteen-year-old Hacker had to travel to Michigan, one of only two states where they could be legally wed. Though they remained married until 1980, the relationship, according to Delaney, "drifted from one aspect to another of low-key nightmare." Michael Emery characterizes Delaney's life at the time: "he was a young black gay dyslexic intellectual married to a white Jewish woman, attempting a low-paying writing career instead of a college degree (which he never seriously pursued), and living a subterranean sexual life on the streets of New York." In his 1988 memoir, *The Motion of Light in Water: Sex and Science Fiction Writing in the East Village, 1957–1965*, Delaney chronicles that subterranean life with disarming frankness. Here he describes his restless and heady nocturnal cruisings among trucks parked along the waterfront at the foot of Christopher Street:

> At one, at two, the activity among the trucks tended to fall off—except for weekends. And even then, there was always some change of tenor.
>
> Sometimes to walk between the vans and cabs was to amble from single sexual encounter—with five, twelve, forty minutes between—to single sexual encounter. At other times to step between the waist-high tires and make your way between the smooth or ribbed walls was to invade a space at a libidinal saturation point impossible to describe to somone who has not known it. Any number of pornographic filmmakers, gay and straight, have tried to portray something like it—now for homosexuality, now for heterosexuality—and failed because what they were trying to show was wild, abandoned, beyond the edge of control, whereas the actuality of such a situation, with thirty-five, fifty, a

hundred all-but-strangers is huge, ordered, highly social, attentive, silent, and grounded in a certain care, if
not community. At those times, within those van-walled
alleys, now between the trucks, now in the back of the
open loaders, cock passed from mouth to mouth to
hand to ass to mouth without ever breaking contact
with other flesh for more than seconds; mouth, hand,
ass passed over whatever you held out to them, sans
interstice; when one cock left, finding a replacement
mouth, rectum, another cock—required moving only
the head, the hip, the hand no more than an inch, three
inches.

At the age of twenty Delaney wrote his first mature novel, a
work of science fiction called *The Jewels of Aptor*. It was published
by Ace Books, where Hacker worked as an editorial assistant.
More novels followed at a furious pace, and accolades as well—by
the time Delaney was twenty-six he had won four coveted Nebula
Awards from the Science Fiction Writers of America: in 1966 for
the novel *Babel-17*, in 1967 for the novel *The Einstein Intersection*
and the short story "Aye, and Gomorrah," and in 1968 for "Time
Considered as a Helix of Semi-Precious Stones." He made little
money on any of these works.

In 1967, Delaney considered abandoning his writing career
in order to become a musician. He performed with the band
Heavenly Breakfast and lived for a time in a commune in the East
Village. When he returned to science fiction in 1970, his books
became more intellectual and challenging. They also became
much gayer in theme. Particularly significant was the influence of
post-structuralist thought on his work. *Dahlgren* (1975) became a
bestseller, and though alienating some of his earlier fans, it
introduced him to a larger audience outside the science fiction
genre. *Triton: An Ambiguous Heterotopia or Some Informal Remarks
Toward the Modular Calculus, Part One* (1976) was hailed as a
masterpiece and vilified as unreadable in its conjuration of a
utopian future where sexual difference is the norm. Between
1979 and 1987, Delaney was occupied with a series of fantastic
tales called *Nevèrÿon*, including *Tales of Nevèrÿon* (1979), *Nevèrÿona*
(1983), *Flight from Nevèrÿon* (1985), and *The Bridge of Lost Desire*
(1987). The third volume in the series paralleled the AIDS
epidemic on earth (and specifically New York City) with a similar

plague on Nevèrÿon. Delaney's other major science fiction work during this time was *Stars in My Pocket like Grains of Sand* (1984), at whose center is a gay relationship between two men.

Samuel Delaney has been extremely influential in the popular genre of science fiction, especially given his double outsider status as both black and gay. In such nonfiction works as *The Jewel-Hinged Jaw* (1977) he has shown himself to be one of science fiction's most important literary theorists, and today he is regarded by some as the father of cyberpunk. His female and androgynous characters consistently defy readers' expectations, and his explicitly gay characters have gone where few gays have gone before—to reach a wide readership that might never otherwise have encountered or considered gay issues in any guise. In recent years Delaney has become increasingly visible and influential as a spokesperson for gay issues, as evidenced by his keynote addresses at the 1991 International Gay and Lesbian Studies Conference and the 1993 Outwrite convention.

Science fiction plays an important role in shaping our culture's sense of possibilities. The genre has always been a way of thinking about the world not only as it is, but as it could be—in all the myriad guises the human imagination can devise. By boldly imagining the fullest range of sexual possibilities, pioneering gay science fiction writers such as Samuel Delaney—and his lesbian counterpart, Joanna Russ—have enlarged our already expanding universe.

97

Ian McKellen

1939–

Ian Murray McKellen was born on May 25, 1939, in Burnley, England. His early education took place at Wigan Grammar School and the Bolton School. He attended St. Catharine's College, Cambridge, where as a student actor he was directed by John Barton, who would later become the director of the Royal Shakespeare Company. McKellen received his BA from St. Catharine's in 1962. He made his stage debut in 1961 as Roger Roper in *A Man for All Seasons* at the Belgrade Theater, Coventry. His London debut in 1964 as Godfrey in James Saunder's *A Scent of Flowers* won him a Clarence Derwent Award for best actor and led to a season with the National Theatre.

In 1967 he played in New York, appearing in Arbuzov's *The Promise*, and in 1968 he received rave reviews for his performance of Peter Shaffer's double bill of *White Liars* and *Black Comedy*. He then consolidated his growing reputation as one of England's finest actors with title roles in WILLIAM SHAKESPEARE's [20] *Richard II* and, in 1969, CHRISTOPHER MARLOWE's [19] *Edward II* (which he claims is his favorite theatrical role).

He helped found the Actor's Company in 1972, a progressive ensemble in which the actors choose their own plays and share equal pay, billing, and leading roles. As Edgar in *King Lear* at the 1973 Edinburgh Festival, he won that year's Drama Desk Award for Outstanding Performance.

In 1974, at the invitation of his Cambridge mentor John Barton, McKellen joined the Royal Shakespeare Company, performing in acclaimed productions of Marlowe's *Dr. Faustus* (1974), Shaw's *Too Good to Be True* (1975), and Shakespeare's *Romeo and Juliet*, *The Winter's Tale*, and *Macbeth* (all in 1976). He left the RSC in 1978 for a role in *Bent*, Martin Sherman's acclaimed drama about gays in the Nazi concentration camps. For his performance, McKellen received the Laurence Olivier Award for Best Actor in 1979. He also began touring his now legendary one-man show, *Acting Shakespeare*. First performed at the Edinburgh Festival in 1977, *Acting Shakespeare* won McKellen the Drama Desk Award, the Elliot Norton Award, and the Antoinette Perry Award. In 1979 he was decorated Commander of the Order of the British Empire.

His 1981 performance as Mozart's jealous rival Salieri in Peter Shaffer's *Amadeus* at the Broadhurst Theatre in New York City garnered him tremendous accolades, as well as the Drama Desk Award for best actor, the Drama League of New York's Distinguished Performance Award, the Outer Critics' Circle Award for best actor, and the Antoinette Perry Award for best actor.

In 1988, Ian McKellen publicly came out, the first major actor to do so. After that, he became an increasingly vocal and visible proponent of gay rights in Great Britain during a time when the Tory government of Margaret Thatcher was busy instituting draconian antigay legislation. Known as Clause 28, the new laws would have recriminalized much gay behavior between consenting adults.

About his coming out, McKellen later observed, "There are

many closeted actors, very ambitious for their careers, who do what I did at their age and keep quiet about their sexuality. I don't have a huge quarrel with that, though I regret it for their own sake. But what I cannot stand is when somebody lies—says they're waiting for the right little woman or right little man to make them happy or gets married and pretends. In my own defense, I never lied. I just avoided the question."

In 1991, in recognition of his long career as Britain's "leading leading man," as he has been called, Ian McKellen was granted knighthood. His decision to accept the honor was bitterly attacked by film director DEREK JARMAN [82], who in a letter to the newspaper the *Guardian* wrote that McKellen should have declined to be knighted by the same conservative government murderously intent on repressing and ostracizing gay people. In the ensuing public debate, McKellen was defended by eighteen prominent film and theater professionals who wrote to the *Guardian* identifying themselves as gay or lesbian and praising McKellen's knighthood as "a significant landmark in the history of the British gay movement." Never again, according to their letter, "will public figures be able to claim that they have to keep secret their homosexuality in fear of it damaging their careers." The signatories included the film director John Schlesinger, producers Cameron Mackintosh and Ned Sherrin, actors Simon Callow, Alec McCowen, and Antony Sher, and actress Pam St. Clement.

Also coming to McKellen's side was playwright Peter Shaffer, writing that the actor had "made no secret of his proper contempt for the government's legal policies regarding homosexuality" and that knighthood "at least represents a recognition of that government of his courage and fearless humanitarianism." Openly gay member of Parliament Chris Smith wrote, " 'Queerbashing' attacks are on the increase. Discriminatory legislation is in the pipeline. The tabloids fulminate offensively. Day by day people are sacked from their jobs or turned out of their homes or charged more for their insurance or refused custody of their children or subjected to abuse simply and solely because of their sexual orientation. In many ways, the difficulties facing lesbians and gay men are getting worse rather than better. Against this tide we can, however, set the brave testimony of people like Ian McKellen—and demonstrate that such openness can at the very least command respect from many millions of people."

Many prominent actors in this century have been gay, among them Sir Laurence Olivier, his lover Danny Kaye, Sir John Gielgud, Tyrone Power, Montgomery Clift, Errol Flynn, Charles Laughton, and of course ROCK HUDSON [63]. In almost every case, however, we have learned they were gay only after their deaths, when the biographical truth comes out. By staying in the closet, these actors haplessly reinforced the notion that to come out would spell the end of one's career. It is for his honesty and courage in publicly coming out, putting his career on the line, and fighting for the rights of gay men and lesbians that Ian McKellen merits his ranking in *The Gay 100*.

98

James Merrill

1926–

James Merrill was born on March 3, 1926, in New York City. The son of Charles Edward Merrill, the founder of the stockbrokerage firm of Merrill Lynch, he was raised in wealthy surroundings and tutored by a governess he called Mademoiselle, a Prussian-English widow who first instilled in him his love of language. When Merrill was twelve, his parents divorced. Mademoiselle was dismissed, and the young Merrill was shipped off to the prestigious Lawrenceville School near Princeton, New Jersey. He began to write poetry and short stories early on, and his first book, *Jim's Book*, was privately published by his father when he was eighteen. In 1943 he entered Amherst College. A two-year stint as a private in the U.S. Army interrupted his education in

1944–45, but after the war he returned to school and graduated summa cum laude from Amherst in 1947. By this time a second collection of poems, *The Black Swan,* had also been privately printed.

In the early 1950s, Merrill traveled extensively in Europe and Asia. In 1953, he met David Jackson (b. 1922), a writer and musician from Los Angeles. The two became lovers and in 1954 settled in Stonington, Connecticut, which was to become the quiet, domestic setting for much of Merrill's poetry. During the 1955–56 academic year, Merrill taught in the English department at Amherst, during which time his play *The Immortal Husband* was successfully produced in New York City. Nineteen fifty-seven saw the publication of Merrill's first novel, *The Seraglio,* and in 1959 he published his first major book of poems, *The Country of a Thousand Years of Peace.*

Like HADRIAN [15] in the first century, WINCKELMANN [21] in the eighteenth, and SYMONDS [10] in the nineteenth, Merrill was drawn to Greece. In 1959 he took a house in Athens and began spending half of each year there. Greece allowed him a double life: he assiduously avoided the company of Americans, and his demotic Greek allowed him to experience the life of the country firsthand. The gay Greek-language poet Constantine Cavafy, who flourished in Alexandria, Egypt around the turn of the century, greatly influenced Merrill's work in these years. Beginning in the late 1970s, Key West, Florida, was added to Greece and Stonington as a place of residence for the peripatetic poet.

Elegant, intimate, introspective volumes of poetry streamed forth at a steady rate in those years, along with increasing recognition: *Water Street* (1962), *Nights and Days* (awarded the National Book Award in 1966), *The Fire Screen* (1969), *Braving the Elements* (winner of the 1972 Bollingen Prize), *The Yellow Pages* (1974), and *Divine Comedies* (winner of the 1976 Pulitzer Prize). Merrill's 1965 novel *The (Diblos) Notebook* was also nominated for a National Book Award.

Merrill's poetry up until this point had been urbane, sophisticated, the gemlike work of a master miniaturist. Beginning in the late seventies that unexpectedly changed, and he brought forth, in several installments, an astonishing work of epic proportions—over five hundred pages—that would become known as *The Changing Light at Sandover.* Consisting of *The Book of Ephraim*

(1976), *Mirabell: Books of Number* (winner of the 1978 National Book Award), *Scripts for the Pageant* (1980), and the coda *The Higher Keys* (1981), the work has been compared to Dante's *Divine Comedy*, to Milton's *Paradise Lost*, to William Blake's *Marriage of Heaven and Hell*. Finally, though, it is unlike anything else: a cosmological extravaganza that balances visionary seriousness with high-camp humor.

In his previous poetry, Merrill had been circumspect about his homosexuality, often adopting the time-worn tactic of addressing love poems to a vague "you." *The Changing Light at Sandover* is unabashedly gay to its very core in both themes and sensibility. The basic scenario is this: through the venerable Victorian parlor game of Ouija, David Jackson and James Merrill, their fingers lightly touching the willowware teacup they use as a planchette on their homemade board, contact the other world. Their first visitor, a spirit named Ephraim, identifies himself as a first-century Greek Jew who was strangled on Capri at the orders of Tiberius, for having been the emperor's nephew Caligula's lover. Ephraim has recognized, in these two twentieth-century lovers, a fellow spirit—and indeed, the poem is a vast hymn to the complex interactive energies of Jackson and Merrill's love for one another. It is love that makes the Ouija work, love that opens for them the secrets of the universe—a universe inhabited by shimmering metaphysical peacocks and strident archangels as well as old friends such as Hans Lodeizen, Maria Mitsotaki, and W. H. Auden. It is also a universe haunted by the crisis of overpopulation and the threat of nuclear disaster.

Since *The Changing Light at Sandover*, Merrill has continued to produce prolifically and is today generally regarded as one of the most important poets in America. I have included him in this ranking on the basis of *The Changing Light at Sandover*, a project of gay soul-shaping, an extravagant and profound and profoundly comic cosmology that promises to resonate in our collective imagination for years to come.

99

Madonna

1958–

Madonna Louise Vernon Ciccone was born on August 16, 1958, in Rochester, Michigan. In high school she excelled in dance and drama, and during her brief stints at college in Michigan and North Carolina trained as a dancer. Through the influence of her boyfriend Steve Bray, a drummer, she became interested in music. Moving to New York City in 1977, she studied dance with Alvin Ailey and worked as a model. After two years, she moved to Paris where, for a short time, she was a backup singer for the French disco star Patrick Hernandez (his big hit was "Born to Be Alive"). Returning to New York, Madonna played in several bands: she was the drummer for Breakfast Club and lead vocalist for Emmy. A demo tape led to a record contract with Sire

Records, and her first single, "Everybody," heavily promoted by her new DJ boyfriend Mark Kamins, became a hit on the club scene in 1982. Although her first full-length album, *Madonna '83,* received mixed critical reviews ("Minnie Mouse on helium"), the album yielded five hit singles, including "Holiday," produced by her latest boyfriend, John "Jellybean" Benitez. The next year saw the release of *Like a Virgin:* both the album and the single of the same name rose to the number one position on the American pop charts.

In 1985, Madonna won unexpectedly good reviews for her acting in Susan Seidelman's film *Desperately Seeking Susan.* A spin-off from the film was the hit single "Into the Groove." Her next film, *Shanghai Surprise* (1986)— in which she costarred with her new husband, Hollywood bad boy Sean Penn—was panned by the critics. That same year she released her album *True Blue* to mixed reviews, though again it proved to be a commercial success. In *Who's That Girl?* (1987, film and album), Madonna began to adopt the mannerisms of Marilyn Monroe with uncanny vengeance.

Madonna found herself at the center of intense controversy in 1989 when her single "Like a Prayer" and its accompanying video, in which she seduces a black saint and receives the stigmata, was condemned by the Vatican. In response, Pepsi-Cola canceled a lucrative sponsorship contract with Madonna. The resultant notoriety, however, turned the album *Like a Prayer* into an international megahit. Following a role in the 1990 film *Dick Tracy,* Madonna embarked on her Blonde Ambition world tour, during which she was threatened with arrest in Toronto for simulating masturbation onstage. Her video for "Justify My Love" was banned from MTV for its portrayal of a pansexual orgy. She was at the height of her powers, and the tour is recorded in the 1991 film *Truth Or Dare: On the Band, Behind the Scenes, and in Bed With Madonna,* in which Madonna cavorts provocatively with her troupe of mostly gay male dancers. A savvy businesswoman throughout her career, Madonna signed a multimillion-dollar deal with Time Warner in 1992, one of the largest of its kind ever.

Unwavering in her support of the gay community, out-spokenly gay positive, generous in her participation in AIDS benefits, Madonna was presented with the Media Award from the Gay and Lesbian Alliance Against Defamation (GLAAD) in 1990.

I have included Madonna in this ranking because I believe she represents an important late-twentieth-century phenomenon, and that she has been made possible precisely because of the influential contributions of all those other individuals who come before her on this list. Writing in Boston's *Gay Community News*, Sydney Pokorny has aptly described the Madonna of the Blonde Ambition Tour as "clothed in the language of heterosexuality" while "soliciting a lesbian gaze": a transformation "from boy toy to gal pal." In a sense, this nominally heterosexual woman (she claims to believe that everyone is bisexual) finds herself at a cultural moment when it is possible to publicly and explicitly adopt the styles of lesbians and gay men for her own purposes. There may very well be something insidious in that appropriation; nevertheless, it is of historic importance that a public figure like Madonna is now able to profit from precisely those identities and styles that have for so long remained anathema. Far from having committed professional suicide by cultivating an ambiguous "affair" with erstwhile lesbian Sandra Bernhardt or by openly cavorting with gay men or by talking candidly about being finger-fucked by her childhood girlfriend, Madonna has in fact only furthered her career. One may certainly criticize her for indulging in a risk-free appropriation: for her, voguing is a luxury; for the young men of the house balls it is sometimes literally a matter of life and death. At the same time, one can argue that no one has done more than Madonna to make images—certain kinds of images—of gay and lesbian life familiar and perhaps even acceptable to millions of people around the world. By exploding preconceptions about gender roles and sexuality, gay and straight alike, Madonna has contributed to a more progressive and tolerant social climate from which gays and lesbians can only benefit.

100

Michelangelo Signorile

1960–

Michelangelo Signorile was born in 1960 in Brooklyn, New York. His parents were first-generation Italian-Americans, and he grew up in a tight-knit Roman Catholic family that discouraged individuality. Nevertheless, he went his own way, eschewing the conventional boyhood involvement with baseball and instead playing with dolls with his cousin Marilu. When he was called sissy and faggot and queer at school, he fought back—going after not only those who harassed him but other boys who had been called faggot as well. As he later wrote, "I became a queer-basher to prove I wasn't queer."

When he was eight, his family moved to Staten Island. He had his first sexual experience at the age of twelve, with a thirty-year-old man who worked in a neighborhood bagel store. "The guilt," he writes, "was insurmountable. I was physically ill for days, throwing up, disgusted over being such a bad Catholic and doing such grotesque things." In an attempt to "cure" himself, he joined the Pee Wee football league and to keep in shape began jogging on the Franklin D. Roosevelt Boardwalk at South Beach. It was under that boardwalk that he discovered dozens of Italian boys his own age who would meet in the afternoons and have sex. "The boys," he writes, "were all in the same boat as I was: None of them would ever have called themselves gay. They were all kids who were trying to deal with this madness that had seemingly taken over their bodies. Most would have said they hated it and wished they weren't that way; all would have said this was just a phase, a time that was going to pass. None of us were ever going to be homos when we got older: We were all going to get married, just like everybody else."

He enrolled in the prestigious Monsignor Farrell High School, where he continued to play football and bash queer-bashers and queers alike. When, after two years of such behavior, he was called into the principal's office for an explanation, he admitted that he got into fights because the other boys called him names. He also admitted that the names he was called might, in fact, be true. For that bit of honesty he was asked to leave the school. He finished his high school education at a public school, where he began to use drugs and, when caught, entered two years of therapy during which homosexuality was never discussed. After graduating, he entered Brooklyn College, but after two years transferred to the S. I. Newhouse School of Public Communications at Syracuse University to study journalism. There, for the first time in his life, he was able to come out of the closet and live openly as a gay man. "I was the happiest I'd ever been, as if I'd finally found that fantasy world I'd always dreamed about. But I also realized how lucky I'd been to make it through those rough years: Thirty percent of the teen suicides in America, I came to learn, are among lesbian and gay adolescents who feel that life has nothing to offer them and that they are freaks."

After graduating from Syracuse he moved to New York City and eventually began working for a public relations firm that planted celebrity "mentions" in gossip columns. Everything seemed fair game in the gossip trade except, Signorile noticed, for homosexuality. In fact, homosexual celebrities were constantly disguised—by their agents, their studios, the gossip columnists themselves—as heterosexuals in what began to look to

Signorile like a vast conspiracy of silence around queer identity. It marked the stirring of a political consciousness in this otherwise apolitical gay man who, in the mid-1980s, was far more interested in what was going on in the trendy Manhattan clubs like Area and Palladium than any developments in the political arena. It was one of his closest friends during this time, *Village Voice* columnist Michael Musto, who made him aware of the deep denial that was fueling the gay scene—denial of the terrifying specter of AIDS. By the late 1980s, its presence could no longer be denied. As Signorile writes, "close friends of mine began getting sick. Old boyfriends were calling me up to say they'd tested positive." He sloughed off the glamorous stupor he'd been living in and, in 1987, began attending meetings of ACT UP. Through his participation in civil disobedience and in publicizing the activities of ACT UP, he came to realize that *not only was being out of the closet absolutely essential, but advertising homosexuality through the media and utilizing the media to show the face of AIDS were even more essential.*

When Gabriel Rotello asked him, in 1989, if he was interested in starting a magazine that would shake people up, Signorile immediately said yes, and the controversial gay and lesbian newsmagazine *Outweek* was born. As features editor, Signorile presided over the publishing phenomenon that would come to be known, courtesy of *Time* magazine, as "outing"—the public identification of closeted gay or lesbian public figures. He writes, "Contrary to popular preconception, outing was a *by-product* of a revolution rather than a conscious invention of that revolution....No matter how much some older and more conservative activists wince at the thought of it, outing was a natural, inevitable outcome of the work that everyone in the larger lesbian and gay movement had done for over twenty years. By 1990, outing was the next logical step. In that way, there was no one factor that made me out [recently deceased] multimillionaire press magnate Malcolm Forbes in March of that year, except the something inside me that told me it had to be done, that it was the right thing to do."

Not surprisingly, the straight media reacted with consternation, refusing for several weeks to report on the outing of Forbes, and only then by blanking out his name. Signorile was accused of McCarthyism, fascism, and invasion of privacy by both gays and straights alike. His editor, Gabriel Rotello, defended him, however, explaining that outing—or "equalizing," the word he and Signorile prefer—simply aims "to treat homosexuality as equal to heterosexuality." As Signorile has argued, "if the media are going to report heterosexual love affairs—whether that is right or not—it is simply homophobic for them to refuse to report on homosexual ones. By not reporting about famous gays, the message the media sends is clear: Homosexuality is so utterly grotesque that it should never be discussed."

The firestorm over Malcolm Forbes was nothing compared to what Signorile unleashed in 1991 when, in *The Advocate*, he outed Pete Williams, the senior civilian Department of Defense spokesman and protégé of Defense Secretary Dick Cheney. That the Pentagon, which bars gays from serving in the military and regularly ousts them whenever they are discovered, should have as its chief spokesman a gay man was a hypocrisy that was lost on few. Nevertheless, the abuse of Signorile poured in.

Signorile eloquently outlines his case for outing in his 1993 book, *Queer in America: Sex, the Media, and the Closets of Power*. The strategy of outing is, for better or worse, here to stay and will influence countless lives. Signorile invokes a poignant way of thinking about its possible effects when he conjures "a sad thought: If [closeted celebrities such as] ROCK HUDSON [63], Perry Ellis, Barry Diller, Liz Smith, David Geffen and Malcolm Forbes had held a joint press conference back in 1982 at the beginning of the AIDS crisis, think of the effect it would have had. Think of the power it would have unleashed. Think of the visibility it would have created. THINK OF THE LIVES IT MAY HAVE SAVED."

You should read Signorile's defense of outing and make up your own mind. And you should consider whether a book like *The Gay 100* would be possible without all those people down through history who had the courage not only to face but to tell the truth.

SELECT BIBLIOGRAPHY

General Interest

Boswell, John. *Christianity, Social Tolerance, and Homosexuality: Gay People in Western Europe from the Beginning of the Christian Era to the Fourteenth Century*. Chicago: University of Chicago Press, 1980.

Cooper, Emmanuel. *The Sexual Perspective: Homosexuality and Art in the Last 100 Years in the West*. London: Routledge, 1986.

D'Emilio, John. *Sexual Politics, Sexual Communities: The Making of a Homosexual Minority in the United States, 1940–1970*. Chicago: University of Chicago Press, 1983.

Faderman, Lillian. *Odd Girls and Twilight Lovers: A History of Lesbian Life in Twentieth-Century America*. New York: Penguin, 1991.

Faderman, Lillian. *Surpassing the Love of Men: Romantic Friendship and Love Between Women from the Renaissance to the Present*. New York: Morrow, 1981.

Foster, Jeannette H. *Sex Variant Women in Literature*. New York: Vantage, 1956.

Katz, Jonathan. *Gay American History: Lesbians and Gay Men in the U.S.A.* New York: Harper, 1976.

Marcus, Eric. *Making History: The Struggle for Gay and Lesbian Equal Rights 1945–1990*. New York: HarperCollins, 1992.

Richards, Dell. *Superstars: Twelve Lesbians Who Changed the World*. New York: Carroll & Graf, 1993.

Rowse, A. L. *Homosexuals in History*. New York: Macmillan, 1977.

Biographies

Albertson, Chris. *Bessie Smith: Empress of the Blues*. New York: Stein and Day, 1975.

Ashton, Dore, and Denise Broume Hare. *Rosa Bonheur: A Life and Legend.* New York: Viking, 1981.

Bach, Steven. *Marlene Dietrich: Life and Legend.* New York: William Morrow, 1992.

Barry, Kathleen. *Susan B. Anthony: A Biography of a Singular Feminist.* New York: New York University Press, 1988.

Bartlett, Neil. *Who Was That Man?—A Present for Mr. Oscar Wilde.* London: Serpent's Tail, 1988.

Bell, Quentin. *Virginia Woolf.* New York: Harcourt Brace Jovanovich, 1972.

Bockris, Victor. *The Life and Death of Andy Warhol.* New York: Bantam, 1989.

Caffrey, Margaret. *Ruth Benedict: Stranger in the Land.* Austin: University of Texas Press, 1988.

Callow, Phillip. *From Noon to Starry Night: A Life of Walt Whitman.* Chicago: Ivan Ace, 1992.

Carpenter, Humphrey. *Benjamin Britten.* New York: Charles Scribner, 1992.

Clements, Robert J. *The Poetry of Michelangelo.* New York: New York University Press, 1965.

Cook, Blanche Wiesen. *Eleanor Roosevelt, Volume One 1884–1933.* New York: Viking, 1992.

Crompton, Louis. *Byron and Greek Love: Homophobia in 19th-Century England.* Berkeley: University of California Press, 1985.

DeSalvo, Louise, and Mitchell Leaska. *The Letters of Vita Sackville-West to Virginia Woolf.* New York: William Morrow, 1985.

Ellman, Richard. *Oscar Wilde.* New York: Alfred A. Knopf, 1988.

Friedman, Susan Stanford. *Psyche Reborn: The Emergence of H.D.* Bloomington: Indiana University Press, 1981.

Furbank, P. N. *E. M. Forster.* New York: Harcourt Brace Jovanovich, 1979.

Glendinning, Victoria. *Vita: The Life of Vita Sackville-West.* New York: Alfred Knopf, 1983.

Goldsmith, Margaret. *Christina of Sweden.* Garden City, NY: Doubleday, 1935.

Grosskurth, Phyllis. *The Woeful Victorian: A Biography of John Addington Symonds.* New York: Holt, Rhinehart and Winston, 1964.

Hodge, Andrew. *Alan Turing: The Enigma.* New York: Simon and Schuster, 1983.

Jay, Karla. *The Amazon and the Page: Natalie Barney and René Vivien.* Bloomington: Indiana University Press, 1988.

Kennedy, Hubert. *Ulrichs: Life and Works of Karl Heinrich Ulrichs, Pioneer of the Modern Gay Movement.* Boston: Alyson, 1987.

Lambert, Royston. *Beloved and God: The Story of Hadrian and Antinous.* New York: Viking, 1984.

Leppman, Wolfgang. *Winckelmann.* New York: Alfred Knopf, 1970.

Mavor, Elizabeth. *The Ladies of Llangollen.* London: Michael Joseph, 1971.

Miller, Jim. *The Passion of Michel Foucault.* New York: Simon & Schuster, 1993.

Nicolson, Nigel. *Portrait of a Marriage.* London: Weidenfeld & Nicolson, 1973.

Painter, George D. *Marcel Proust: A Biography,* 2 vols. London: Chatto & Windus, 1959–65.

Pequigney, Joseph. *Such Is My Love: A Study of Shakespeare's Sonnets.* Chicago: University of Chicago Press, 1985.

Richardson, Joanna. *Verlaine.* New York: Viking, 1971.

Roscoe, Will. *The Zuñi Man-Woman.* Albuquerque: University of New Mexico Press, 1991.

St. John, Christopher. *Ethel Smyth: A Biography.* London: Longmans, 1959.

Schwartz, Barth David. *Pasolini Requiem.* New York: Pantheon, 1992.

Shilts, Randy. *The Mayor of Castro Street: The Life and Times of Harvey Milk.* New York: St. Martin's Press, 1982.

Siciliano, Enzo. *Pasolini: A Biography.* New York: Random House, 1982.

Smith, Jane S. *Elsie de Wolfe: A Life in the High Style.* New York: Atheneum, 1982.

Starkie, Enid. *Arthur Rimbaud.* New York: New Directions, 1961.

Summers, Claude J. *Christopher Isherwood.* New York: Ungar, 1980.

Timmons, Stuart. *The Trouble with Harry Hay.* Boston: Alyson, 1988.

Tomlin, Clare. *The Life and Death of Mary Wollstonecraft.* New York: Harcourt Brace Jovanovich, 1974.

Tsuzuki, Chushichi. *Edward Carpenter 1844–1929: Prophet of Human Fellowship.* Cambridge: Cambridge University Press, 1980.

Ward, Carol M. *Rita Mae Brown.* New York: Twayne, 1993.

White, Edmund. *Jean Genet.* New York: Alfred Knopf, 1993.

Williams, Dakin, and Shepherd Mead. *Tennessee Williams: An Intimate Biography,* New York: Arbor House, 1983.

Young-Bruehl, Elizabeth. *Anna Freud.* New York: Summit, 1988.

Yourcenar, Marguerite. *Mishima: A Vision of the Void.* New York: Farrar, Straus & Giroux, 1980.

PICTURE ACKNOWLEDGMENTS

Many of the illustrations in *The Gay 100* are in the public domain. The author thanks the following for permission to reprint.

AP/Wide World: E. M. Forster, Vita Sackville-West and Harold Nicolson, Rita Mae Brown, Martina Navratilova, Mary Renault, Holly Near, Freddie Mercury, Ian McKellen

The Bettmann Archive: Oscar Wilde, Walt Whitman, Edward Carpenter, Susan B. Anthony, Virginia Woolf, Jane Addams, Marcel Proust, Ruth Benedict, Vaslav Nijinsky, Arthur Rimbaud, Rock Hudson, Elsie de Wolfe, Marlene Dietrich, Anna Freud

Reuters/Bettmann: Barney Frank

UPI/Bettmann: Gertrude Stein, Harvey Milk, Michel Foucault, Adrienne Rich, Christopher Isherwood, Pier Paolo Pasolini, Yukio Mishima, H. D., Martin Duberman, Rudolf Nureyev, Samuel Delaney, James Merrill, Madonna

King's College, Cambridge & The Royal Society: Alan Turing

National Anthropological Archives, Smithsonian Institution: We'wha, photo #85-8666

New York Public Library Picture Collection: Sappho, J. A. Symonds, Alexander the Great, Hāfiz, the Amazons

Jerry Bauer: Edmund White

Chris Felver: Judy Grahn

Jean Harvey: Quentin Crisp

Sara Waddell Lewinstein: Dr. Tom Waddell

Fred W. McDarrah: The Patrons of the Stonewall Inn, Andy Warhol, John Cage, James Baldwin, Jean Genet, Larry Kramer, Tennessee Williams, Bayard Rustin, Liberace, Allen Ginsberg, Kate Millet, Francis Bacon, Roy Cohn, Halston

William Moritz: Harry Hay

Margaret Randall: Gloria Anzaldúa

Howard Sooley: Derek Jarman

Michael Wakefield: Michaelangelo Signorile

Jean Weisinger: Cherrie Moraga, Audre Lorde

INDEX